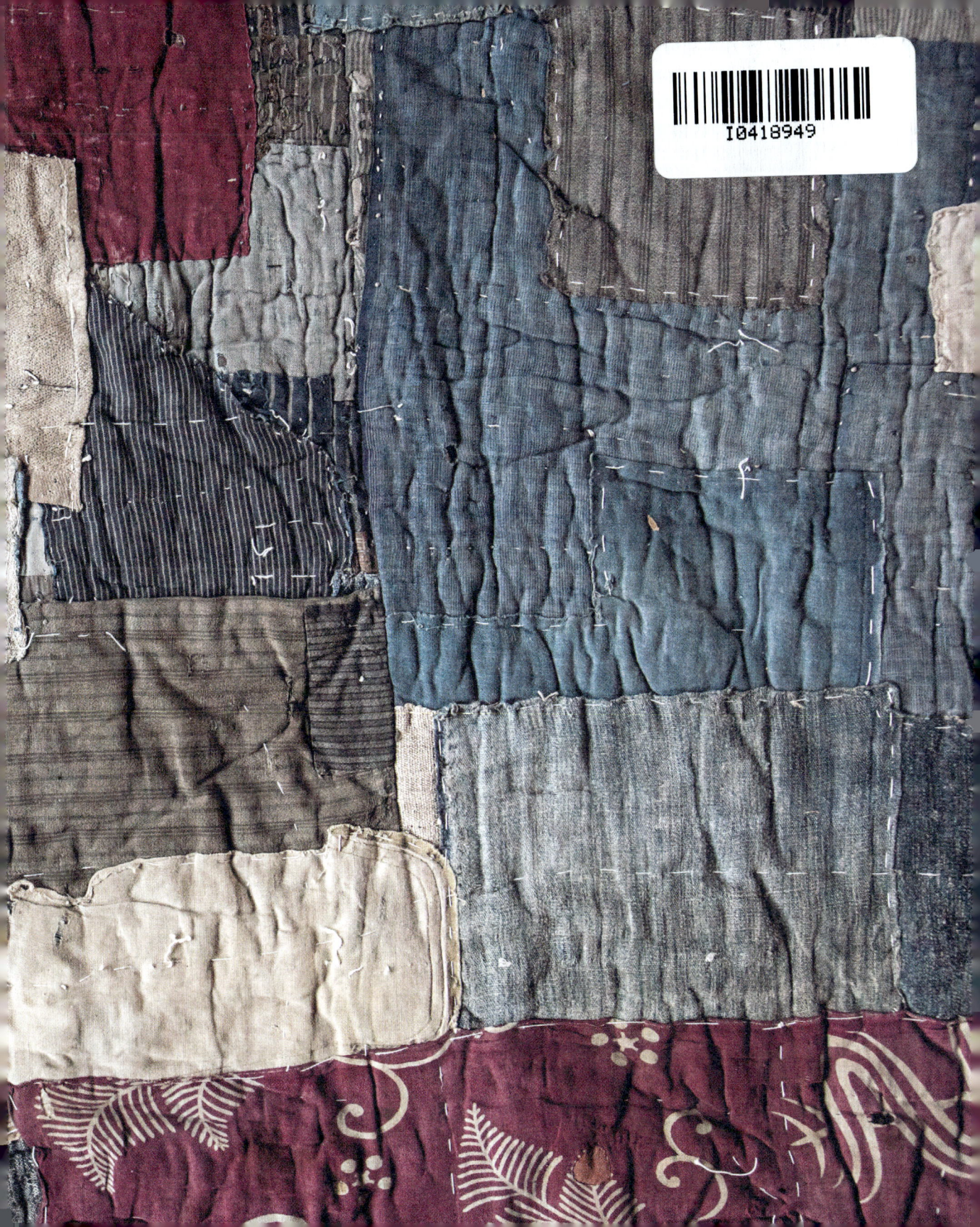

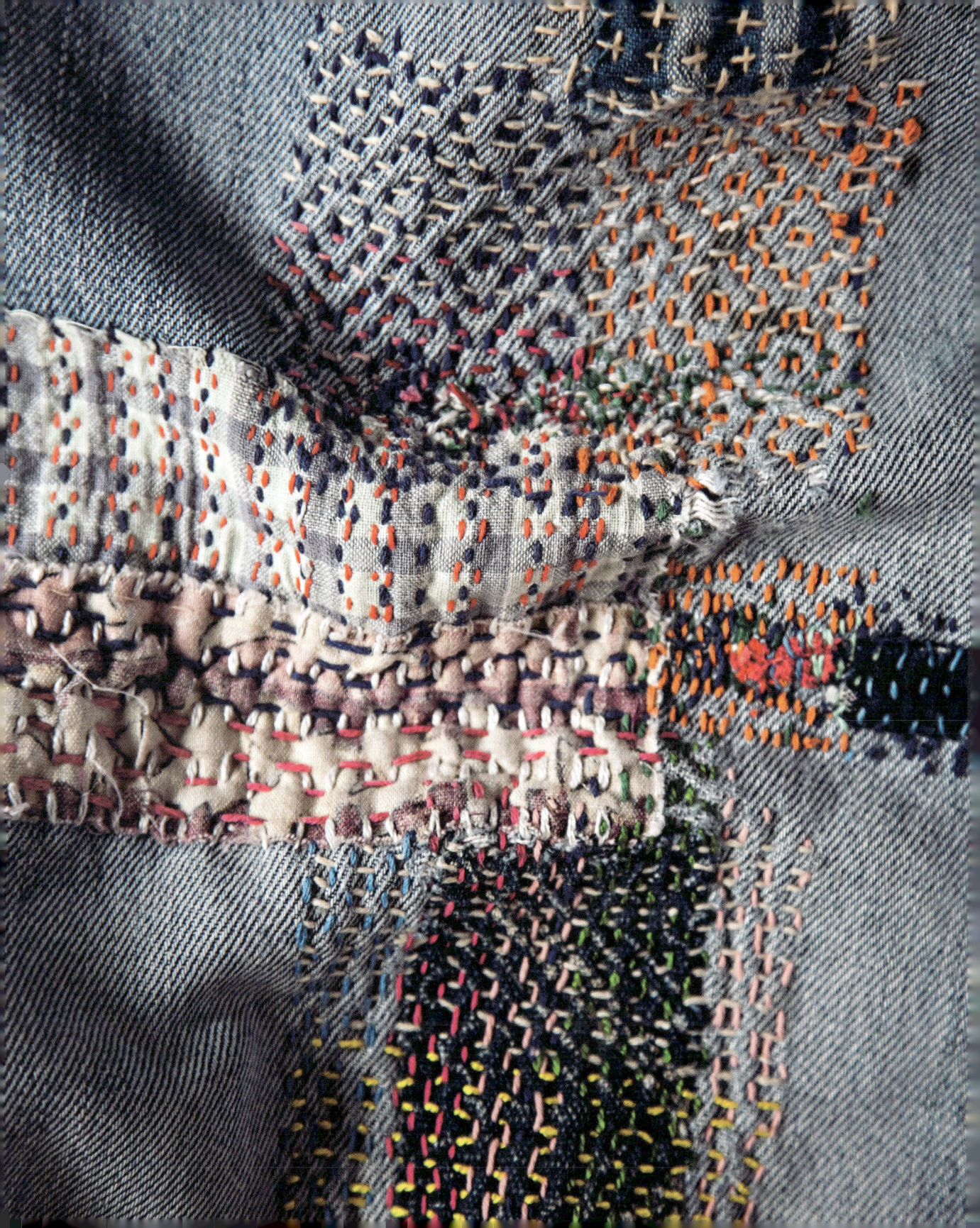

MENDING WITH
SASHIKO

TAKAO MOMIYAMA

KERSTIN NEUMÜLLER

BATSFORD

CONTENTS

Foreword 6
Takao 'Momi' Momiyama 6
Kerstin Neumüller 7
Glossary 8
Sashiko Diary Entries 10
What is Sashiko? 14
Different Types of Sashiko 22
Sashiko Diary Entries 30

TECHNIQUES 34
Mending Clothes with Sashiko 36
Sashiko Diary Entries 54

PROJECTS 58
Mending T-shirts and Socks 60
Mending Jeans 66
Mending Jeans with Hitomezashi 70
Mending a Torn Jeans Hem 74
Mending a Jeans Pocket 78
Mending Stretch Jeans 80
Mending a Handkerchief with Furoshiki 84
Mending a Cushion Cover 89
Mending a Shirt Collar 92
Mending a Blanket 97
Making a Potholder 100
Bodoko - Almost a Patchwork Quilt 105
Mending Tabi 108
Sashiko Diary Entries 110

MOMI'S ARCHIVE 114
Afterword 135

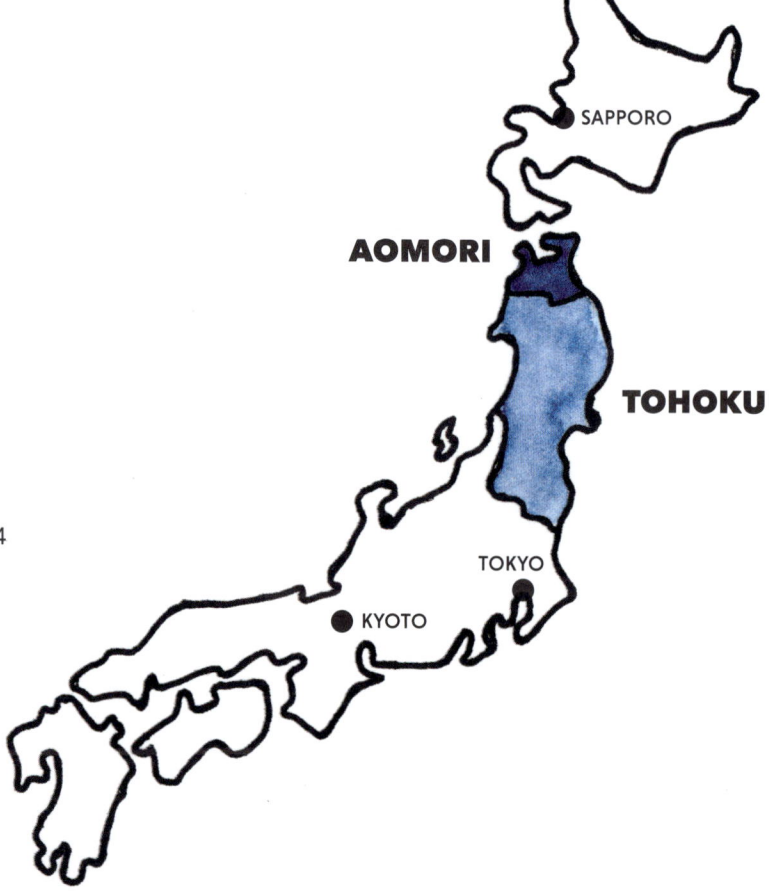

SAPPORO

AOMORI

TOHOKU

TOKYO

KYOTO

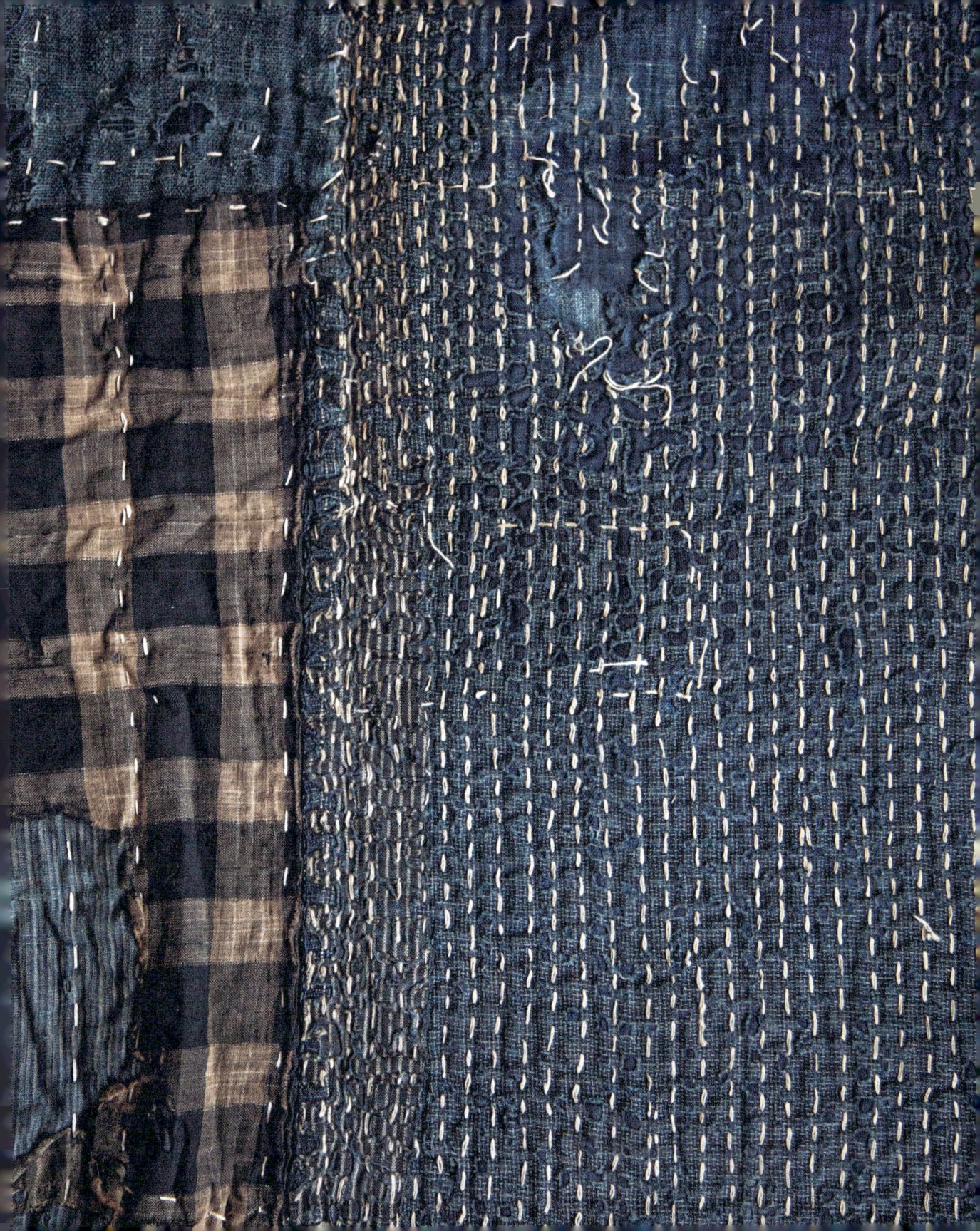

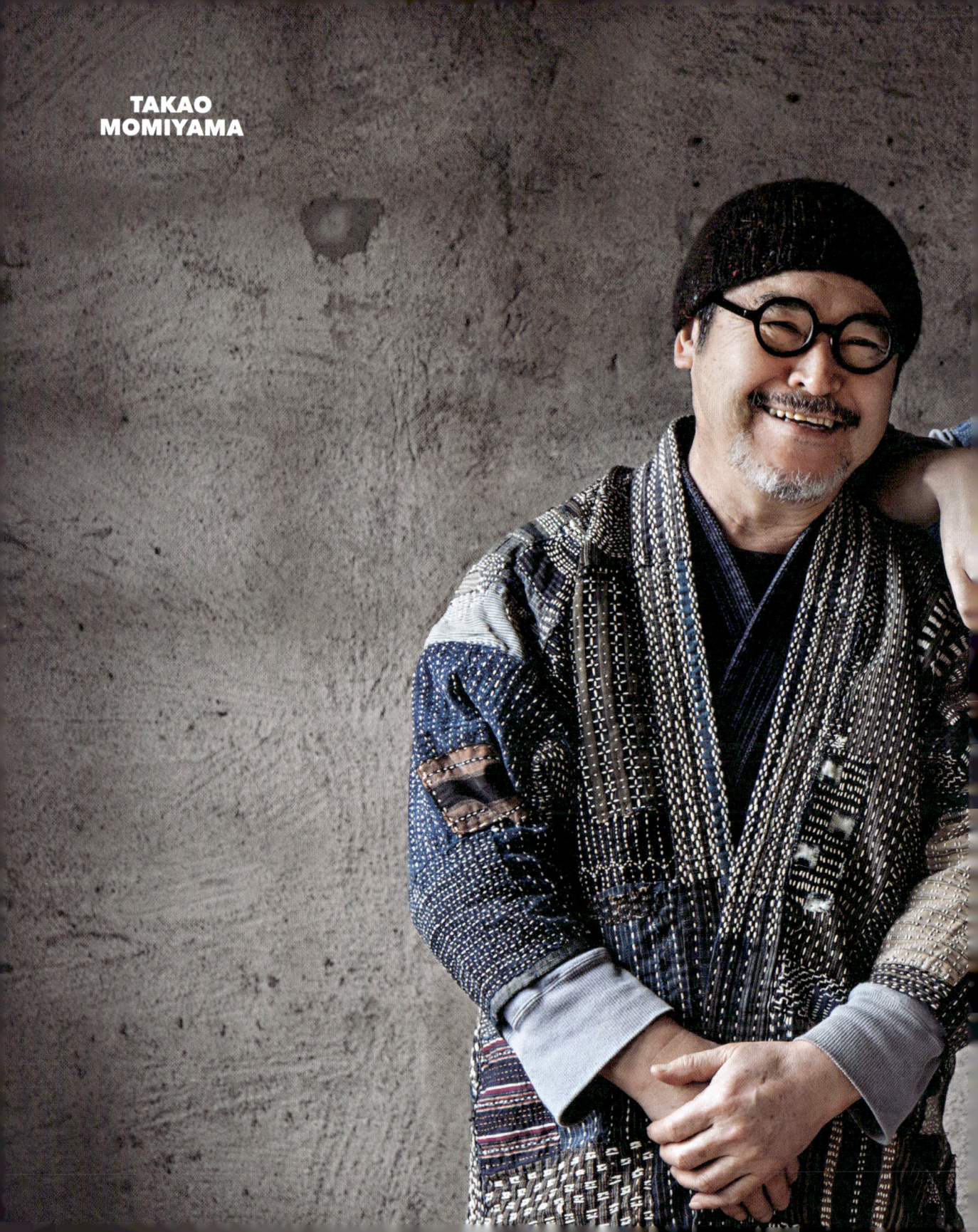

TAKAO
MOMIYAMA

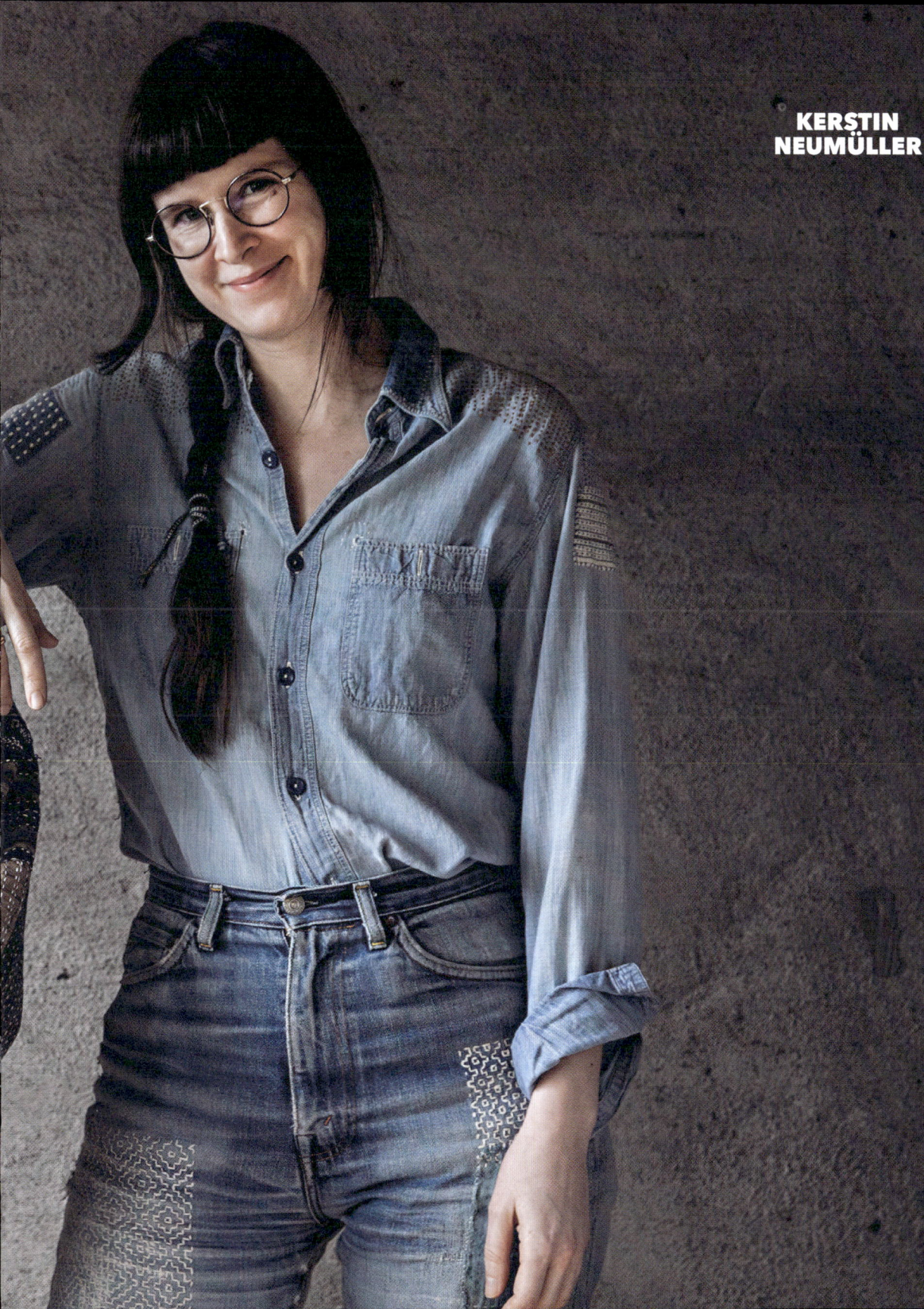

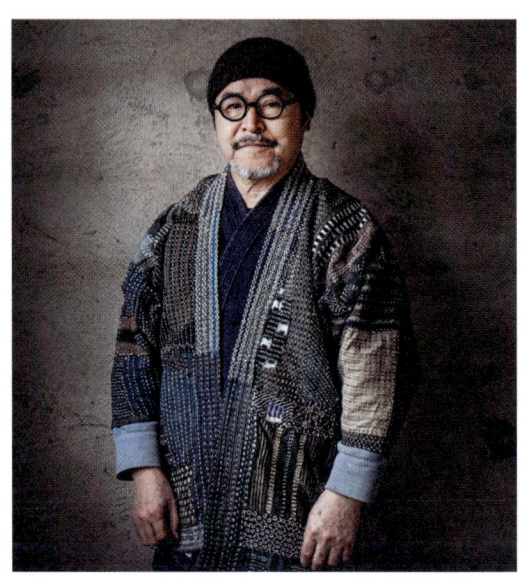

FOREWORD

Sashiko looks so easy at first glance. It's just standard stitches, up and down! But as with all handicrafts, the world of sashiko becomes more and more complicated the closer you look at it. Different patterns have different requirements, and after a while it's easy to get lost in all the complexities associated with the art of sewing those simple stitches.

We are Takao 'Momi' Momiyama and Kerstin Neumüller. We both love sashiko and boro, which tell the story of a fabric's journey and its rebirth through reuse and repair.

We believe that sashiko should be easy and accessible, and for us there aren't any rights or wrongs when you sew – the important thing is that the result is what you want it to be. In this book we show examples of our own handiwork, and our hope is that you as the reader will be able to dive into the book and find your own way of mending clothes with sashiko!

TAKAO 'MOMI' MOMIYAMA

I grew up as a farmer's son 100 kilometres north of Tokyo. My parents worked with hemp and silk, and as a boy I played with my brother among mulberry trees and rice fields. When I was 12 I started practicing Japanese martial arts and eventually became a master in iaido, which can be described as the 'art of drawing the sword'. In the 1970s I moved to Sweden and today I live in the countryside in Scania in the south of Sweden where I have my training studio.

When I practice martial arts in the winter I use 'tabi', the sewn Japanese socks that are divided into two sections with one section for the big toe and one for the other four toes. The socks wear down quickly and my whole mending journey started one winter when I didn't have any money to buy new tabi; I had to try to mend them. Mending tabi using a sewing machine was too difficult so I sewed by hand using the simplest of stitches: running stitch. I still use that first mended pair of tabi today, and mend them when needed.

A move from the city to a house with a garden meant gardening work and more clothes to mend. I worked my way through my wardrobe

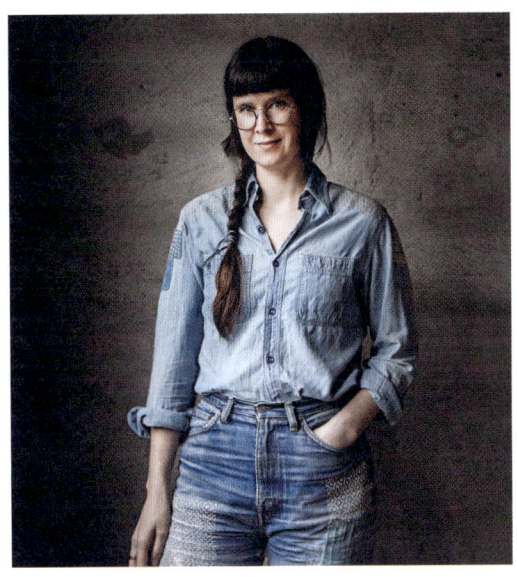

and mended trousers, shirts, jumpers, jackets, socks, t-shirts and so on. I practice the idea of 'mottainai', a Japanese expression for that which is too good to throw away, and my inspiration comes from my collections of patched and mended textiles from north Japan. I study the old textiles and look at how they are sewn, but I don't make exact copies. You can say that I carry on with a tradition but I am not traditional in my method of sewing; instead, I use a specific technique as a springboard and then expand on the expression.

Prolonging the life of textiles through patching and mending is my contribution to the philosophy around mottainai, and I want to pass that on to the next generation. The textile cultural heritage enriches and unites us over both geographical and generational borders and I want to thank the people who started sewing sashiko once upon a time, in particular my mum who showed me how to sew by hand. Now I carry their legacy on.

KERSTIN NEUMÜLLER

Making has always been central in my life. During my upbringing in the countryside, it was about making my world bigger, more imaginative – a way to expand my horizons without having to travel far. I am so fascinated by what feels 'genuine' and it is a continuous search, a red thread through most things that I do, the chase after that feeling that 'this time it's for real'.

When I was around 25, I heard about sashiko for the first time. I had just started my tailor training and saw a picture of dense, white stitches against a blue background – a new world opened before me. What was it, how did it work? I, who already did a lot of hand sewing, soaked up the new technique like a sponge.

A while later I was asked to write my first book. *Indigo* became a recipe collection for indigo dyers, with craft projects as serving suggestions. Over the years I have written more books, and when I was asked to write one about sashiko together with Momi, it was a very easy decision. Of course I wanted to! In this book I am the narrator with focus on Momi's handiwork, but I have also snuck in a few of my own projects.

7

GLOSSARY

BASTING
The art of temporarily attaching a piece of fabric to another one using large stitches that are removed after the actual stitches has been sewn.

BORO
A word that describes something that is worn down and doesn't work.

HAGIRE
Scraps of worn clothes that have been unpicked for reuse.

HEM
A folded edge of a fabric, sewn in place to prevent it from unfolding.

HORIZONTAL
A direction. (4)

KIMONO
A long garment with wide sleeves. (1)

NORAGI
A short work jacket with tapered sleeves. (3)

TABI
Socks with a separate part for the big toe.

UNSHIN
The art of sewing multiple stitches at a time.

VERTICAL
A direction. (2)

YOKOGUSHI
The art of sewing only one stitch at a time.

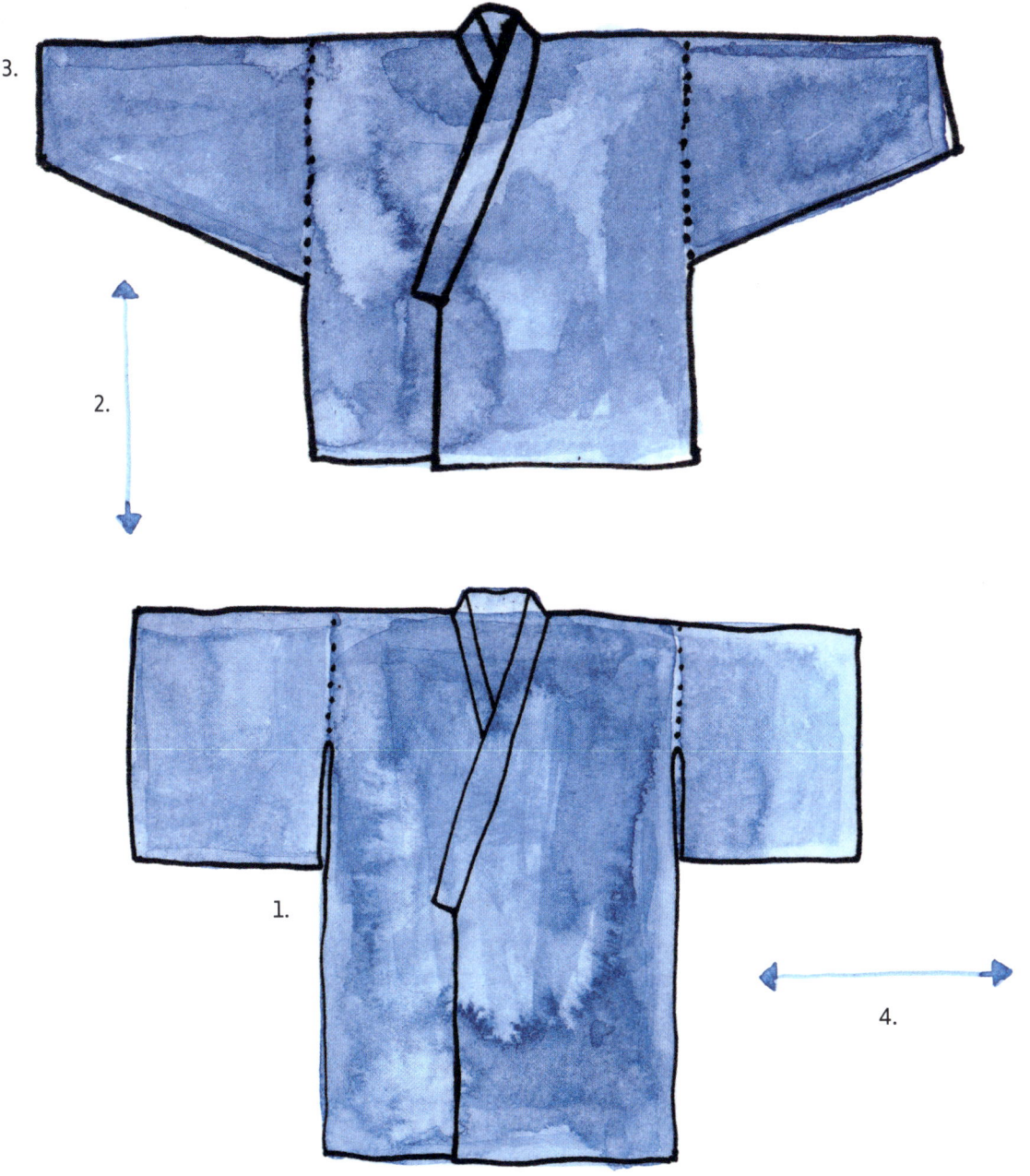

3.

2.

1.

4.

SASHIKO DIARY ENTRIES

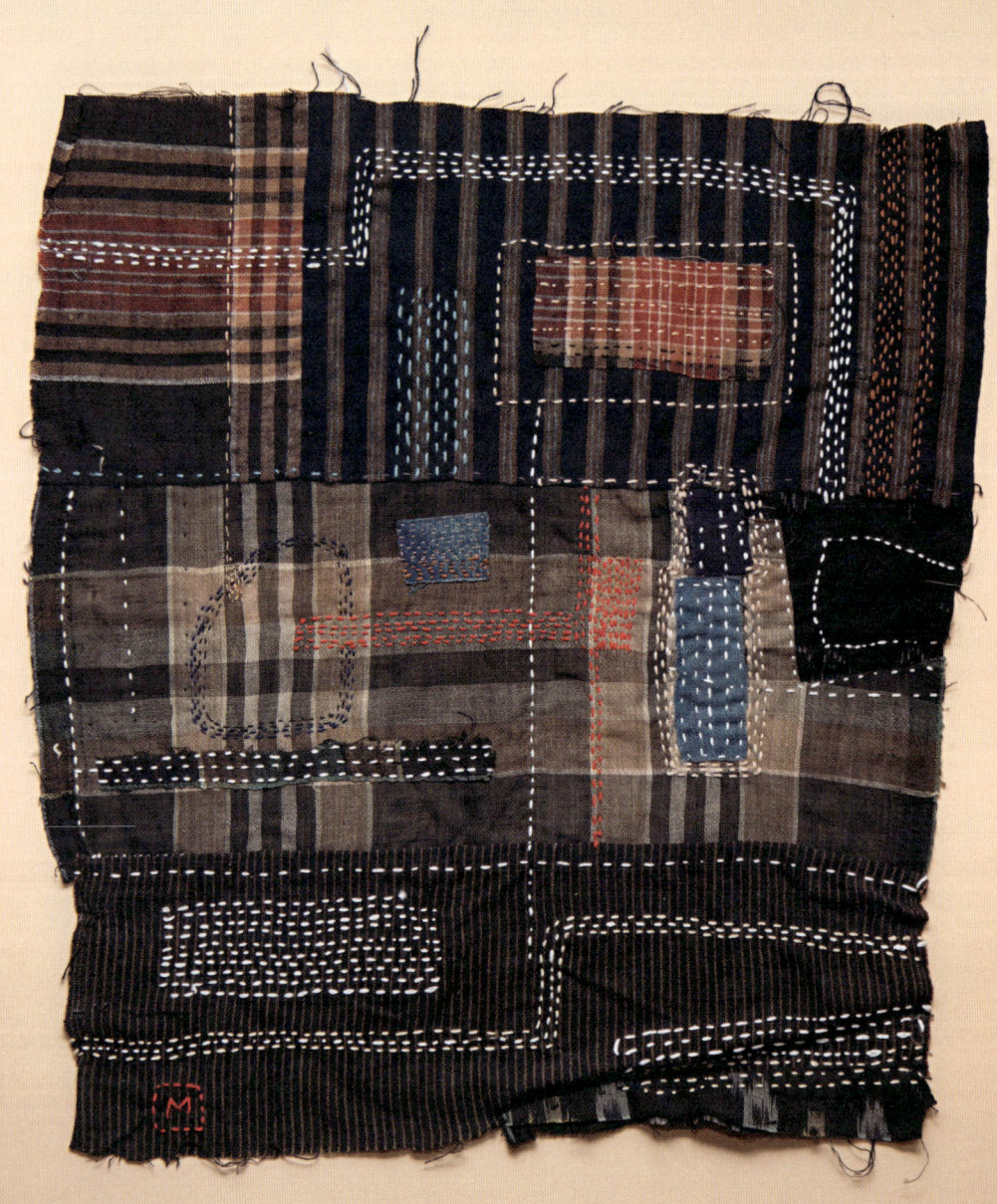

Momi has a routine of sewing sashiko every day. Often, it's to mend something, but sometimes he creates more artistic compositions, fabric pieces on which he tries out new techniques, inspired by a colour or the texture of a fabric scrap. These fabric pieces make up his 'sashiko diary', like a note made with needle and threads.

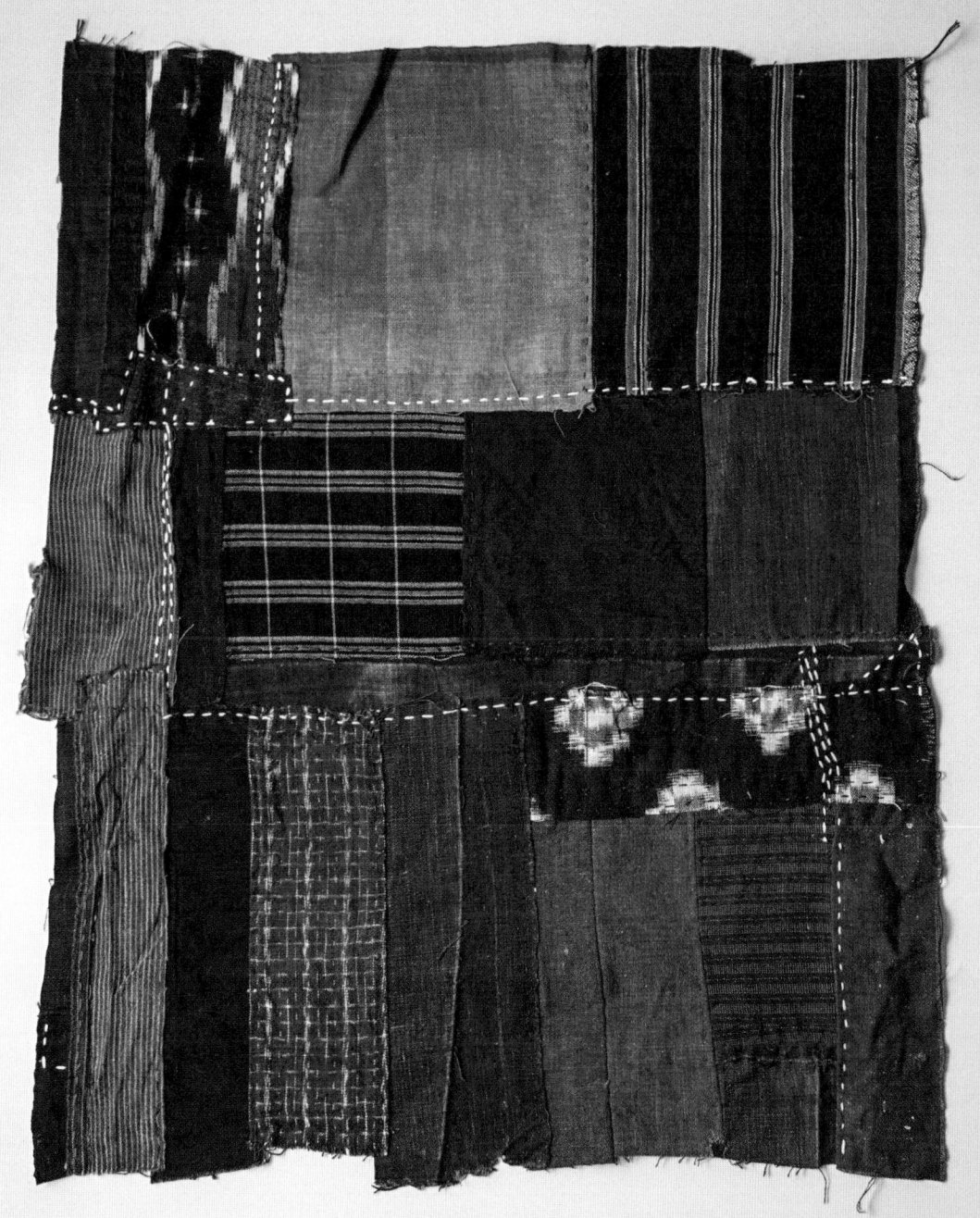

SASHIKO DIARY ENTRY, 14.04.2023
'I wanted to make a series with compositions that resemble the landscape of Österlen,
seen from above. I wanted to capture the feeling of the houses and the fields! And the roads.
The strips of the fabric became fields.'

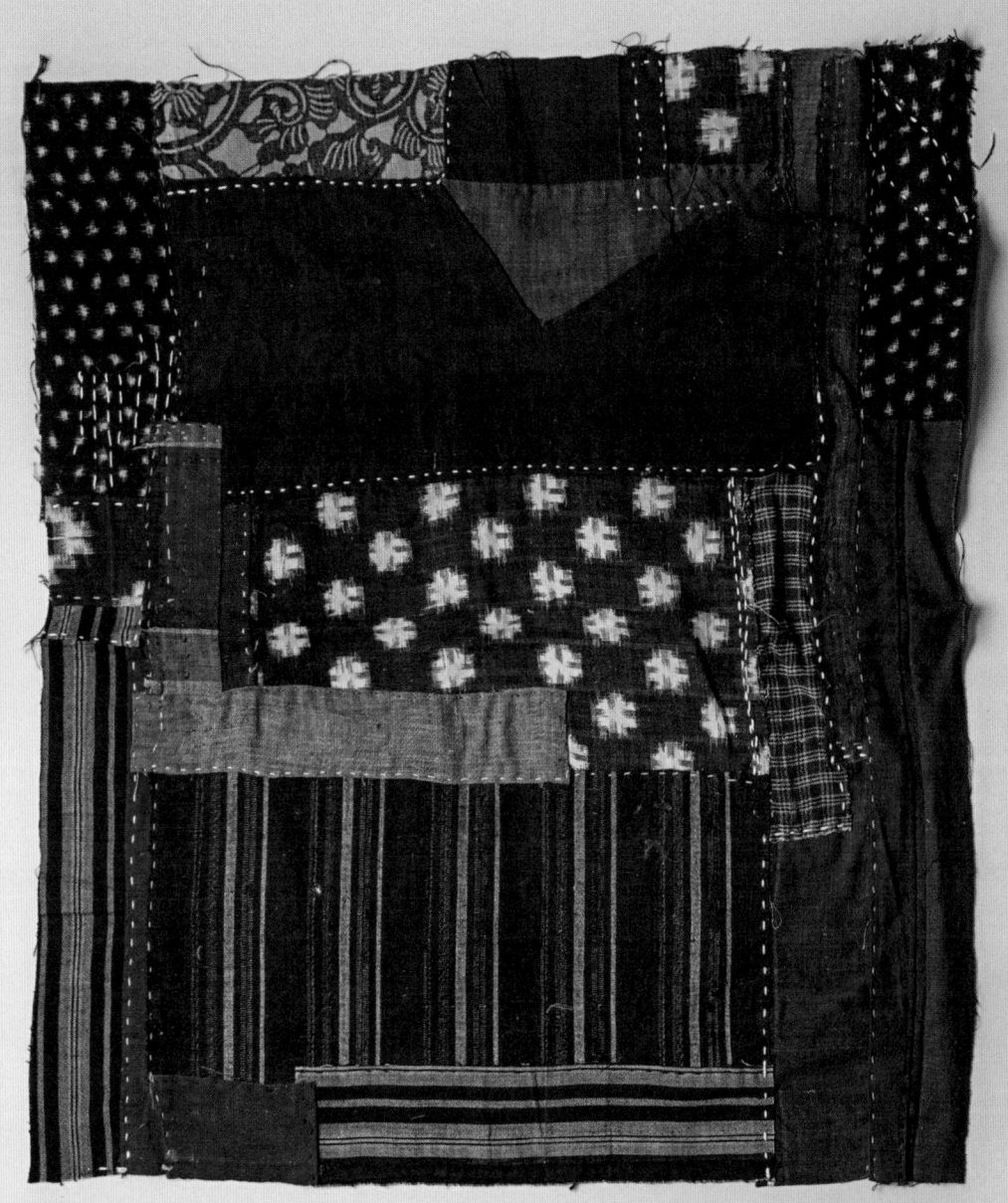

SASHIKO DIARY ENTRY, 01.06.2022
'In this blue landscape I wanted to mix different Japanese techniques.
Here are katazome, kasuri (two fabric-dyeing methods) and woven strips together.'

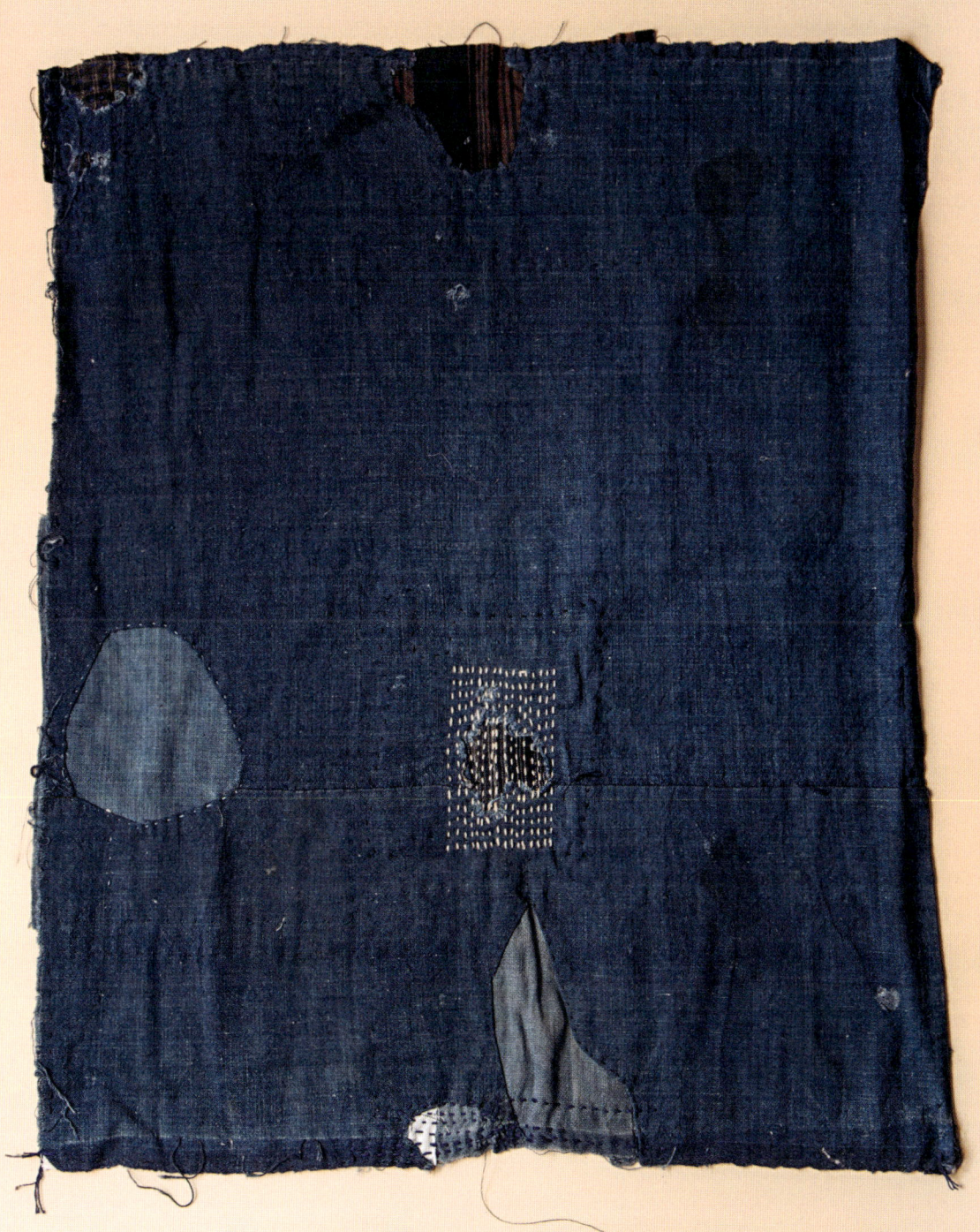

SASHIKO DIARY ENTRY, 17.03.2021
'This is almost an abstract painting.'

WHAT IS SASHIKO?

Sashiko originates from Japan and has become associated with embroidery and mending but, in essence, it's neither one nor the other. The word means 'little stab' and involves sewing small stitches onto a piece of fabric. In the beginning, these stitches had two purposes: to hold several layers of fabric together and in this way create warmer garments, or to reinforce a piece of fabric to make it more durable. You can say that sashiko in its original form is a proactive mending technique; you'll know from experience where the fabric will wear down and can then reinforce it even before a hole has appeared. Therefore, the closest we come in England to explaining what sashiko really is, would be to call it 'a sewing technique' rather than embroidery or mending. But, of course, you could say 'a sewing technique that is used for embroidery or mending' if you like. Over time, people have started to use the concept that is associated with sashiko for everything from mending clothes, sewing decorative embroideries and transforming printed patterns, to decorating everyday items and using it in art.

You could say that sashiko is constantly evolving, but in its original form sashiko is a hand-sewing technique. You only use one type of stitch: running stitch. It's not just the Japanese who sewed with a running stitch; similar techniques can be found all over the world, and perhaps the most prominent one is the Indian 'kantha', which involves sewing worn-down sari fabrics in layers to create new textiles. What is distinctive for sashiko, however, is that in its original form it is often sewn with white thread onto a blue base. Sometimes the stitches form geometrical patterns, but they can also be free flowing and form figures such as flowers, or *mon*, which are symbols for different families, similar to a coat of arms.

It's difficult to pinpoint exactly when the tradition of sewing sashiko appeared, but by the time the 19th century had passed it had been long-established and different local variations had evolved. The end of the Edo period (1868), the opening up of Japanese society for trade and foreign ideas and eventual industrialization were factors that radically changed the lifestyle of the Japanese. The countryside population's habit of making what they needed themselves or relying on local craftspeople was replaced by paid work that generated money with which you could buy mass-produced goods. In that society, sashiko no longer had a natural place, and by the end of the Second World War only a few practitioners remained.

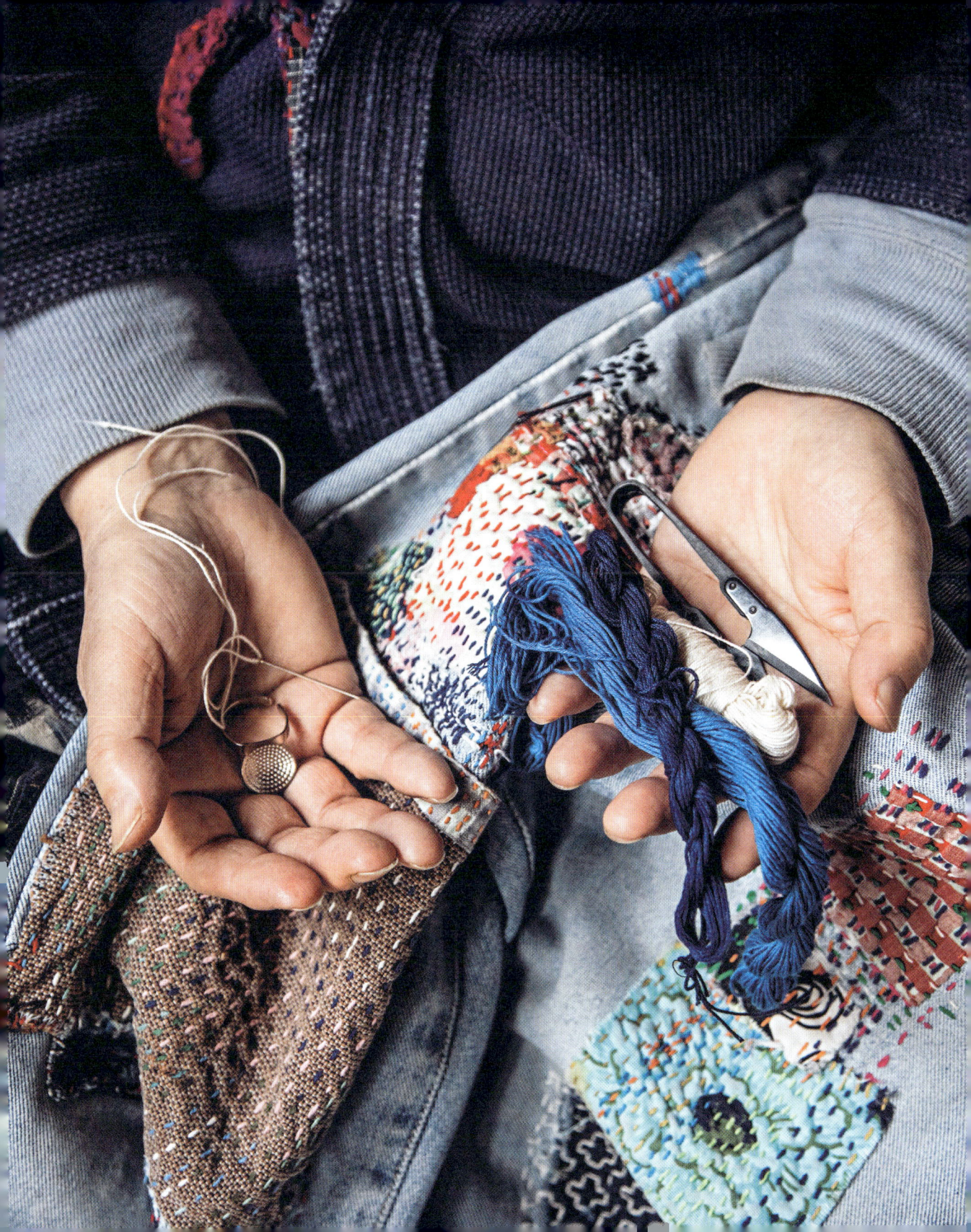

'First you think you know everything. Then you realize that you hardly know anything at all. After that you can start learning about the subject.'

PRESERVATION OF THE CULTURAL HERITAGE

Just as in Europe, industrialization gave rise to a resistance movement in Japan. The counterpart of the Arts and Crafts movement came to be known as *mingei*, a word that can closest be translated as 'folk craft'. The man behind the movement was called Yanagi Sōetsu and he wanted to preserve the craft that he regarded as genuine, natural and pure: created by unknown craftsmen who produced beautiful objects from natural materials, not because it would bring them fame and elevate them to artists but because it was their job.

Yanagi collected craft from all corners of Japan and founded Nihon Mingeikan, a museum for Japanese folk art, where he among other things exhibited garments sewn with sashiko. It was of course not only Yanagi's effort that led to the art of sashiko being preserved for future generations, but it was clearly a contributing factor.

With time, the Japanese interest in sashiko was revived and was eventually also spread beyond the country's borders. The technique was picked up as an embroidery pattern for neat little bags and wall hangings, and resourceful sellers of craft materials put together kits with needle, thread and fabrics with printed sashiko patterns ready to be filled in. Sashiko was back in the game, albeit in a new form!

When the *mingei* movement began to gather the folk art they were going to preserve, they faced a choice: what is worth preserving? Some objects were regarded as too simple and uninteresting, or as having too many untypical qualities to fit in. Sashiko textiles where luckily regarded as a category worth preserving.

When you pick up a tradition and place it in a display case to present it to an audience, you inevitably remove it from its context. Often, only one example of each pattern or design is shown, and with that misconceptions occur: I see, in Tsugaru the sashiko embroideries look exactly like this. This must mean it's the only right way of sewing sashiko.

This is the curse of conveyors of knowledge. To be able to share information about a culture we must simplify it until it's possible to grasp for those who don't have a lot of pre-existing knowledge. You can't tell the story of sashiko, for example, by talking about all different varieties of the hemp leaf pattern, how it has been sewn in different ways in different villages and that it has also varied over generations. It will simply be too much information to take in in one go. Unfortunately, this leads to new craft practitioners often holding the belief that there is only one way of doing things, or that a craft must look a certain way. It's often not true. If you take the time and effort to read up on a craft, the following often happens: first you think you know everything. Then you realize that you hardly know anything at all. After that you can properly start learning about the subject.

Why do we say this? Because there are many who like to have an opinion about sashiko. What sashiko is, how it should be sewn, what is right and wrong and who is even allowed to sew sashiko are questions that have been frequently raised in discussion forums over the past few years.

Our stance is that the objects that were created during the period before the Second World War, when the tradition of sewing sashiko was a natural and integrated part of society, are the key. We can look at them to see how they were made, and no one should come and say that you aren't allowed to make knots when sewing sashiko if there are knots at the back of the sashiko of the old fishermen's wives, for example. That said, there is nothing that stops us today from sewing our own sashiko without knots if we want to!

SASHIKO THROUGH HISTORY

In the north of Japan, the temperature can reach -10°C in the winter, but since there weren't any sheep, the people didn't have any wool clothes to keep them warm. Before industrialization, they used clothes made from strong hemp, warm cotton and beautiful silk. Silk, however, was reserved for society's upper classes, and cotton was also banned during certain periods from use in the lower classes in some areas, for example in Aomori. What people were left with was hemp and other plant fibres that are strong and durable but not particularly warming. These fibres have similar qualities to linen, our favourite cool material here in the Nordics.

The tradition of sewing sashiko was developed from a need partly to make clothes stronger and partly to make them warmer. By sewing many layers of hemp fabric together you could get clothes that kept fishermen and farmers, if not directly warm, at least alive. These seams and stitches were originally sewn with hemp thread and has developed to what we today call sashiko. At the end of the 18th century, cotton thread started to appear among traders' goods in Aomori and the new, soft thread turned out to be much easier to sew beautiful patterns with. Just as there are different dialects, so there are also regional craft traditions, and sashiko came to look different in different parts of the country.

SASHIKO TODAY

The idea of sashiko has spread all over the world in recent years and every time it meets new creative people, new variations appear. There are countless specially manufactured products for sewing with sashiko, such as special thread in all the colours of the rainbow, special needles, chalk, pens, paper patterns and fabrics with printed patterns that you can fill in with stitches. Using sashiko for mending denim is particularly popular, perhaps because denim fabric dyed with indigo in some way resembles the old traditional Japanese indigo fabrics.

We separate the modern sashiko from the historic and let the modern be a technique that can be used both for repairing clothes and for decorative embroidery.

BORO

Among modern sashiko practitioners, boro and sashiko have become synonymous with each other but, in fact, they are two separate concepts. Boro describes something that is worn down and doesn't work. You can say that a car that is mended with duct tape is boro, but what we think about when we hear the word are textiles that are patched and mended in many layers. Also these textiles belong in Aomori, and unlike the rich city dwellers' habit of getting rid of worn-out garments and buying new ones, Aomori's population held on to what little they had, and the textiles were handed down the generations and were patched and mended in perpetuity.

In fact, before industrialization, Japanese towns had incredibly well-developed systems for sorting waste. Rubbish heaps didn't exist, as all refuse was sorted and bought up by dealers who sold it on: household ash for making lye, paper for recycling, faecal matter as fertilizer on the fields and textiles were baled up and sent to the countryside where they were sold to farmers and fishermen.

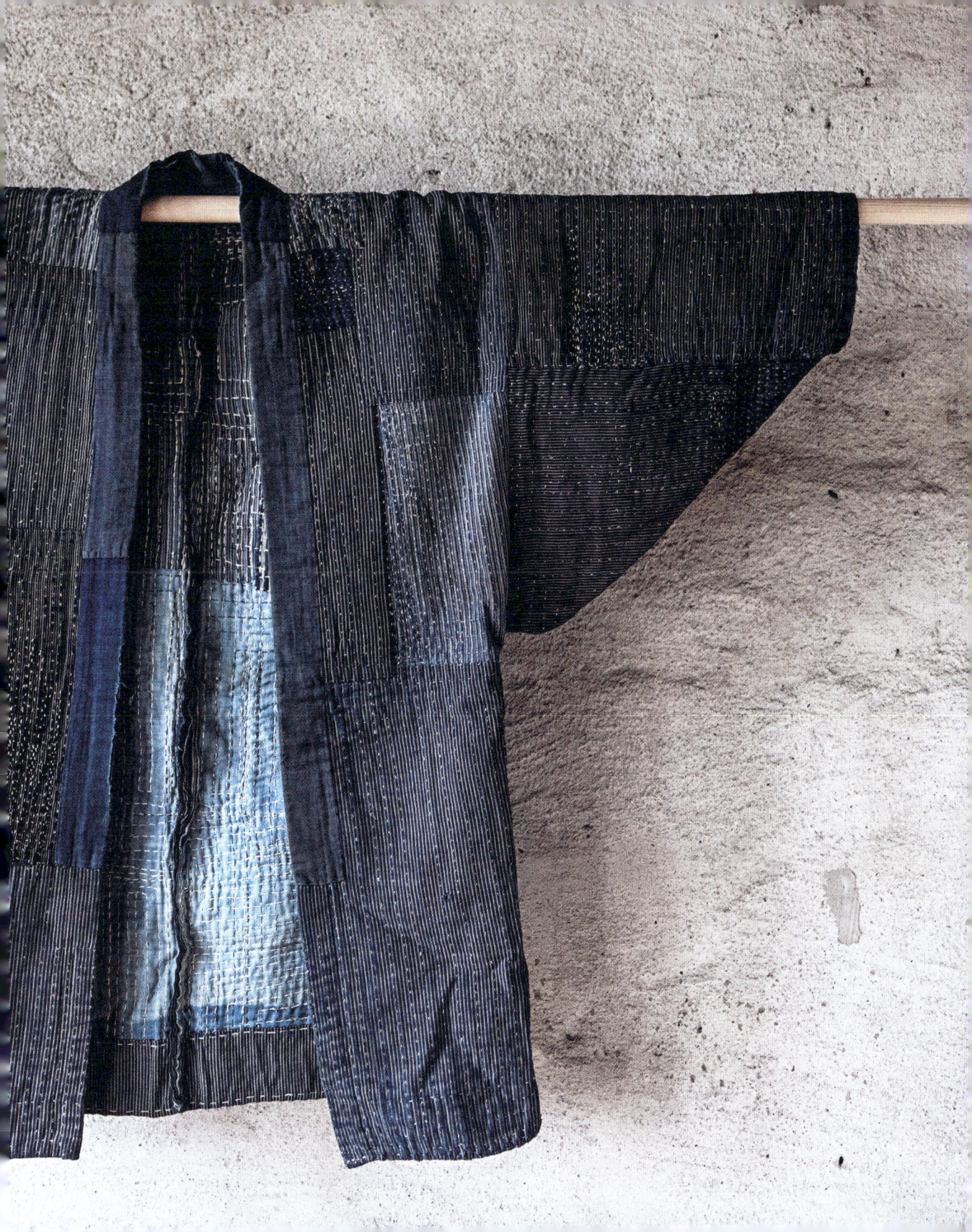

'In traditional Japanese society, the worn-out boro textiles weren't anything you wanted to show off.'

Japanese society had enormous class differences during this time, and even into the 1930s there were many who couldn't afford new cotton fabrics. There are heart-wrenching stories of funerals that escalated into fights over who should inherit the deceased's only set of clothes, which gives a clear signal as to how highly valuable textiles were.

When the old, worn-out clothes from the towns reached Aomori, the women in the poor villages came together and bought a bale to share, and those who had a little bundle with saved patches made from cotton were regarded as rich. The cotton patches were washed and could then be sewn onto worn clothes made from home-woven hemp fabric, or sewn together into bigger pieces that became new garments.

In traditional Japanese society, the worn-out boro textiles weren't anything you wanted to show off. In fact, they were often made so that one side was a relatively whole fabric that the patches were then sewn onto. When it comes to garments, it's almost always the inside that's mended, unless the garment has deteriorated so much that it's necessary to put patches on the outside as well.

Today, the fashion world has discovered boro, and when you see people wearing old, worn-out garments they usually wear them inside out to show off the colour play of the patches and the beautiful stitches that keep them in place. What traditional Japanese society would have thought if we came and pranced around the fishing villages wearing their work clothes, inside out no less, combined with modern accessories, we can only guess. They would probably think we'd gone mad.

This is what's nice about being inspired by history. We can choose to take inspiration from a style or tradition without having to embrace the lifestyle that comes with it unless we want to. But the inspiration will always become more multifaceted the more we know about the history surrounding it!

WHY IS EVERYTHING BLUE?

When you look at older sashiko and boro you might soon start to wonder why everything is blue. Of course, it's lovely, but ... where are the other colours?

There are many explanations as to why most of these textiles are blue. Among other things, sumptuary laws were in place that regulated which colours were permitted for the different classes, and blue was a colour that the poorest were allowed to wear. You could also highlight indigo's relatively good colourfastness in comparison to other plant dyes. Another factor could be the selection process that took place when things were preserved for future generations. For example, in southern Aomori, green noragi jackets with sashiko embroideries existed, but since the blue ones were more common, they are usually the ones being displayed.

MOTTAINAI

Mottainai is a phrase that roughly translates to 'too good to be wasted' or 'worth keeping'. It can be applied to many different things, for example a worn-out shirt that can be used to repair another garment. The phrase can also be used to convey a loss – for example if a person who was an asset to the community passes away, you can say 'mottainai', this person will be missed. One story that has long circulated describes how in north Japan in the past, they were so thrifty that not a single piece of fabric was to be wasted. If it was large enough to wrap around three beans, it was 'mottainai'; good to have, in other words, and should be kept.

Mottainai is a theme that permeates Momi's life. After he began mending his martial-arts clothes, he started to collect old textiles and mend all his clothes. Today he is fascinated by how much can be done by hand with needle and thread, without electricity or expensive equipment.

DIFFERENT TYPES OF SASHIKO

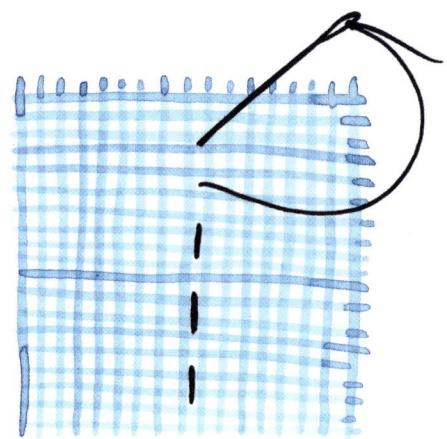

The tradition of sewing sashiko developed in north Japan where people often lived fairly isolated lives and weren't exposed to many outside influences. In places like these, specific local traditions often appear, for example dialects, different ways of cooking – or sewing sashiko. You usually talk of three main categories of sewing sashiko: *hitomezashi, moyozashi* and *kogin-zashi*.

We have chosen to write sashiko when we talk about the whole group of techniques, but -zashi when we talk about a specific technique. It can seem confusing, but it lies closer to the Japanese pronunciation than writing -sashi.

HITOMEZASHI

Hitomezashi is a technique that involves forming geometrical patterns by sewing different layers of stitches on top of each other. For example, sew all vertical stitches first and then all horizontal. Sometimes you also sew a layer of diagonal stitches and, depending on how the stitches in the different layers are placed, you can make different patterns. One common rule to stick to is that the stitches should all be of equal length, and the gaps in between them should also be of equal length. If the stitch is 5mm (¼in) long, the gap before the next stitch should also be 5mm (¼in). This is a rule that can sometimes be broken, but it's good to stick to when you start off sewing hitomezashi.

How do you make the stitches even? If you have sewn hitomezashi all your life you'll get even stitches automatically (see 'Sewing patterns without a ruler', page 46), but if you're not used to it there are a few good tricks you can use.

For coarse fabrics with plain weave, you can count the threads. Then you can, for example, sew over two threads and under two and so on. You can also draw up a grid on the fabric, with chalk or a water-soluble textile pen that you can wash off once you're finished.

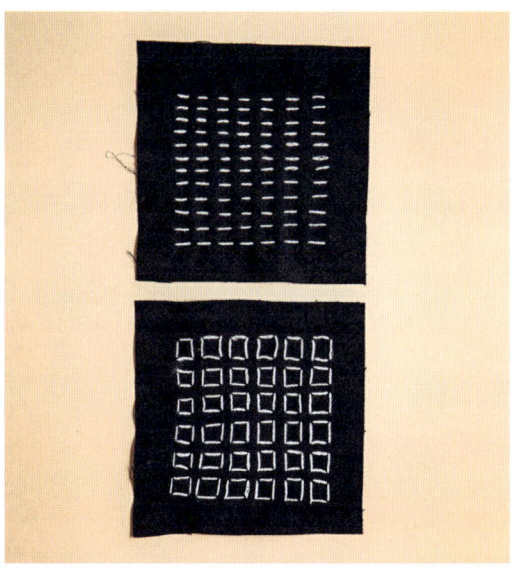

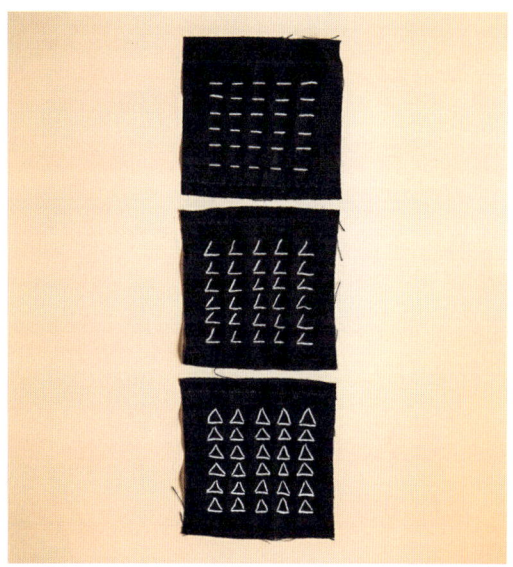

LITTLE SQUARES

All hitomezashi patterns start with sewing all stitches in one direction first. Here Momi has started with horizontal rows that are placed parallel to each other.

When all the horizontal stitches are sewn, you can sew all the vertical stitches. Momi turns the fabric 90 degrees (see page 42) so that he can keep working from right to left, and then he sews new rows. Now the new stitches will bind together with the ones he sewed in the first layer, so that they together form a square.

TIP! If the stitches in the first layer are longer than the second layer, the squares will become rectangular.

TRIANGLES

The horizontal stitches for a triangle pattern are sewn the same way as for little squares, in parallel rows of horizontal stitches. When you have finished this layer you can turn the fabric 45 degrees and sew a layer of diagonal stitches, and finally you finish off by turning the fabric again and sewing another layer of diagonal stitches.

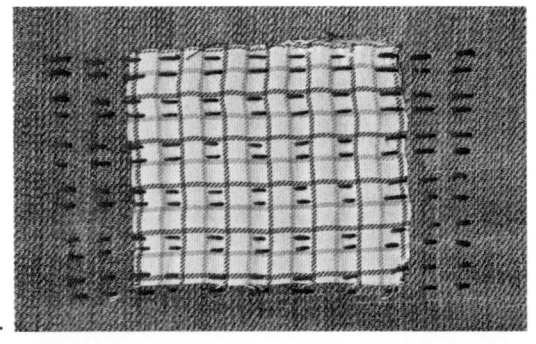

1.

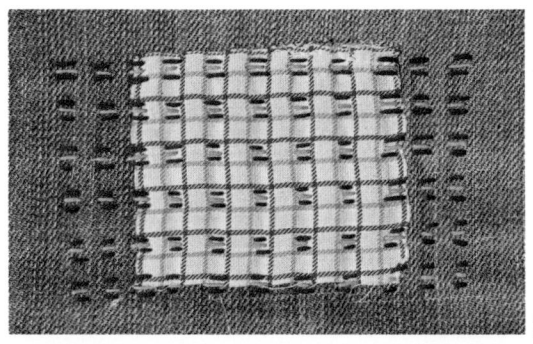

2.

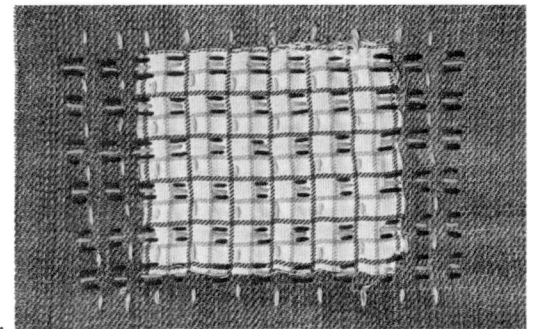

3.

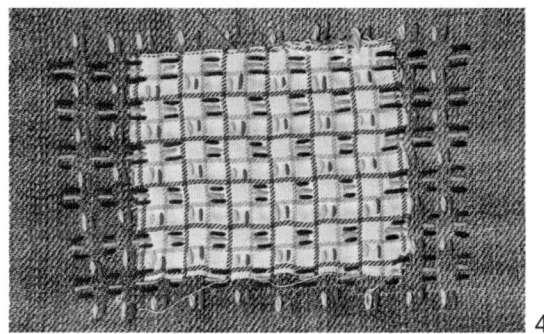

4.

MULTICOLOURED HITOMEZASHI

Momi has developed his own way of sewing hitomezashi where he creates a complex pattern by simply sewing with different coloured threads onto a checked fabric. This way a visual effect is built up from the squares of the fabric, the placement of the stitches and the colour of the thread. He often lets the stitches continue outside of the edges of the patch and tries to stick to the same stitch length that he used to sew the patch onto the checked fabric.

METHOD

Start by sewing stitches with black thread in horizontal lines. The checked pattern of the fabric will determine the length of the stitches, and in this case, the stitches are placed parallel, two within the same square. (1) Now you can sew a row of stitches with pink thread between the two black threads of each pair. (2)

The next step is to sew vertical stitches. Momi starts with lines of green stitches that also follow the checked pattern of the fabric. Can you see that they are not placed in the middle of the square, but slightly off-centre? (3)

When it's time to sew the final layer of vertical stitches, Momi chooses a red thread. (4) He places the stitches parallel with the green ones and keeps within the same square of the fabric's pattern as them.

24

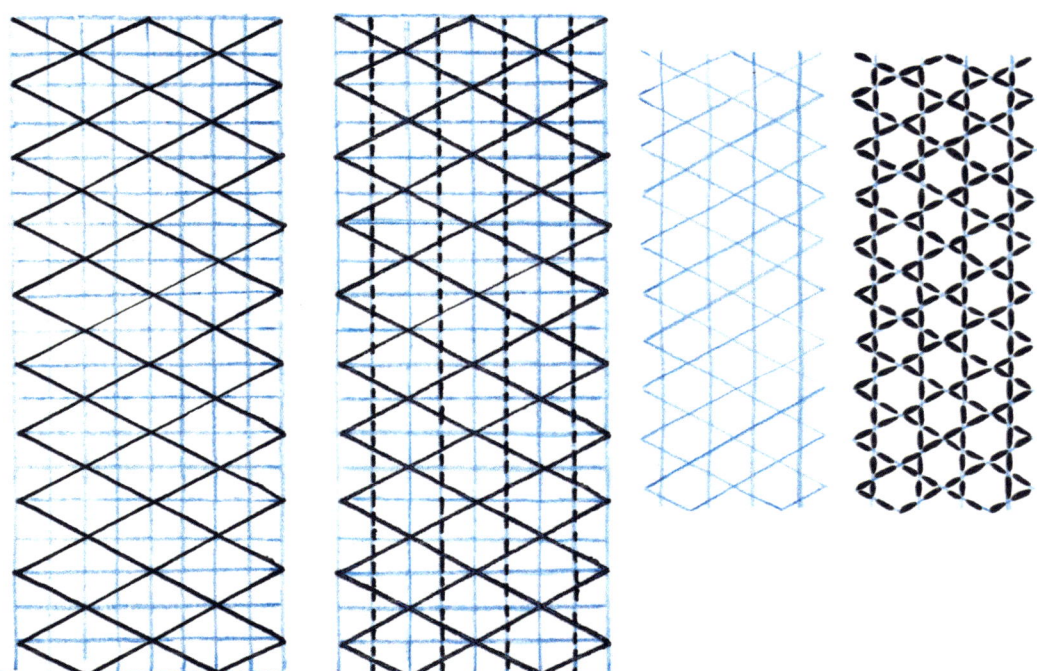

ADVANCED HITOMEZASHI PATTERNS

When you look at old garments from pre-industrial Japan you find an abundance of hitomezashi patterns, and in modern times even more have been invented: a search on the internet won't leave you disappointed. Here are two examples of typical older patterns.

KAGOME, WOVEN BAMBOO PATTERN

The kagome pattern breaks the rule that the stitches should have a gap between them as long as the stitches themselves. Instead, you bring the needle up only a millimetre (about the thickness of a fabric thread) from where you inserted it, which results in a very small gap before the next stitch. The pattern resembles a coarsely woven bamboo basket and is built up of vertical rows that meet two diagonal rows.

METHOD

The basic structure for the kagome pattern is built on rhombuses. Draw them out on a squared paper if you want them to be the exact same size!

The star shape will appear by adding two vertical lines.

The pattern will look nice if you place the gap between the stitches exactly where the lines meet.

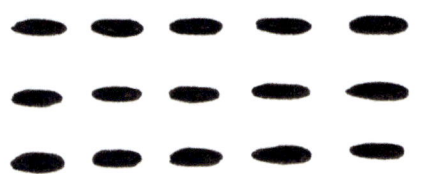

PARALLEL STITCH ROWS

OFFSET STITCH ROWS

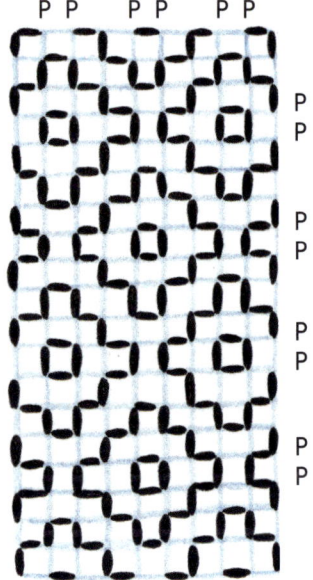

KAKI NO HANA

KAKI NO HANA

This pattern resembles a persimmon flower and is built on the same basic principle as the little squares (see page 23), but instead of sewing all vertical stitches in parallel rows, you sew two rows of stitches with offset stitches before the next parallel row.

The trick to working out how this type of pattern is built up is to figure out which stitch rows are parallel and which ones are offset in both the vertical and horizontal stitch layers! It can sound complicated but it really isn't. In the chart, the parallel rows are marked with a 'P' and all other rows are offset.

The incredible thing with this pattern is that it changes character depending on how many offset rows of stitches you place between the rows of parallel stitches, and this is fun to experiment with! The more offset rows, the more 'rings' around the centre of the flower you will get, and if you just place one single parallel row, surrounded by offset stitches you will get one single enormous flower.

MOYOZASHI

Moyozashi is the version of sashiko that most closely resembles western embroidery. In this technique you sew stitches in lines that together form a pattern, and it's very common to draw out the pattern onto the fabric before you start sewing. You can use multiple moyozashi patterns for the same garment, or let one pattern cover the whole surface. Moyozashi has also been used for embroidering single designs, such as family crests or other symbols.

In some villages where moyozashi was used, it was extremely important that the stitches didn't touch or cross over each other, and in other places it wasn't important at all. You can work this out from looking at the old textiles.

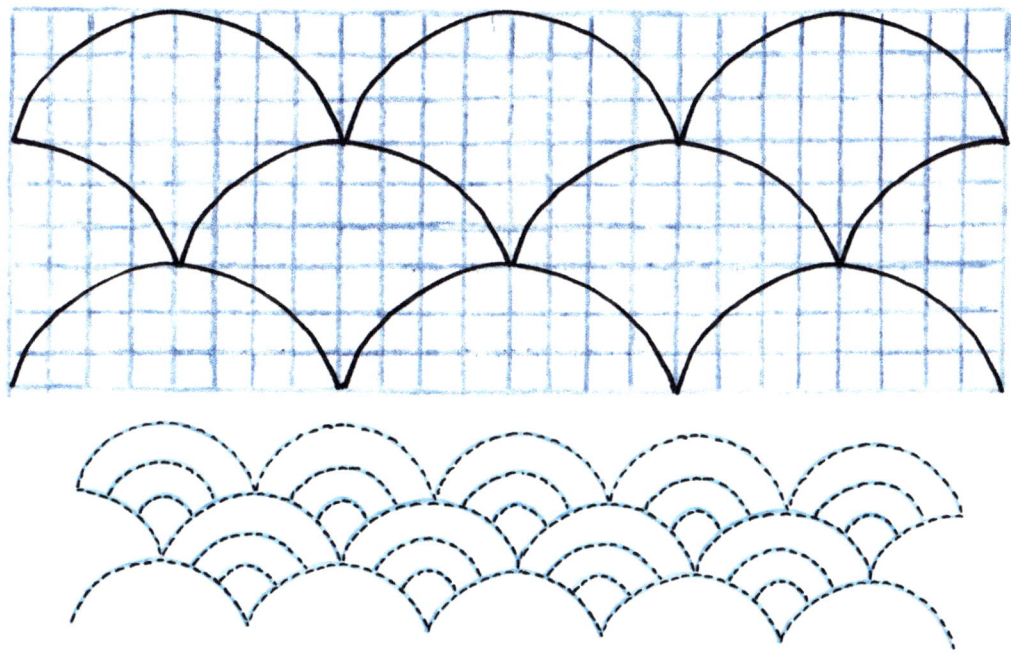

SEIGAIHA-MON

This rolling pattern depicts the movement waves make on the surface of water. It's fairly simple in its construction, and in its purest form it is built on semicircles that are placed on top of each other. You can sew more, smaller semicircles inside of the first ones if you want a denser pattern.

METHOD

For this example, one basic shape is three squares high and eight squares across. It makes the semicircle slightly flattened, and the pattern gets a more fluid appearance than if you were to draw it over 4 x 8 squares. But you can do that as well of course – try it out and see what you like best!

Draw a horizontal row of semicircles. When you are ready to start with the second row, you offset it against the first row. If you think it's difficult to draw even circles, you can use a circular object or cut out a template from card that you can then draw around.

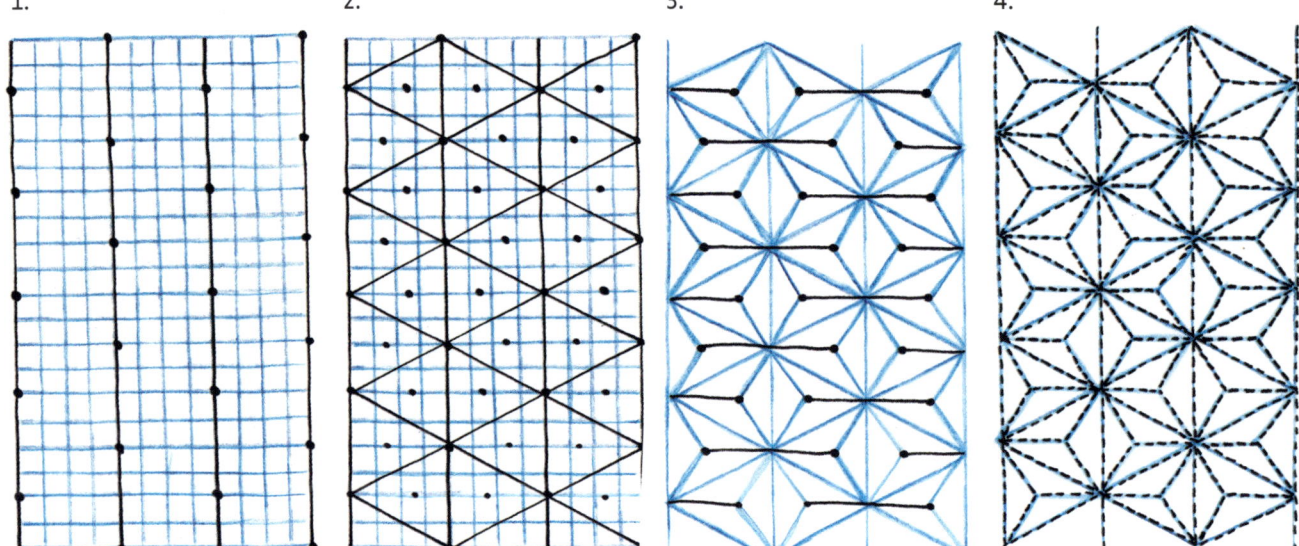

1. 2. 3. 4.

ASANOHA

The hemp plant is very important in Japanese society, since its fibres are very useful for making clothes. 'Asanoha' means hemp leaf, and the pattern is often used for children's clothes with the intention that the children should grow just as strong and fast as the hemp.

METHOD

Start by deciding on a standard measurement (from now on abbreviated to 'SM') which will define how large a hemp leaf will be. A leaf is made up of 2 SM and it is convenient if you choose an even number! Here, SM is 4 squares.

Draw out vertical lines with 1 SM gap in between each one. Then draw out dots along the lines. The dots will become junctions for the lines of the leaves, and they should sit with 1 SM gap in between. Place the dotted lines offset to each other. (1)

Join the dots with diagonal lines and then draw a dot in the middle of each triangle. (2)

The basic shape for this pattern is an isosceles triangle, and you should now draw a straight line from the dot in the middle of the triangle to the triangle's pointiest angle (black line). (3) Then you can draw another two lines from the middle dot out to the triangle's other corners (blue lines). This forms the shape of the leaves.

When you are sewing asanoha, you can either take care to make sure the stitches never meet in the middle of the leaf shape, or you can decide not to worry about whether the stitches cross over or not. It will look great regardless. (4)

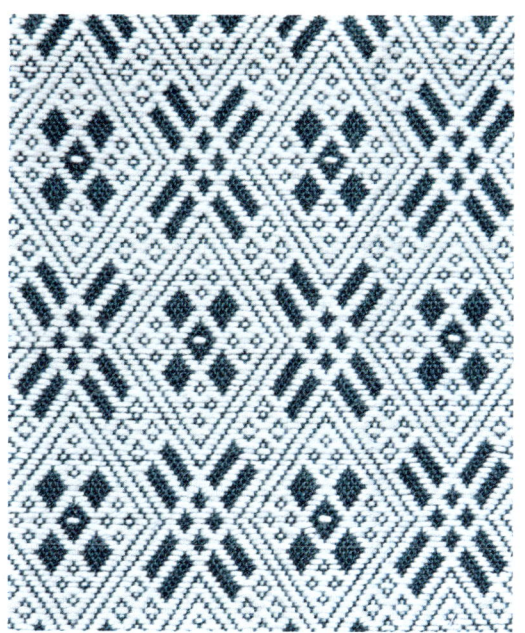

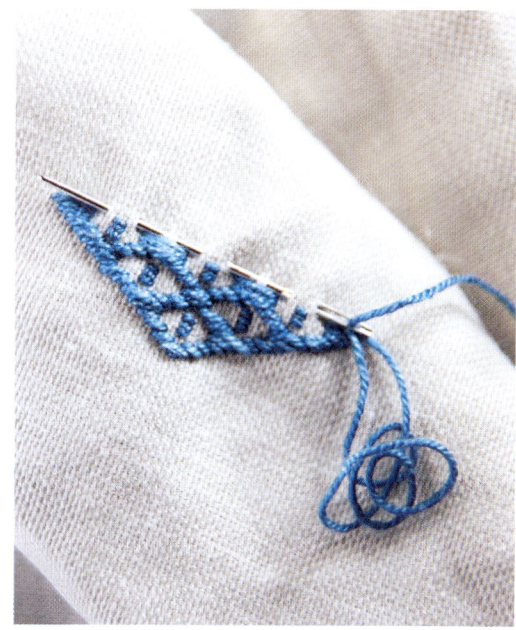

KOGIN-ZASHI

Kogin-zashi is sewn so densely that you might think the pattern is woven, but in reality it's sewn with cotton thread onto a fabric that is so sparsely woven that you can count the threads in it.

Traditionally, the technique was used to reinforce the parts of a work garment that are exposed to a lot of wear and where you might need a little extra padding, for example over the back and shoulders.

This is actually a very simple technique, but it requires a high level of meticulousness. Here all stitches run in the same direction, sewn in horizontal lines, and you continuously count the threads of the base fabric to know where to insert and bring up the needle. You could say you work in a similar way to a digital printer!

On the older garments that have been preserved, kogin-zashi covers large areas; you almost feel dizzy when you consider that someone sat down to sew the intricate patterns in a little village in the 19th century. But they did.

Today it's not very common that those who do sashiko sew whole garments covered in kogin-zashi. Instead you often see that people isolate single pattern designs and sew them as little freestanding decorations onto fabric-covered buttons, small bags or other smaller textile objects. We haven't included any mending using kogin-zashi in this book, but the technique is still definitely worth mentioning.

TIP! Kogin-zashi has a sister technique that is called hishizashi that is sewn densely together with colourful wool yarn in small repetitive patterns. It's well worth an internet search!

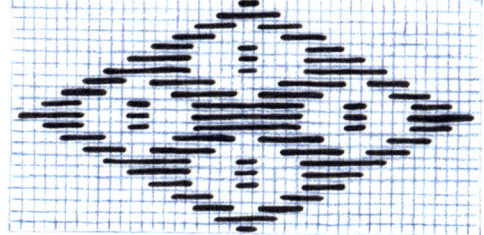

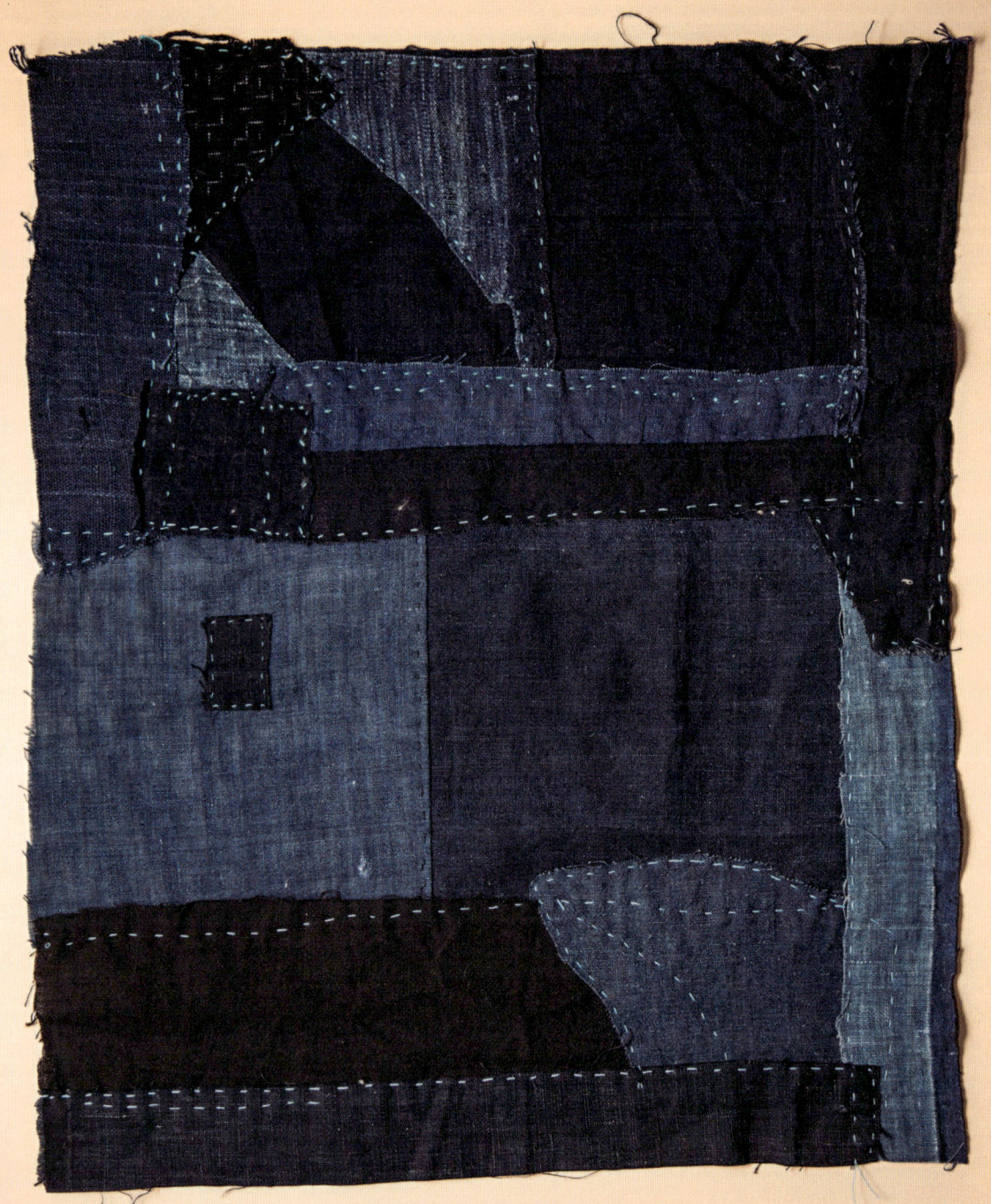

SASHIKO DIARY ENTRY, 20.03.2021
'Indigo fabrics that have worn unevenly into different hues become a composition of ageing.
It's not only pieces of fabric that cross over each other, but also different times that meet!'

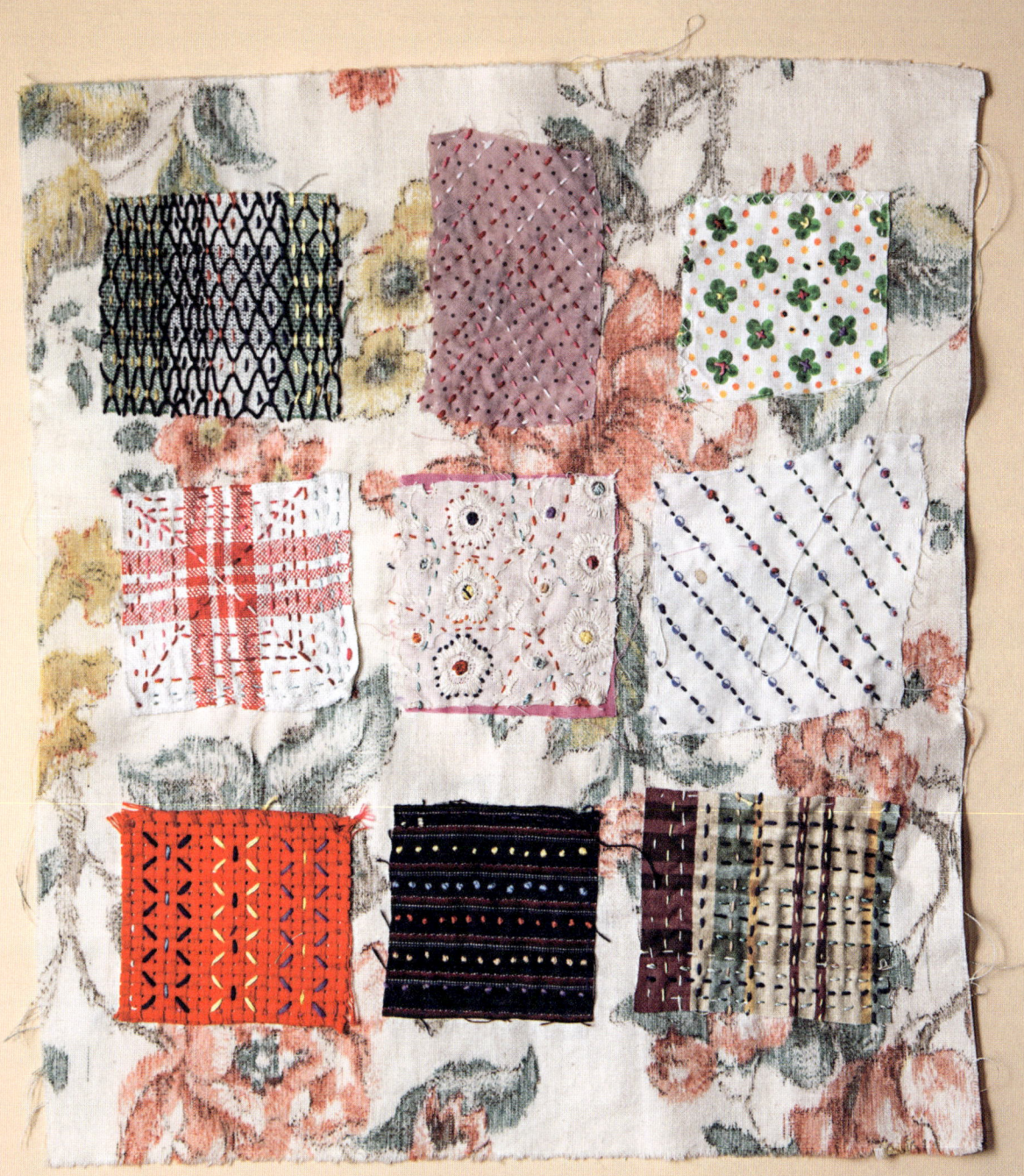

SASHIKO DIARY ENTRY, 17.08.2021
'I sewed this in preparation for a sashiko workshop to show the students.
Now it's important for me as well, as I often go back to it for inspiration.'

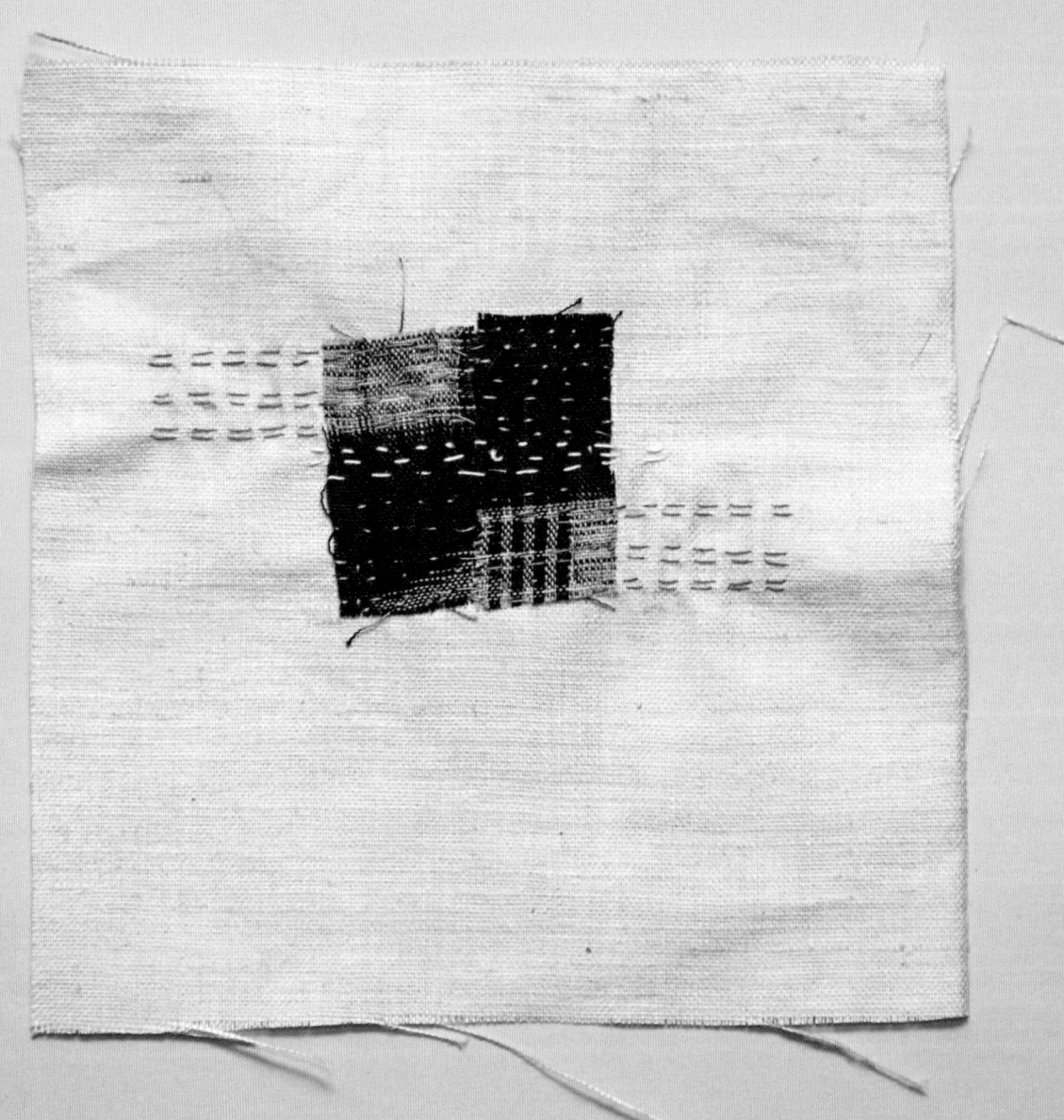

SASHIKO DIARY ENTRY, 30.06.2023
'A 15-minute sketch. You don't need to cover the whole area with stitches to get a nice result!'

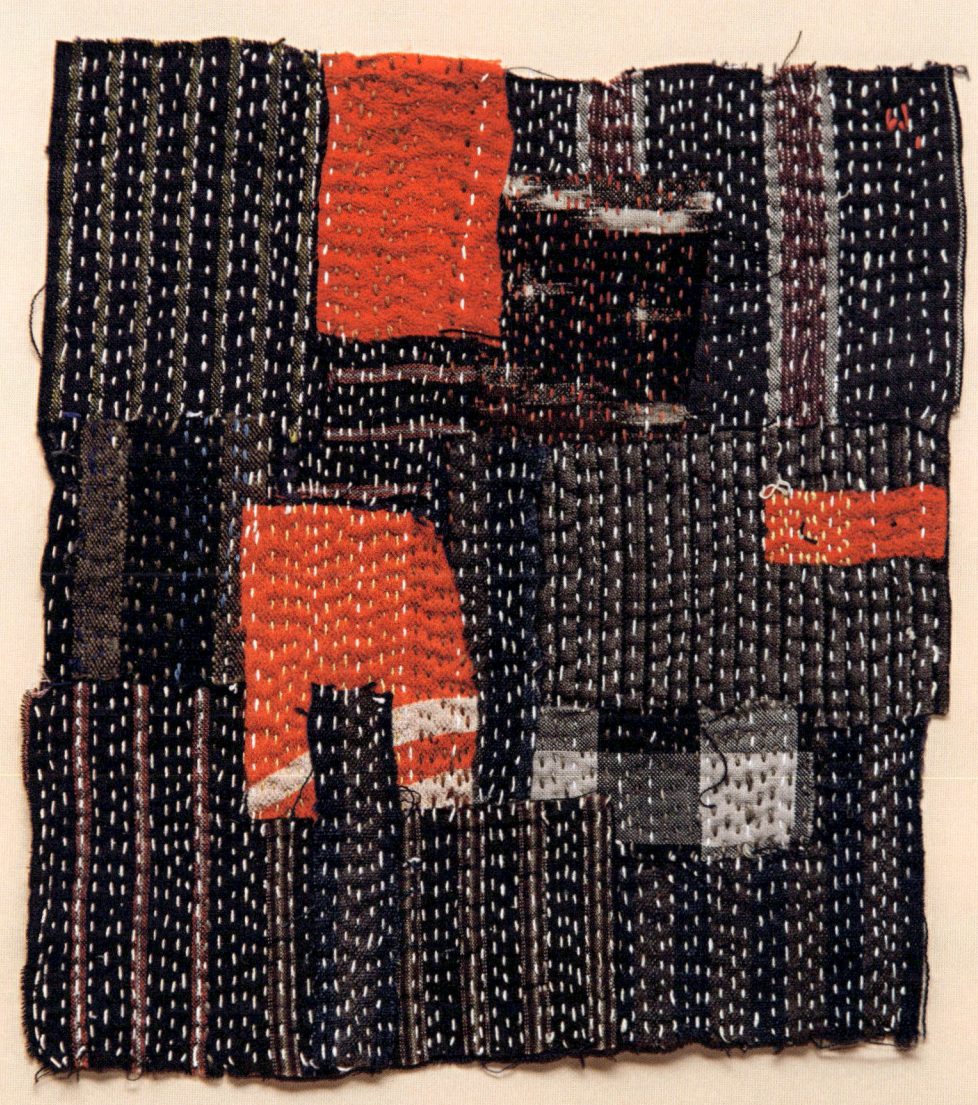

SASHIKO DIARY ENTRY, 25.12.2023
'When I travel to teach budo, I can sew on a patch for several days.
This came with me to Hamburg, Copenhagen and Budapest, but when I came home I realized
something was missing and added the red pieces. Then it was finished.'

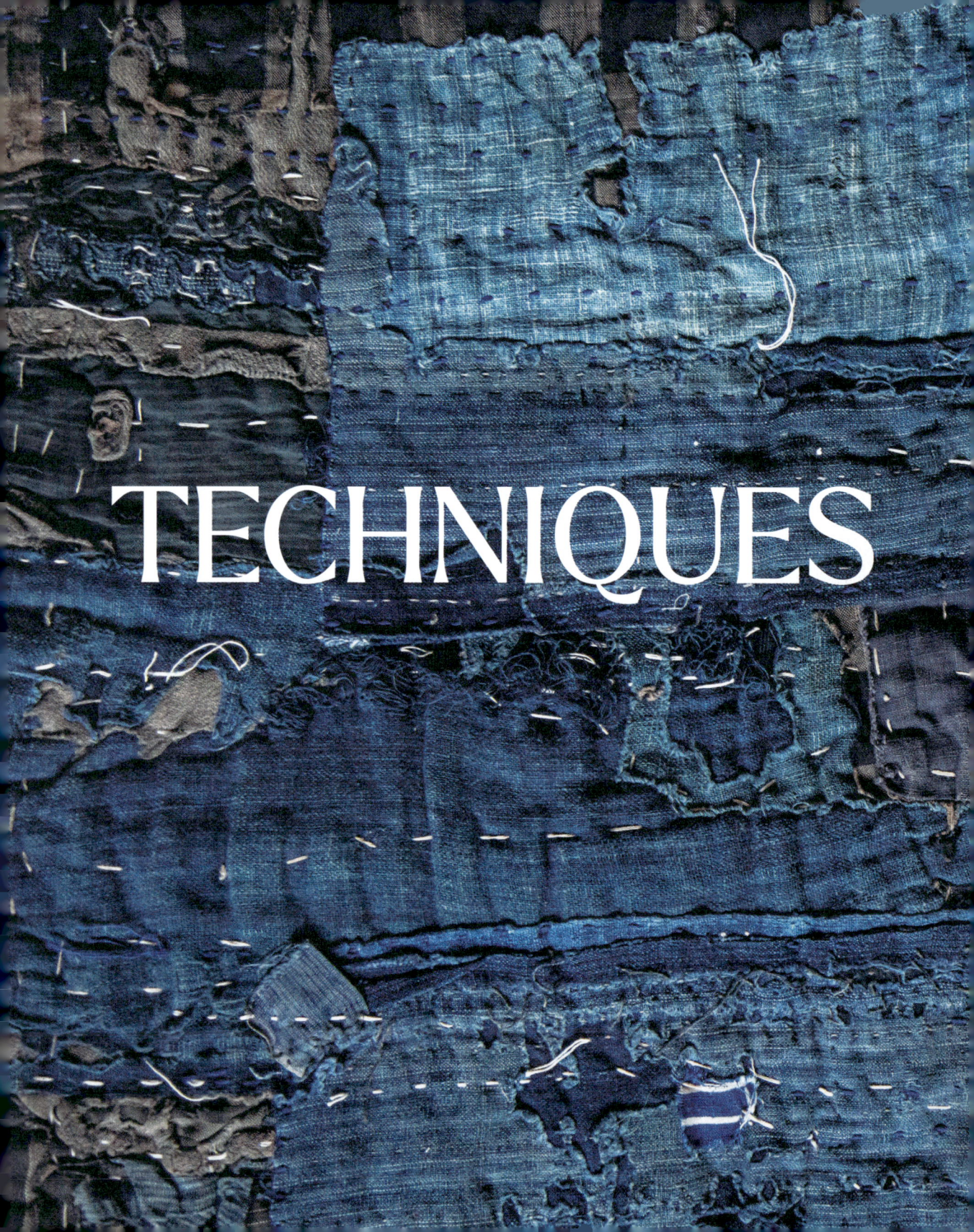

TECHNIQUES

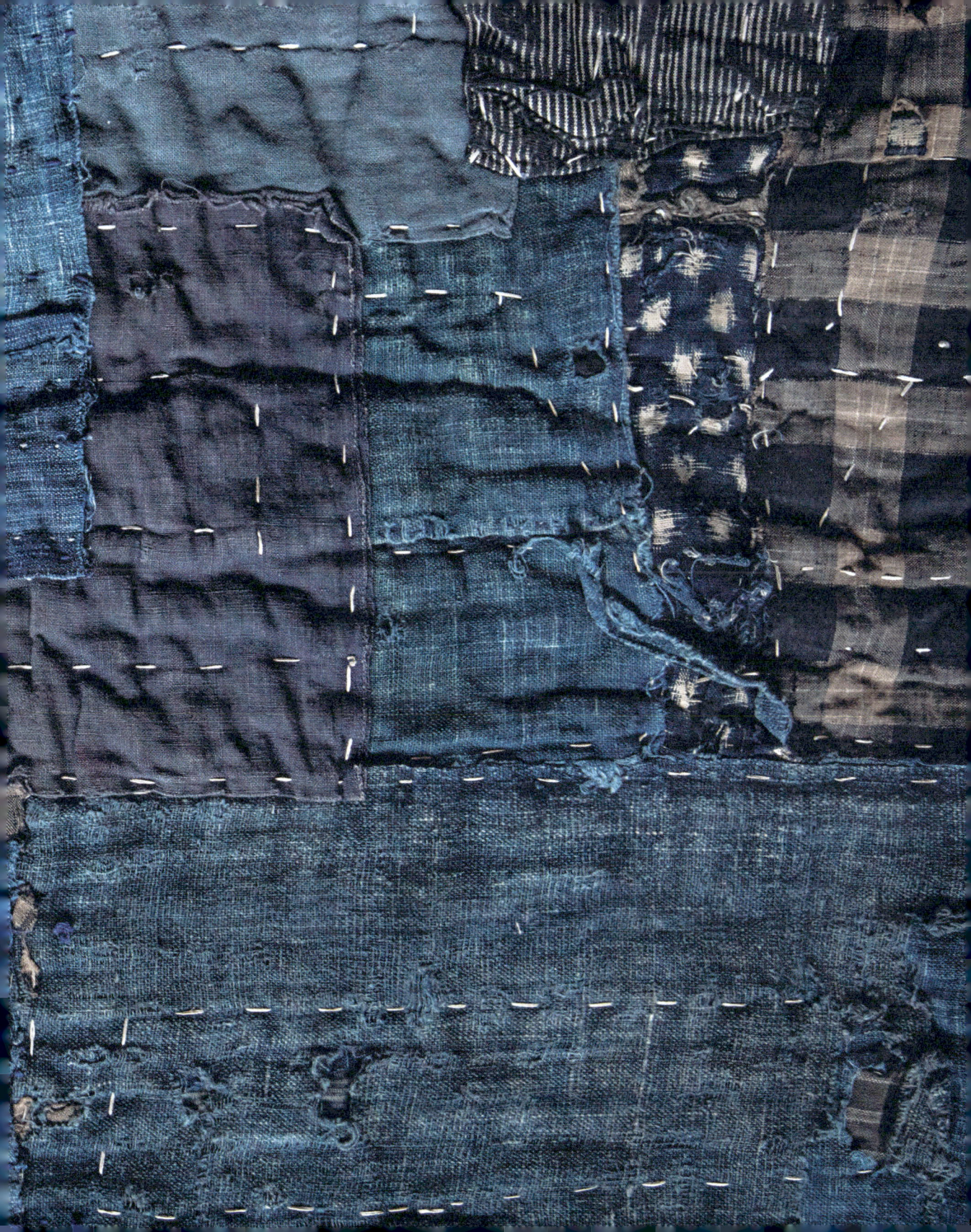

MENDING CLOTHES WITH SASHIKO

When we mend clothes with sashiko you can say that we combine both boro, which is the patching up of the clothes, and sashiko, which is the geometrically arranged stitches. There are a few tips and tricks that make the mending easier, and this chapter contains our best tricks for achieving neat and durable mending!

TOOLS

The sashiko tradition is born out of folk culture and a use-what-you-have mentality. It means that from the beginning, there weren't any specific sashiko needles, sashiko threads or similar, which we think is rather good. This means you won't need a pair of scissors that look exactly like Momi's, even if they're pretty. You can actually use any pair of scissors. Momi's mending box contains:

SCISSORS

PINS

SEWING NEEDLES: with large eyes, so the thread fits through.

THREAD: sewing thread, specially imported sashiko thread and a hank of flea-market yarn. All are welcome in the sewing kit.

JAPANESE RING THIMBLE AND THIMBLE: see how they're used on page 45! You can also cut one out yourself from a piece of leather.

WHAT'S THE DAMAGE?

Holes on clothes usually appear for a couple of different reasons: either from long-lasting wear and tear or because you got stuck on something so the fabric was ripped apart. In the latter case, the damage is limited to the rip itself, but if the hole appeared because the fabric has been worn down and eventually torn, you might have to mend a much larger area than just the hole itself. In this case, you will also need to reinforce the area around it that has become worn thin.

If you are unsure whether a garment is worn thin or not you can hold it up against a light source and check whether it shines through anywhere. Wherever you see the light the strongest, the fabric will be thinner!

A good rule of thumb is that a mending patch should be between one and two centimetres (⅜–¾in) bigger than the hole and the worn-down area around it. This way you can be sure that the edges of the patch are sewn onto undamaged fabric, and then you won't get a hole right next to the patch as soon as you have finished mending and started to wear the garment again.

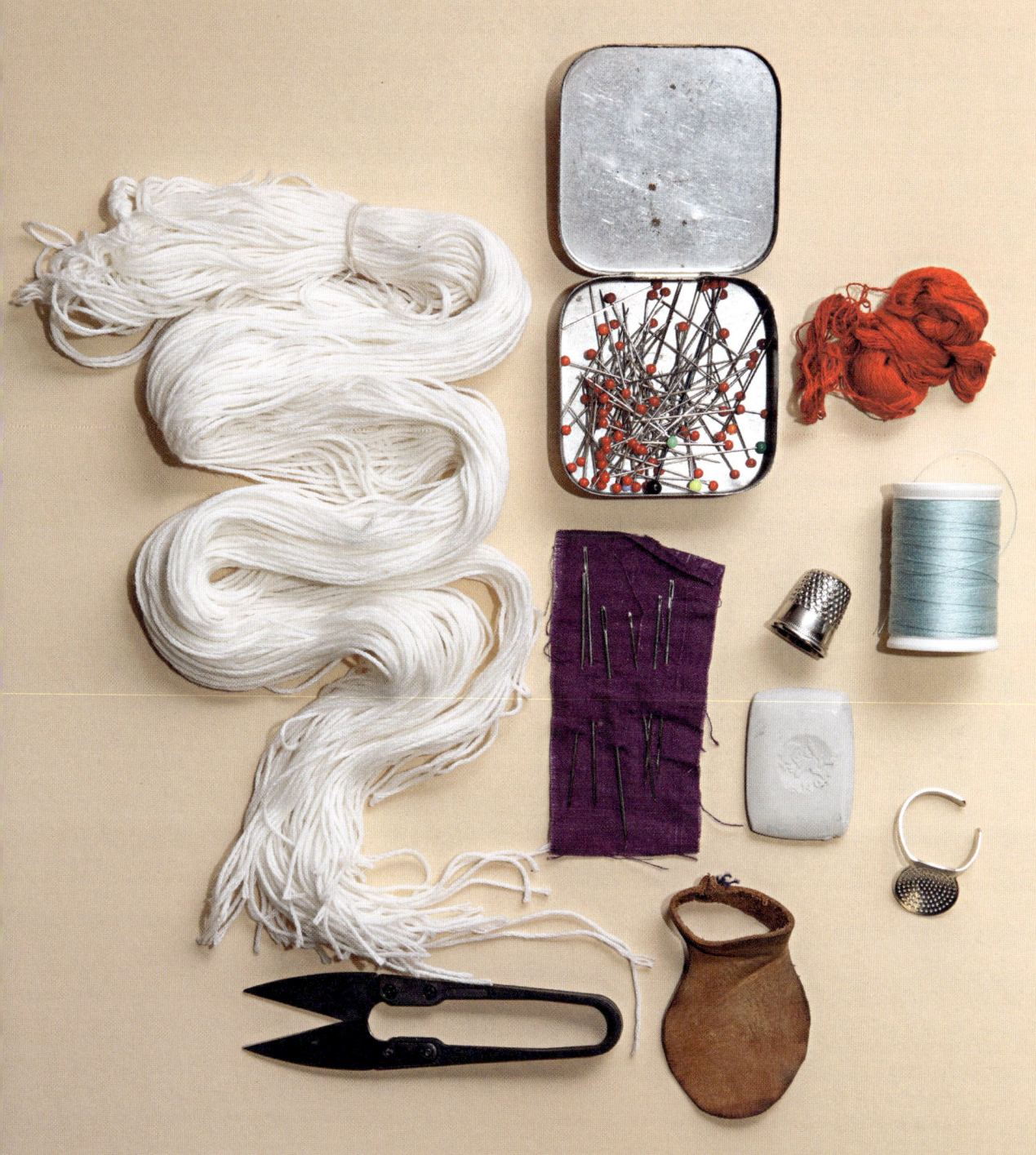

'A good rule of thumb is that a mending patch should be between one and two centimetres (⅜-¾in) bigger than the hole and the worn-down area around it.'

MEND WITH THE SAME MATERIAL

Are you unsure what material you should use for your mending? A good rule of thumb is to mend with the same type of fabric that the garment is made from and to never use thicker or heavier fabric than the garment fabric either. If you don't know which material the garment is made from you can do a simple burn test. Remove a small amount of fibre from the damaged part and set it alight. The way it burns and how the smoke smells will tell you what fibres you've got on your hands!

WOOL: goes out quickly, smells like burnt hair.
COTTON: doesn't go out, smells like burnt paper.
VISCOSE: can look like silk, doesn't go out, smells like burnt paper.
LINEN: doesn't go out, smells like burnt grass.
POLYESTER AND ACRYLICS: don't go out, smell like burnt plastic.
SILK: goes out quickly, smells like burnt hair with a meaty note.

If you can't be bothered to do a burn test and just want a few simple guidelines, here are some:
Don't use wool for mending unless the garment is made from wool, since the mended area can shrink in the wash otherwise.
Don't mend with fabric that is thicker than the garment's fabric, or the mended area will become thick and bulky.

ARE SYNTHETIC MATERIALS BAD BY DEFINITION?

It's easy to think that fabric and thread that are made from plastic automatically are worse than using a natural fibre, regardless of the situation, but Momi doesn't agree. 'What already exists should be used: if I am buying something new, I will pick a natural material but if I have a piece of polyester, I won't throw it away just because it's made out of plastic!'

Even if we both love natural materials, it's a fact that synthetic materials are usually more durable. And as Momi says, if it already exists, we should use it! The damage of producing textiles from crude oil is already done, and it won't help anyone that you avoid using a piece of fabric just because it happens to be made from polyester. Instead, think about how you can maximize it! Perhaps it's good for adding to a jacket that gets holes from your backpack rubbing against it?

WHAT IS WORTH MENDING?

Sometimes we hear that garments haven't cost a lot and aren't worth mending, since the investment it takes to replace the garment isn't very big. But there are many arguments for mending your clothes, regardless of how much you spent on them!

The textile industry is incredibly straining on the environment. Paradoxically, it's usually the cheapest clothes that affect our environment and the people who produce them the most, not just because of how many chemicals are released into the environment during production, but also the extremely poor working conditions and the transportation of them that in turn generates exhaust fumes. So if you've bought a batch of cheap socks, there is a good case for mending them a few times before they're thrown away.

Perhaps you like this garment in particular! It might be your most comfortable, favourite jeans or a jumper that your mum always used to wear on summer nights. Those kinds of garments can't be replaced by buying new ones, but you can mend them if they get damaged so that you can continue using them.

Mending something for yourself can also be a way to be nice to the person you're guaranteed to spend the rest of your life with, yourself.

DO YOU HAVE TO MEND EVERYTHING?

You decide yourself what you think is worth mending and what isn't. A shirt so worn down that the whole fabric feels like paper, and that gets a new hole every time you wear it regardless of how much you mend it, is perhaps not worth struggling on with. Or you do just that and eventually the whole shirt is made out of patches – a new garment is born!

You can also use old worn-out garments for mending other clothes that aren't as damaged. One good example is jeans: they can seem thoroughly worn-out, but the fabric below the knees is usually nice and whole. You can use that for mending other jeans, and the cycle continues.

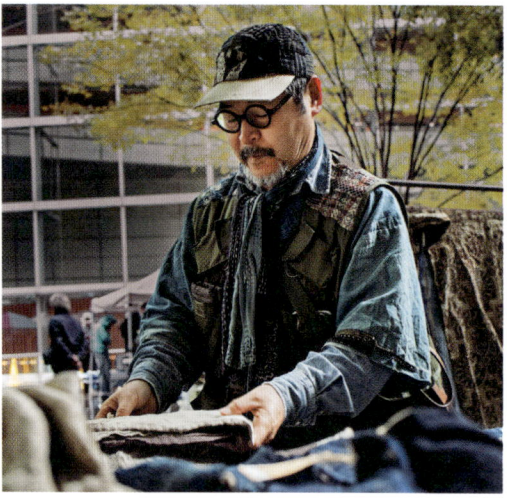

MENDING WITH JAPANESE FABRICS

There's something special about old Japanese cotton fabrics. They are woven from thin threads and often dyed blue with indigo that has become worn to show different hues. Mending where these have been used is often super nice. But how do you even get hold of them and is it really okay to mend your clothes with antique fabrics?

Small pieces of fabric from old cut-up kimonos are called 'hagire', a word that means abandoned fabric scraps. We often use these fabrics for mending our own clothes, and it's easy to find both hagire and old Japanese work clothes such as nogari and other boro garments for sale on the internet. But it's most fun to buy them on location in Japan of course! There are both antique shops that specialize in textiles and pop-up flea markets where textile retailers or members of the public who have had a clear-out can make an appearance.

When you go out on your flea-market hunt it's good to remember to bring cash and that you can often haggle the price down 10–20 per cent if the price of the garment is more than 3000 yen. Being indifferent and demanding will rarely work in Japan, but if you are nice and polite it might work.

ARE YOU REALLY ALLOWED TO DO THAT?

Where does the boundary fall between preserving an object for future generations and it being okay to cut it up and sew it onto your shopping bag? Unfortunately, this question has no easy answer. We think that if there is a lot of material that looks the same and is already preserved in museums and archives, it's okay to use the rest of the material. But even here it's not black and white! We would, for example, not take apart an antique garment unless the garment was so worn down that it was closer to a rag than a garment. On the contrary, opening up a shikimono (see page 131) to check what's hiding in it feels okay. Sure, it can seem odd that it's okay to use the fabric if a rag-and-bone man in Japan has cut open a garment and sold it to us, but it's not okay doing it ourselves, but humans don't always follow logic!

At the end of the day, you have to make your own judgement as to what feels right or wrong. Spare a thought for all the work that has gone into the fabric and remember that a stack of hagire could be an enormous asset in a poor Japanese village.

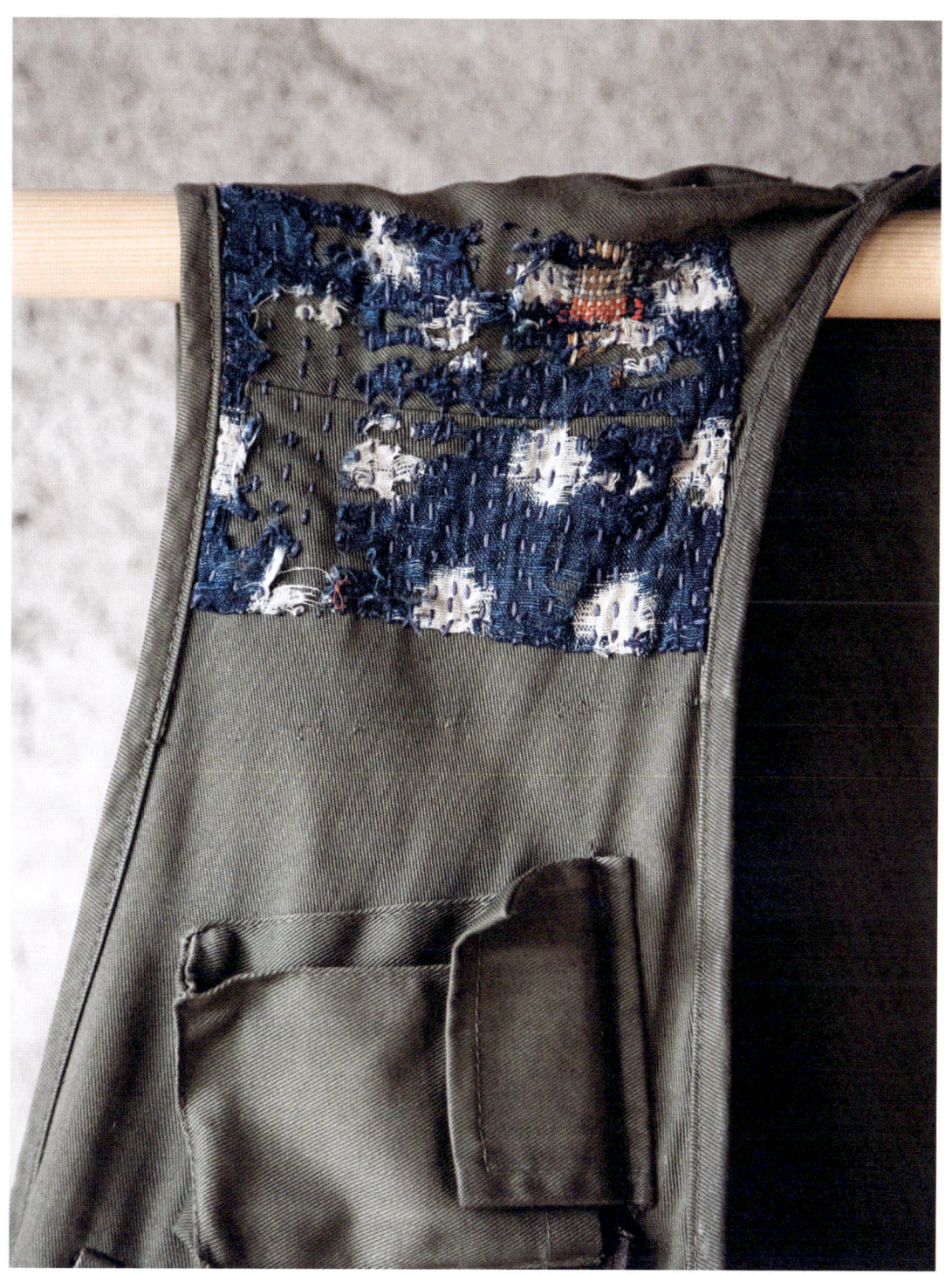

RUNNING STITCH

1.

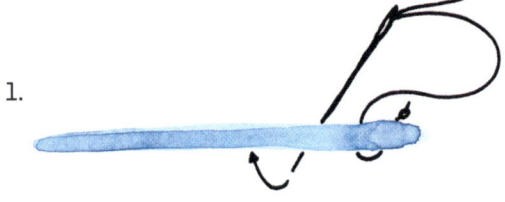

2.

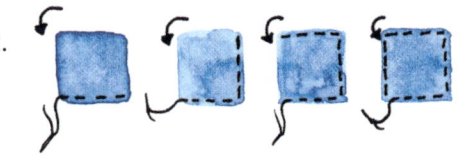

3.

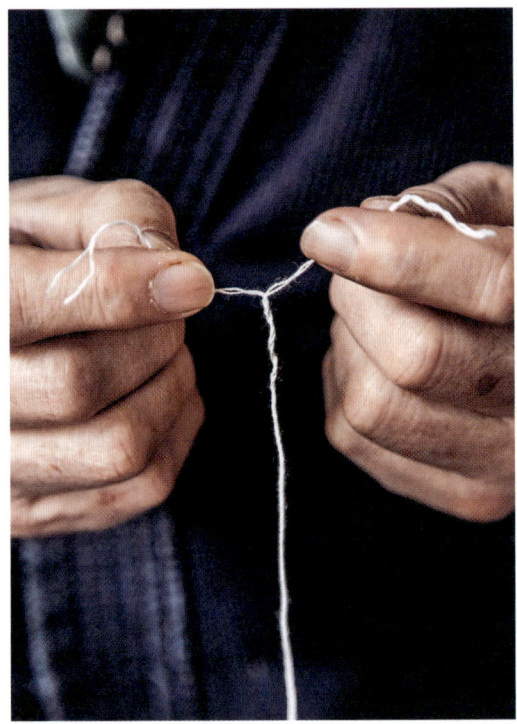

THE STITCHES

The stitches that are used when sewing sashiko are called 'running stitches' in English. It's one of the most common stitches in the whole world and we dare to claim it's also the simplest one to sew! We're talking about straight up-and-down stitches. (1)

If you are right-handed it's most common to sew from right to left, and a good tip is to turn the fabric as you sew instead of starting to sew in all kinds of directions.

If you are sewing a square for example, you don't have to first sew from right to left, then up, then from left to right and down again. Instead, turn the fabric 90 degrees every time you want to change direction, and you can keep your hands in the same position. (2)

Another good tip for keeping the mending soft and flexible is to leave a small loop at the back of the work when you sew sharp corners. (3)

THREAD

Momi uses all kinds of threads for his sashiko. His favourite is rug warp, which you can find cheap at flea markets! He often splits the rug warp to make it a bit thinner and softer for sewing with. Momi also uses Japanese sashiko thread, silk thread and sewing thread. The latter he likes to use double or quadruple.

If a yarn is made from many threads that have been twined together, you can make it thinner by splitting it. Make sure to have at least two threads left in the part you want to use for sewing; single threads will break easily when sewing with them.

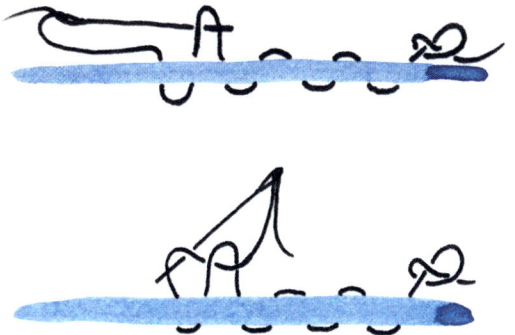

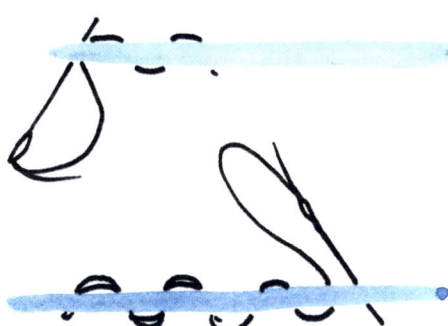

HOW LONG SHOULD THE THREAD BE?

When sewing by hand you usually use a thread that is no longer than your arm.

It can be easy to think that you should use a longer thread so that you don't have to bother with securing it so many times, but threads that are longer than your arm have a tendency to tangle a lot and it will often take more time to untangle it than the time saved from not having to secure the thread so often.

SECURING THE THREAD

The most common way to secure a thread is to first make a knot at one end before you start sewing. Then thread the needle and pull the ends so that the end with the knot is the longest. Insert the needle through the fabric from the back of the work. When you pull the thread through, the end with the knot will stay in place at the back.

When you have sewn so much that you only have around 10cm (4in) of thread left, it's time to secure the end with a knot. Sew once through a stitch at the back of the work to create a loop that you insert the needle through. Pull to form a knot. If you want, you can sew another knot in the same place before you cut the end of the thread.

Sometimes you want to secure the threads without any visible knots. Then you can do the following: start a small distance in front of the place where you intended to start sewing, and 'reverse' back to that point. When you have reached this point you can sew forwards following your own stitches. The thread needs to run double for at least two stitches, and when it does you don't need a knot.

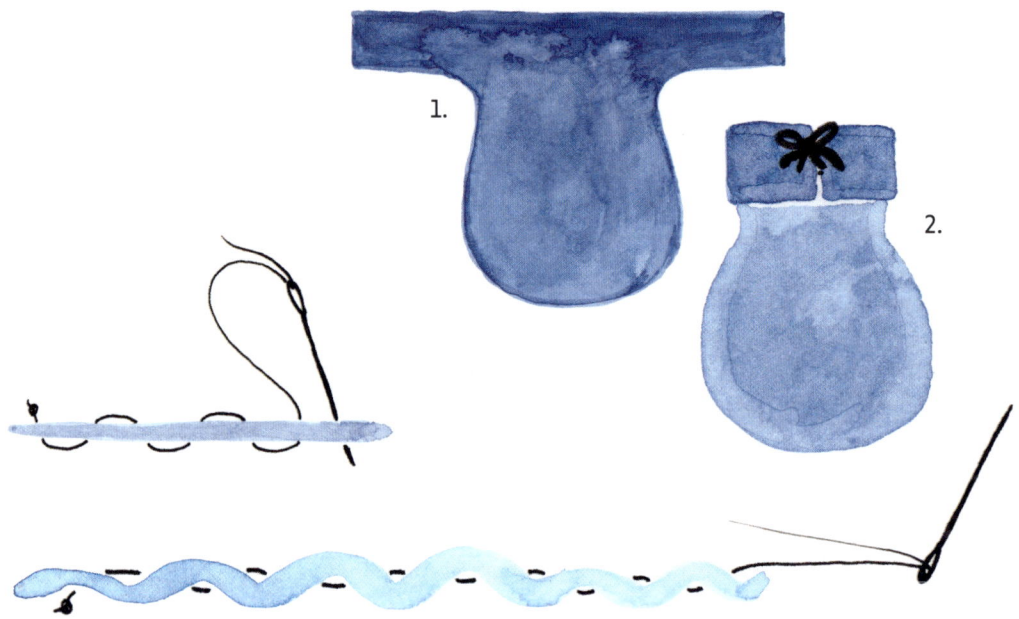

SEWING LOOSE STITCHES

When sewing by hand, and particularly when you mend something, it's easy to think that you need to pull the thread tightly to get a good result but this isn't true. That final little pull might seem solid and reassuring, but try to avoid it! When sewing sashiko it's important not to pull the thread too tightly, since the fabric will start to pucker. You can say that the thread should conform to the fabric, not the fabric to the thread.

The size and density of the stitches will also have an effect on the end result. The more and smaller the stitches you sew, the firmer the mended surface will be. If you place a patch on a garment that isn't just worn thin but also has a hole in it, the patch should also cover the area that's worn thin by a few centimetres (about ¼in). Then, when you sew, you can choose to place stitches more sparsely over the area where the patch extends over the worn fabric, but on the part that covers the hole you can sew smaller and denser stitches to compensate for it only being a single layer of fabric there.

THIMBLES & RING THIMBLES

There are many ways to hold a sewing needle depending on what you're sewing, but regardless of how you hold it, pushing the needle through fabric can mean that your hand becomes sore after a while! It's mainly the part of the hand that pushes the needle through the fabric that is at risk, and therefore different thimbles and thimble rings have been developed in different parts of the world.

In Japan it's common to have a ring thimble with a plate that is placed at the base of the middle finger. The needle is supported against the plate and is gripped with the index finger and the thumb while you sew with a movement that includes pushing the fabric onto the needle with the left hand (if you are right-handed).

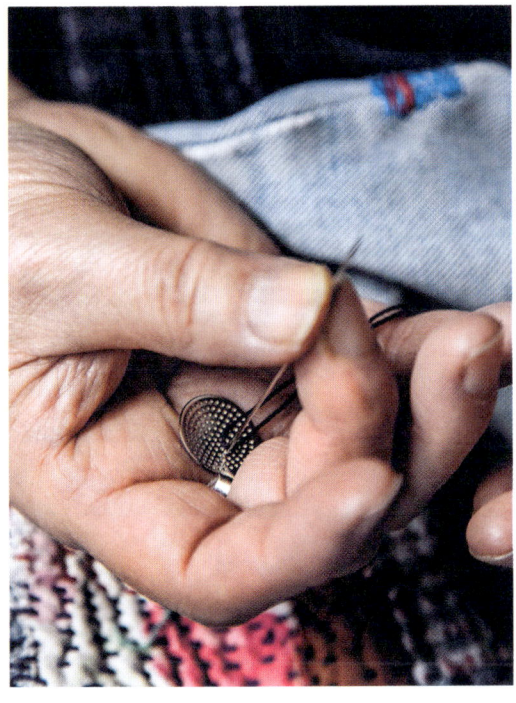

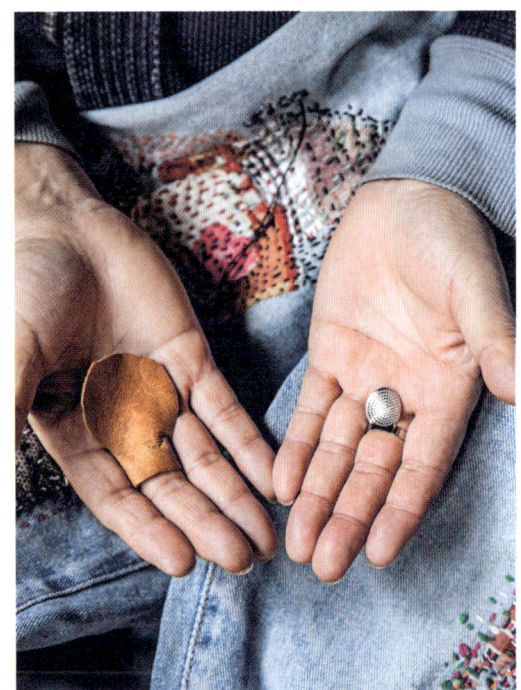

In Europe, thimbles placed on the tip of the middle finger are more common. You hold the needle with the thumb and the index finger, and when sewing you push the needle with the side of the middle finger that is protected with the thimble.

There aren't any rules that you have to use a thimble if you think it's awkward, but when your hands start feeling sore and you want to continue sewing, it can be worth a try.

1. The Japanese ring thimble forms a support for the back tip of the needle.
2. It's possible to make your own ring thimble from a piece of leather.
3. The European thimble is placed on the middle finger and can then be used to push the needle through the fabric.

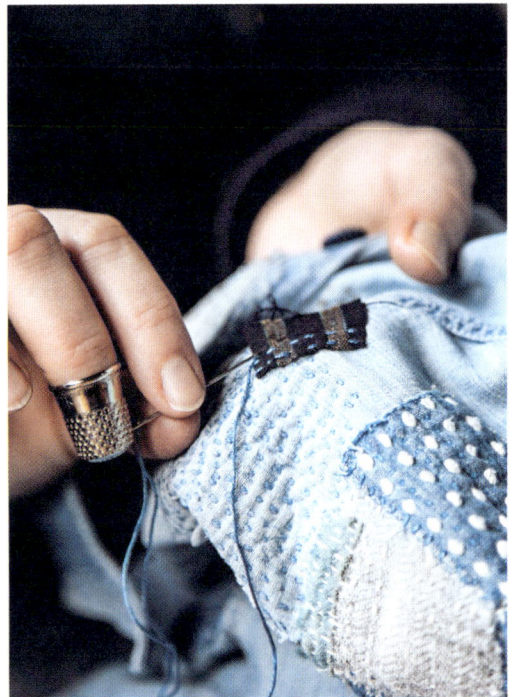

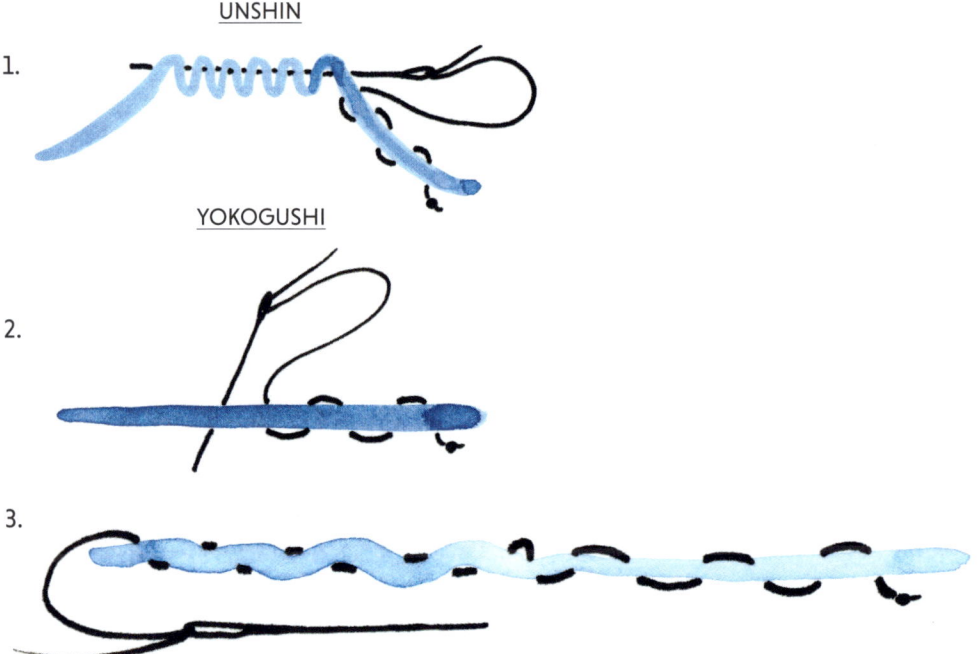

UNSHIN

1.

YOKOGUSHI

2.

3.

ONE OR SEVERAL STITCHES

Sewing sashiko takes time, but there are tricks to speed it up. Momi often uses the unshin technique (1) which involves threading several stitches onto the needle before you pull it through the fabric. It's a lot quicker than sewing yokogushi (2) which involves inserting the needle through the fabric (from the front to the back or the other way around) and pulling through the needle and thread before you make the next stitch.

Unshin is quicker, but there is a chance that the stitching will pucker the fabric. You won't notice it straight away, but after you've worked a while, you'll see that the fabric is wavy and puckered. Avoid this problem by leaving a small loop of the thread as you pull the needle through. The extra length will spread across the thread and will prevent the work from puckering. (3)

With yokogushi it's possible to make very small and dense stitches. The technique is suitable for thick fabrics or when you sew through many layers. It's easier to control how tightly you pull each stitch and the technique is better suited for beginners.

SEWING PATTERNS WITHOUT A RULER

There are many contemporary sashiko practitioners who rely fully on fabrics with drawn-on patterns. There are even fabrics on which each stitch has been printed so you only have to fill in the pattern with thread! These are good tools if you want to sew a completely perfect pattern. We avoid pre-printed patterns when possible however. It just feels very far removed from the original Japanese tradition to draw on the fabric with washable textile pens; drawing intricate patterns with chalk is bound to end in disappointment (the chalk will get rubbed off if you handle the fabric too much) and those pre-printed fabrics with exact stitches give a result that doesn't feel particularly lively.

So how should you go about achieving those exactly equal-length stitches when sewing hitomezashi, or embroidering intricate moyozashi patterns?

Sewing by hand involves a lot of muscle memory. A bit like learning how to walk: in the

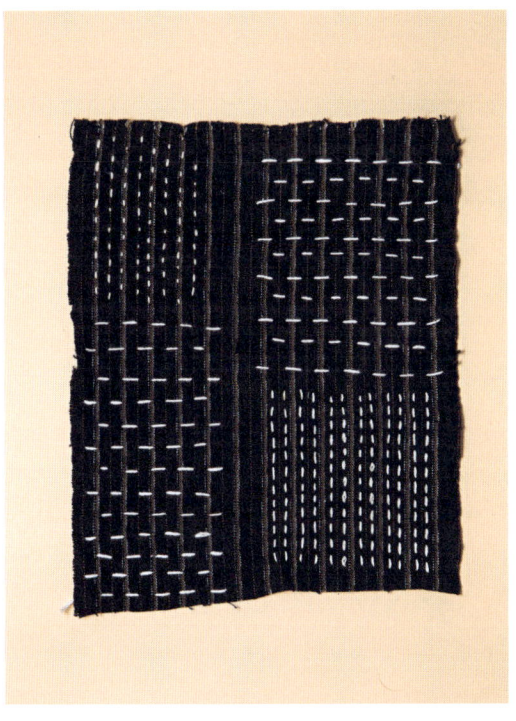

1.

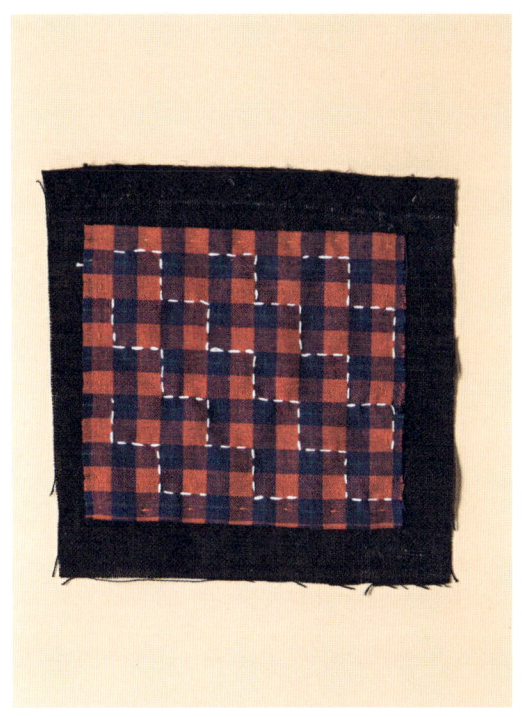

2.

3.

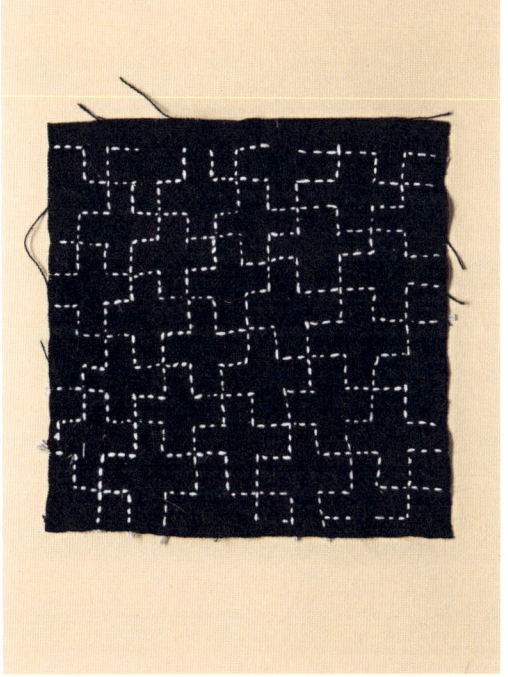

beginning all steps are a different length, you lose momentum, sway to one side ... but you practice and practice and eventually you stop focusing on the act of walking. The muscle memory becomes activated, and after a while you don't need to think all about how long your steps should be.

It's the same with sewing. You can practice making consistent stitches by sewing on checked or striped fabrics, to get the hand's muscles used to the feeling!

1. Striped fabrics offer a good guide for those who want to sew by hand.
2. Checked fabrics offer a lot of possibilities!
3. Momi likes to sew his sashiko without drawing up the pattern. Instead, he counts stitches: three up, three to the right, three up and so on. This pharmacy cross pattern is based on a similar step-like pattern as in picture 2, but with either the horizontal or vertical lines elongated. It is also in two layers, one of which is mirrored.

47

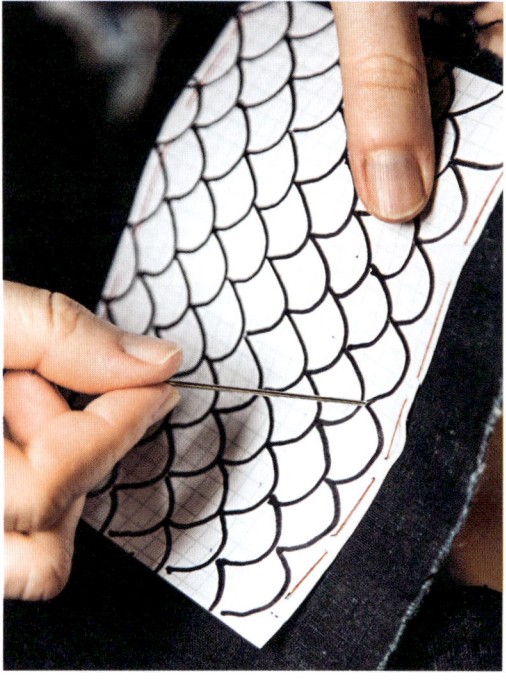

1.

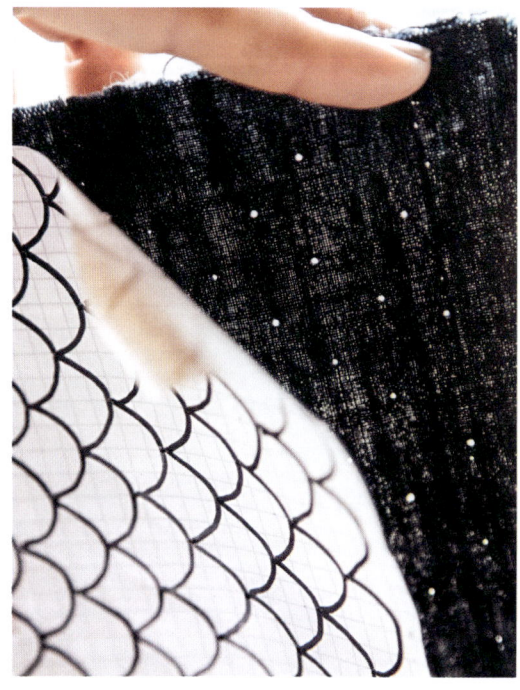

2.

3.

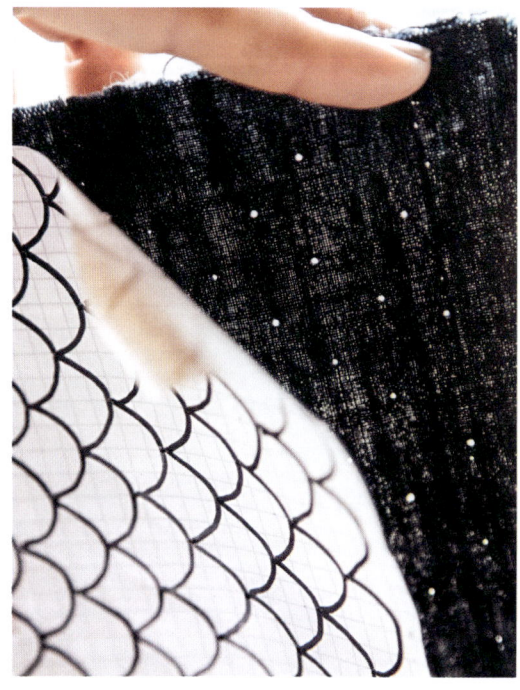

MARKING PATTERNS

Sometimes you do want to mark your pattern on the fabric. A good option is to draw the design onto paper, secure the paper with pins or basting stitches to the fabric in question and then insert a thick needle through the paper where the lines meet, creating small holes in the fabric. These holes are not made out of torn threads, but from threads that have been pushed to one side. This can be good to know if you are worried that the fabric will get damaged! Then you can sew your pattern using the holes as the starting point. This works well for densely woven cotton fabrics.

1. Baste or pin the sketch to the fabric and insert the needle through the paper and fabric at the points where the lines cross each other.
2. Remove the paper and hold the fabric up against a light source and you will see exactly where the holes are.
3. You can draw your pattern with a textile pen/ chalk if you want, or do like Kerstin and sew the pattern freehand with the dots as a guide.

48

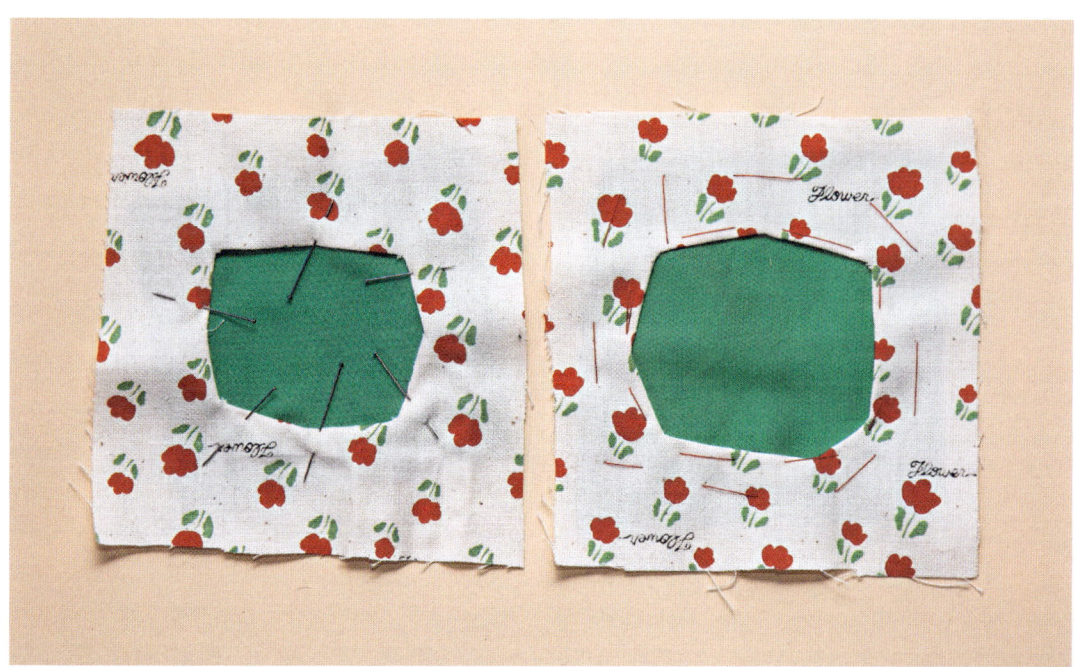

BASTING OR PINNING

When you are sewing on a patch it will need to be kept in place while you're stitching. You can do this with help from your thumb if it's a very small patch, but often it still gets a bit wonky as you work. To avoid this, it's common to attach the patch with pins. Some prefer safety pins instead since they will keep the patch in place on the fabric and you don't risk pricking yourself on them.

Another way to keep things in place is to baste. With this technique you sew the fabric pieces together with long, temporary stitches (1.5–2cm (⅝–¾in) is a good length). Then you sew your 'real' stitches and remove the basting stitches as you sew, or when you're finished with your sashiko.

Baste with large running stitches (the same stitches as for the sashiko itself, but longer) and secure the thread by making two small stitches about 5mm (¼in) long, in the same place.

If you are sewing on a small patch, up to around 5 x 5cm (2 x 2in), basting once around the edges of the patch is enough. If your patch is larger than that, it is a good idea to add a few rows of basting stitches that cover the surface of the patch as well. Alternatively, to help prevent the layers from slipping, you could use diagonal tacking stitches as shown on page 81.

The benefit of basting instead of using pins is that you don't risk pricking yourself while you sew, and it's also more workable than using safety pins. It can feel like a waste of time to sew stitches that you are going to remove, but try it out. Once you're used to it, it will feel much more convenient than fiddling with pins!

THE ART OF SEWING ON A PATCH

When you are new to sewing you often want to zigzag all raw fabric edges to stop them from fraying, but you often don't need to do this when you use fabric patches for mending. On old boro textiles from Japan, we often see that the edges have been left raw and that the mending stitches continue outside of the edge of the patch. This way the threads at the edge are locked into place and won't fray. If you want, you can fold the edges of the fabric under before you sew, so they sit protected inside of the patch when you're finished. Often, it's enough to just fold them and iron them, and they will remain folded, but sometimes you might need to baste the edge into place.

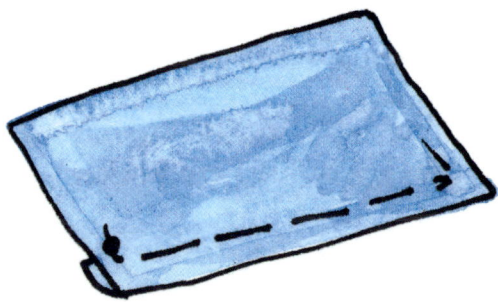

MENDING WITH A PATCH ON THE OUTSIDE

Placing a patch on the outside of a garment is a quick and effective way to mend a hole.

1. Start by choosing a mending patch. It should be larger than the hole itself – somewhere between 1–3cm (⅜–1¼in) is a good margin.
2. Attach the patch with pins, or as here, basting stitches. If the garment you're mending is creased (perhaps it's been waiting in a mending pile for some time) you might need to iron it flat before you attach the patch.
3. Sew the patch in place. If it's a very small patch, say 1–2cm (⅜–¾in) a couple of rows of stitches around the edge of the patch are enough, but if it's larger the mend will be better if you sew stitches all over the patch. They can be placed in a pattern, as shown opposite, or just sit in rows – it doesn't make any difference when it comes to the durability of the patch.
4. At the back of the mend, the edges of the hole will be sewn down by the stitches you cover the patch with. This way, the mend is built up by both the patch and the stitches it's attached with. Here you can see that Momi has sewn the edge of the patch in place with dark thread and then covered the whole patch with white hitomezashi stitches.

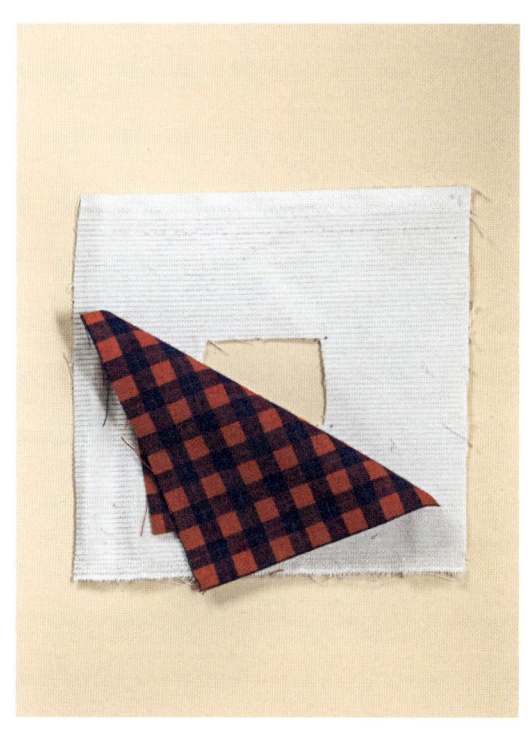

1.

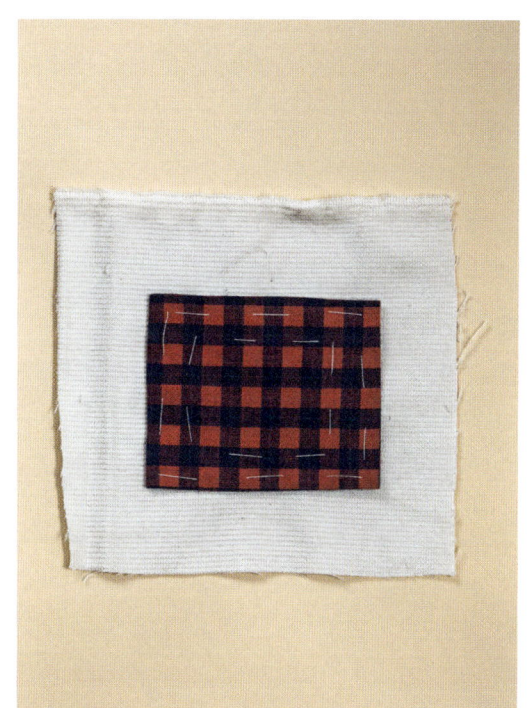

2.

3.

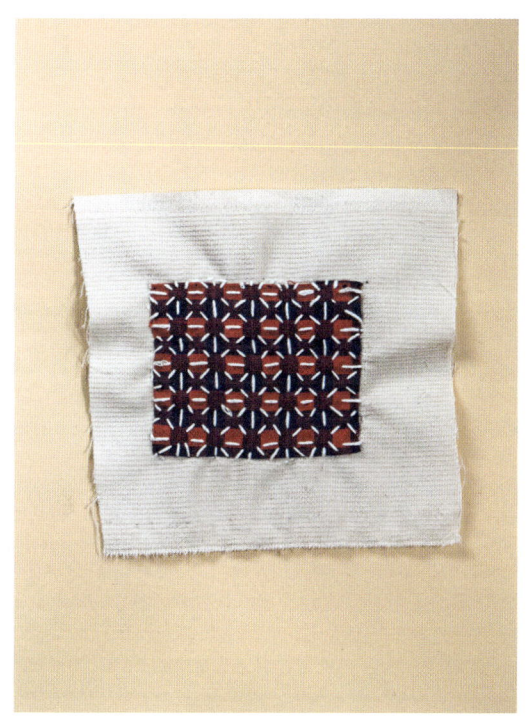

4.

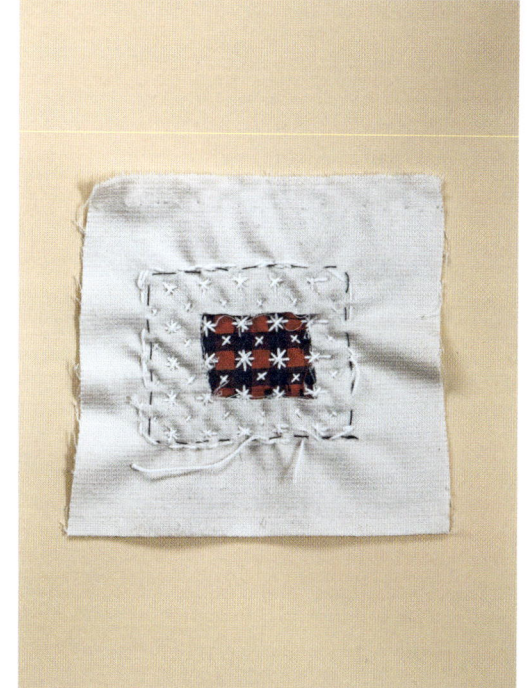

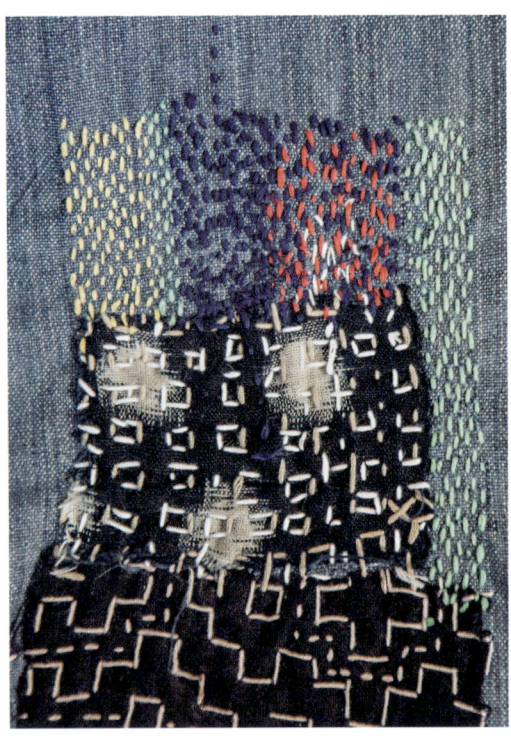

MENDING WITHOUT A PATCH

If the fabric around a hole is worn thin but your patch isn't large enough to cover the whole thin area, a good alternative is to reinforce it with dense stitches.

MENDING WITH A PATCH ON THE INSIDE

Sometimes you might prefer placing your patch on the inside of the garment. The benefit of this is that it will cover less of the surface of the fabric and will therefore not be as visible. Well, if you use a patch in a similar hue to the fabric of the garment that is! On pages 89-90, you will see in a more detailed way how to mend using this technique, where we have used it to mend a hole in a torn cushion cover.

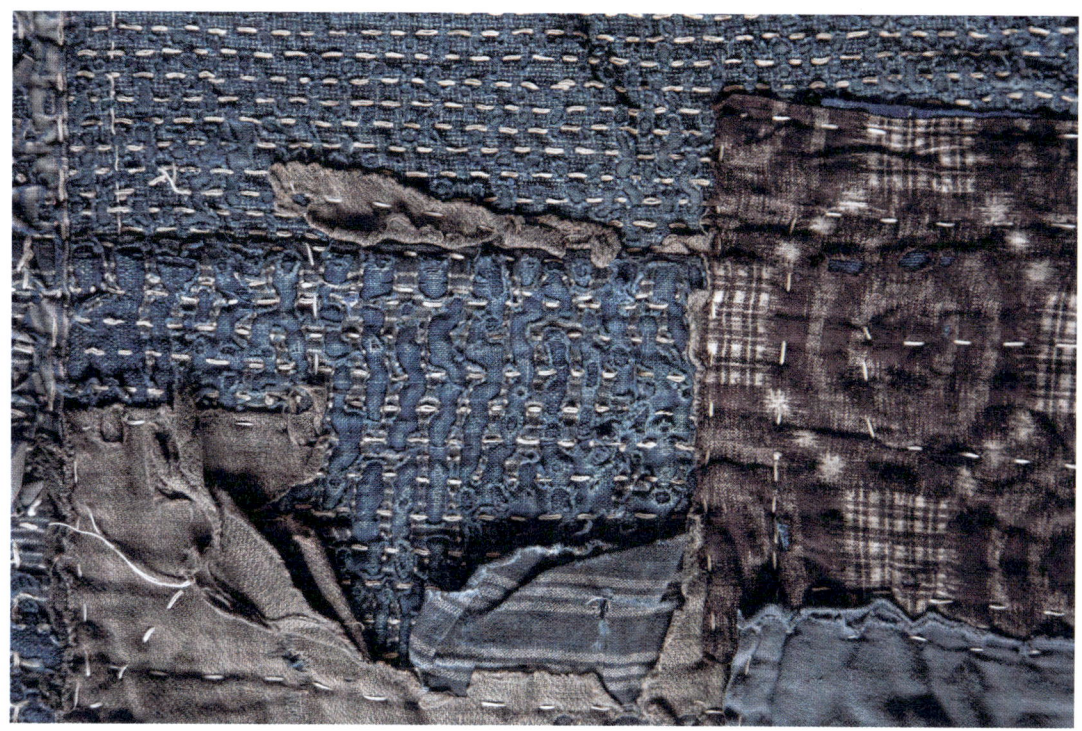

LAYERED MENDING

We often meet newly converted mending enthusiasts who want to start patching garments that aren't damaged, just because it looks nice. And preferably many patches at the same time! You can, of course, do this if you want, but one thing is for sure: that special feeling that boro has is difficult to achieve in one day. If you mend things when needed instead, use the garment and continue to mend it as necessary, the expression will become more varied and natural, since the oldest mending will fade and wear down as you use your clothes.

The same applies when you are choosing fabric for mending: you can't go into a fabric shop and buy ten nice new fabrics, sew them onto each other with sashiko stitches and hope you'll get that lovely feeling. If you don't already have a box with 'nice pieces of fabrics that are good to have' it's time to start collecting them now! In our own stashes are worn clothes, tea towels with monograms, stains and holes, Japanese hagire pieces, scraps from old craft projects and holey socks. Most things can be used for mending – it's just about matching the right patch to the right mend!

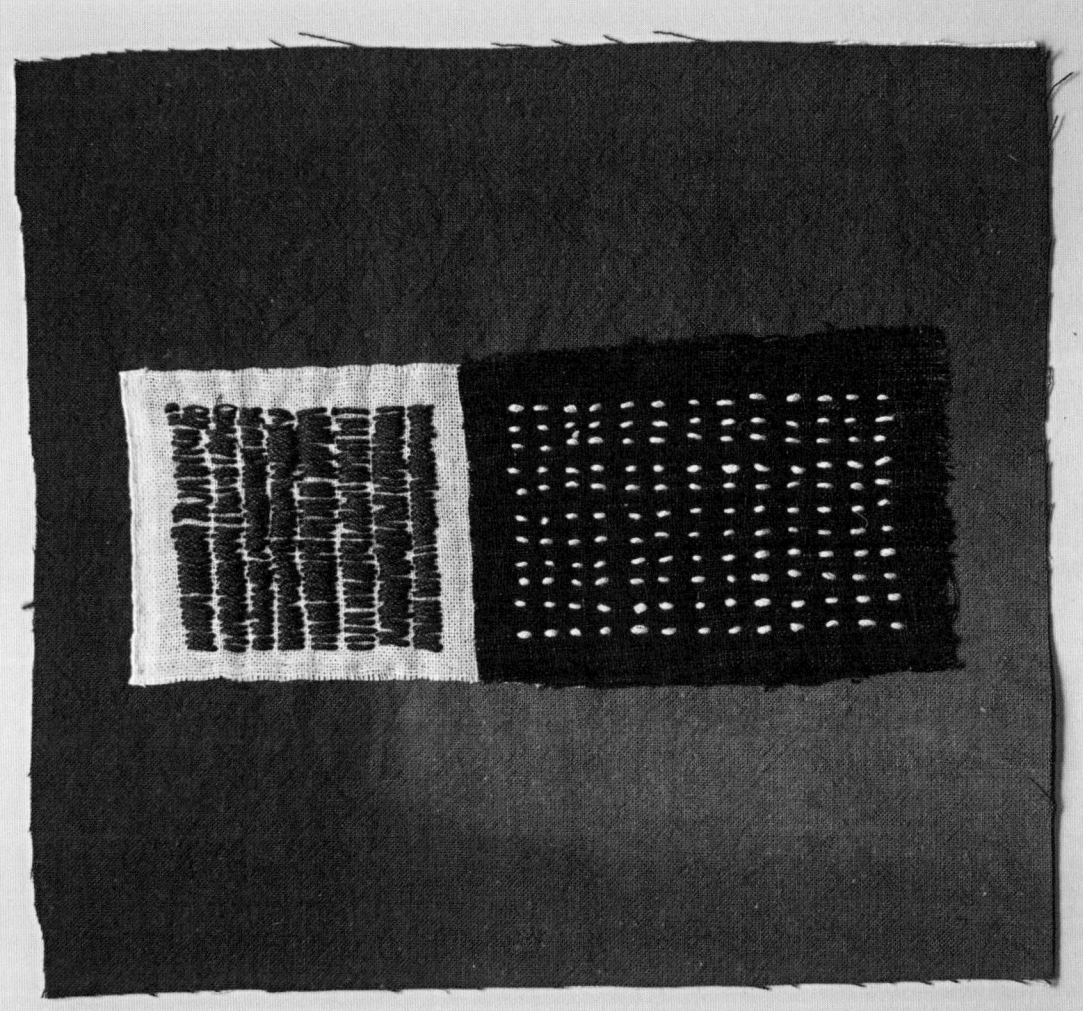

SASHIKO DIARY ENTRY, 14.03.2016
'I was inspired by kogin-zashi and hishizashi. But my philosophy is that it should be simple!
I started sewing rows of stitches and counted the threads in the fabric, but lost count.
Still, I continued, because there is a freedom in imperfect lines too.'

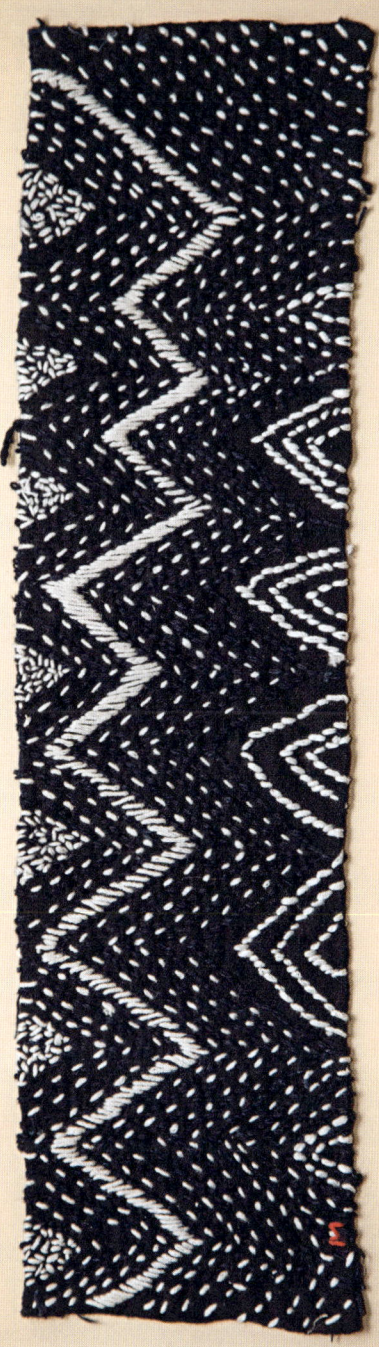

SASHIKO DIARY ENTRY, 02.04.2016
'I was working on the graphic design for a knitting pattern
at the same time as I was thinking about kogin.'

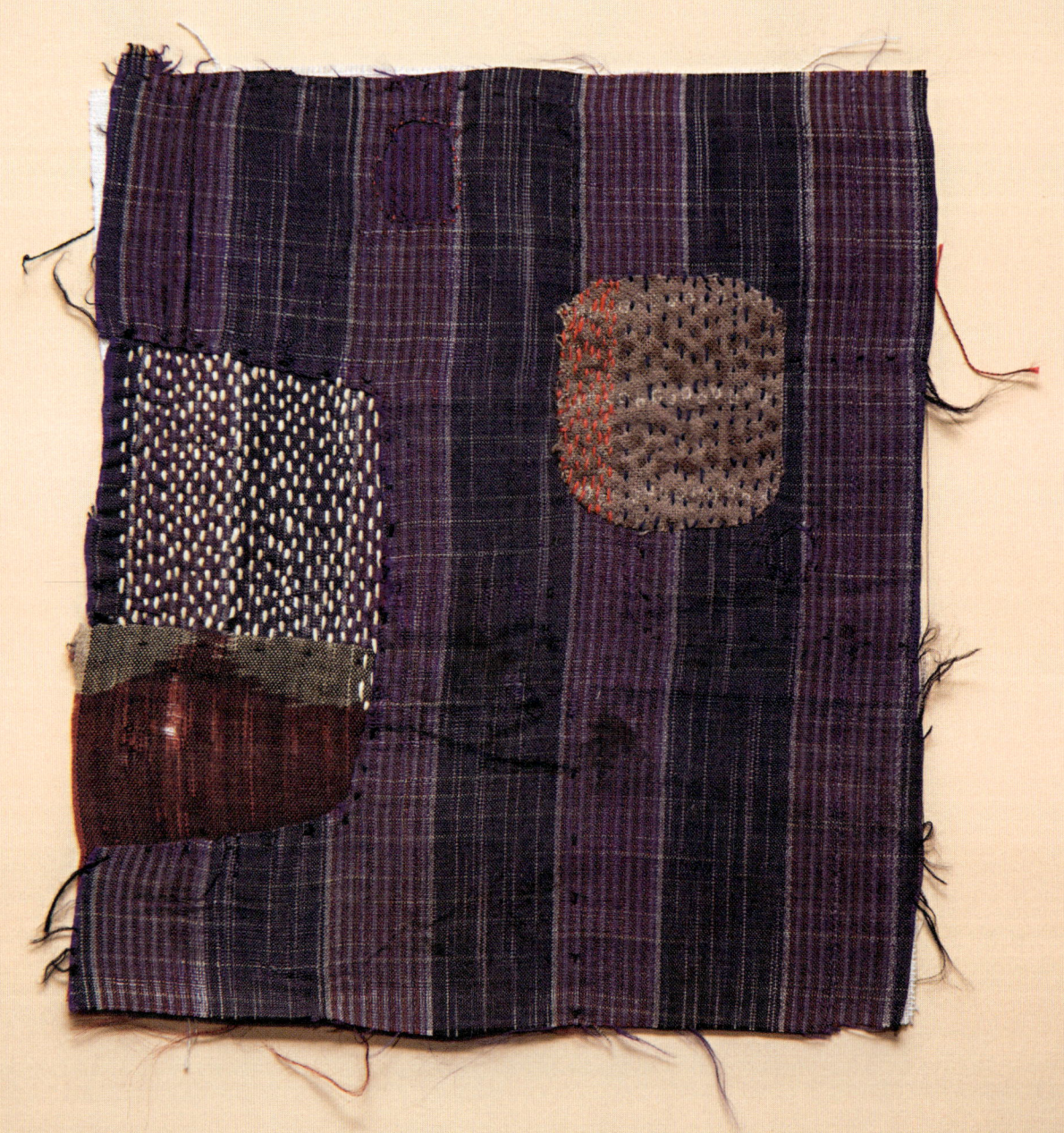

SASHIKO DIARY ENTRY, 10.04.2023
'I was practising making as small and dense unshin stitches as possible.
It resulted in a few classic mends, but also in art!'

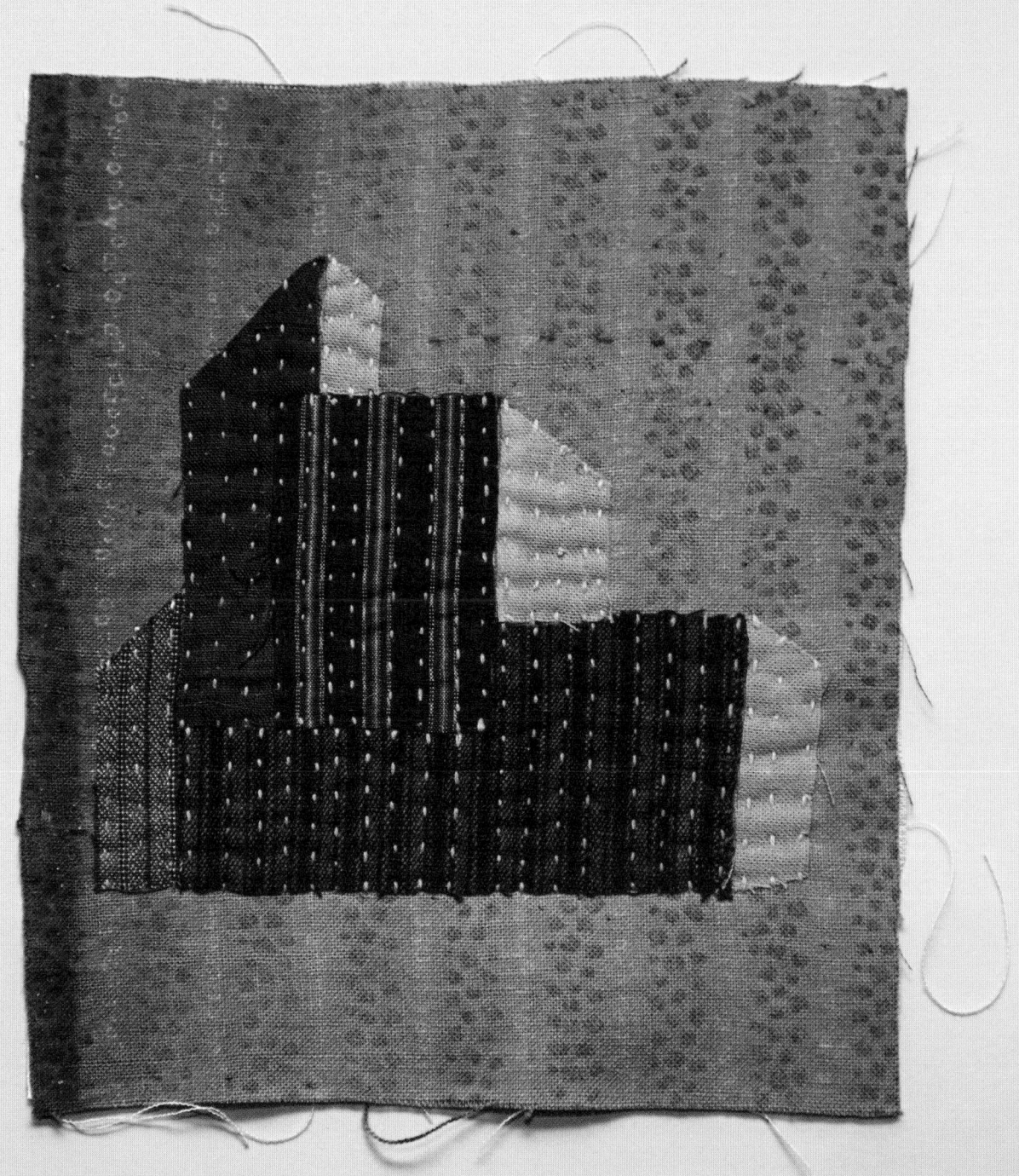

SASHIKO DIARY ENTRY, 02.01.2023
'I dream about living in a house that looks like this. It should be situated deep in a Nordic forest.'

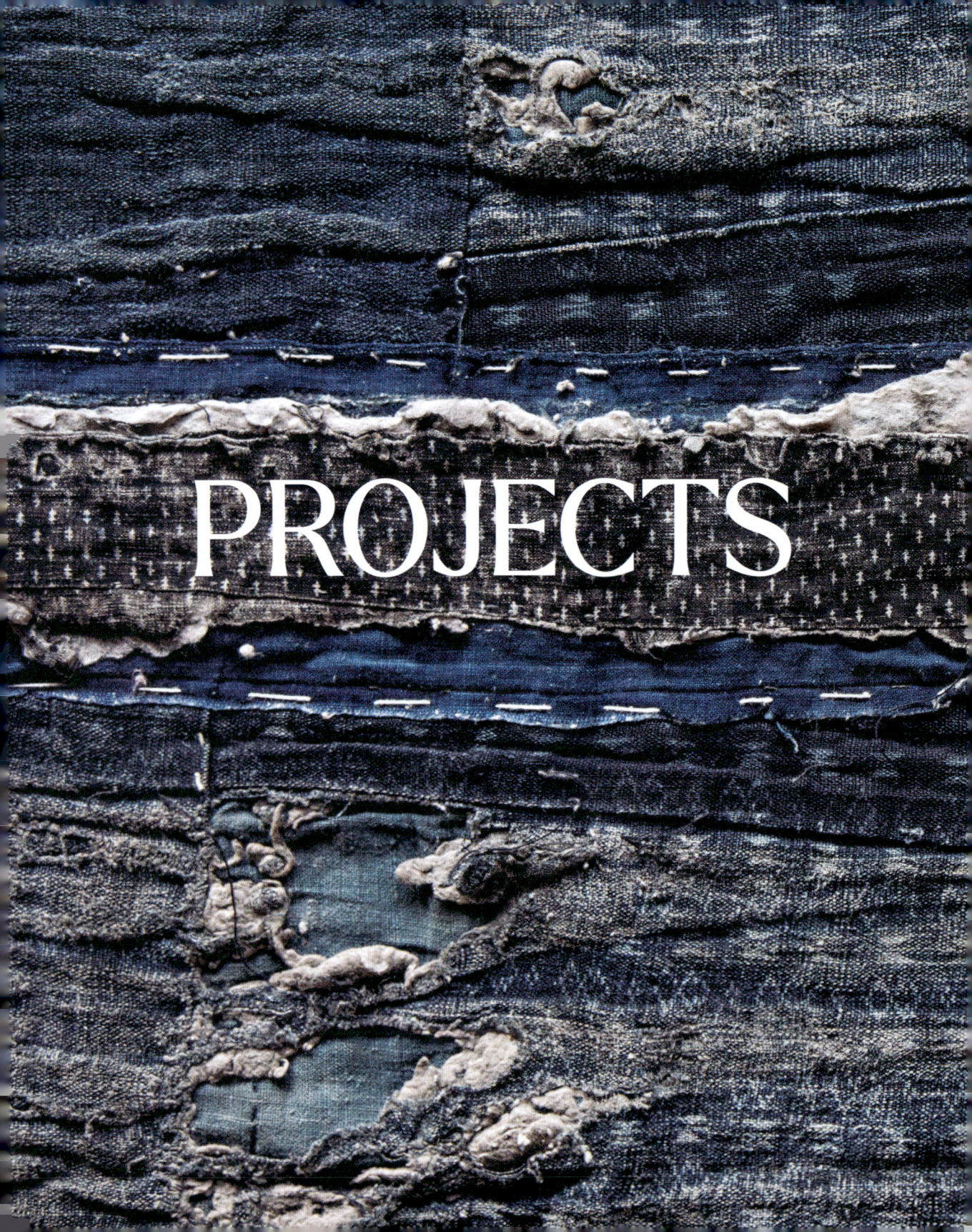

PROJECTS

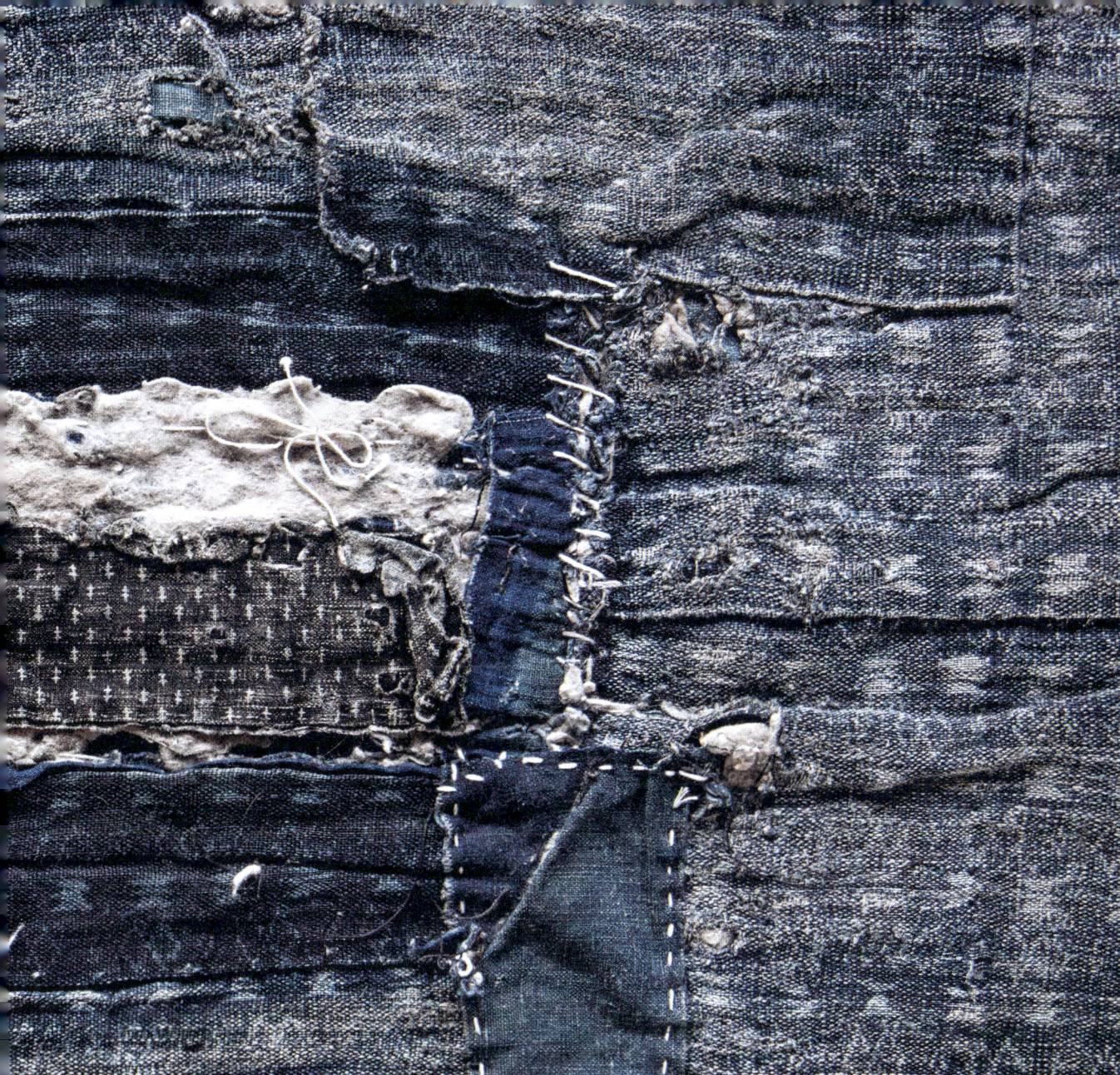

MENDING T-SHIRTS AND SOCKS

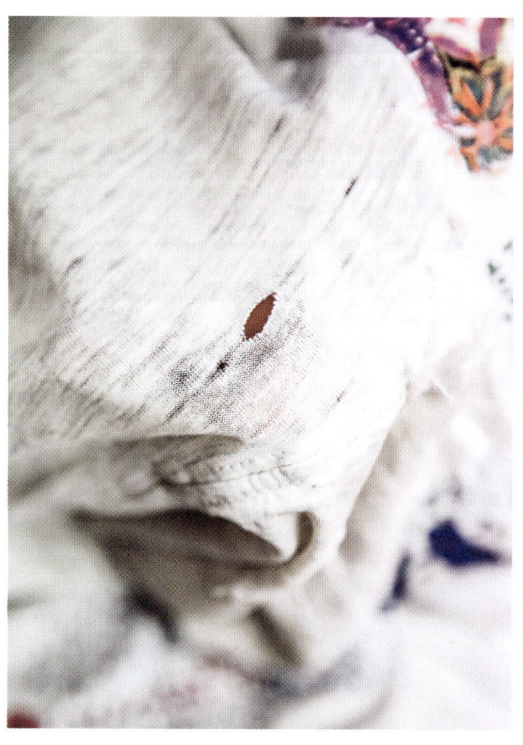

Mending knit fabrics can be a bit tricky since the sashiko stitches aren't stretchy, but it's usually fine and Momi mends both his t-shirts and socks! A trick to achieve a soft mend with a little bit of stretch is to sew loose stitches. The thread shouldn't sit in loops over the fabric, but almost. The smaller the area that is being mended, the fewer stitches you need. For these mends it's good to use a loosely twined 6-ply sashiko thread or double sewing thread made from cotton.

WHAT'S THE DAMAGE?

T-shirts will often get small round or oval holes when one of the threads in the knitted fabric breaks.

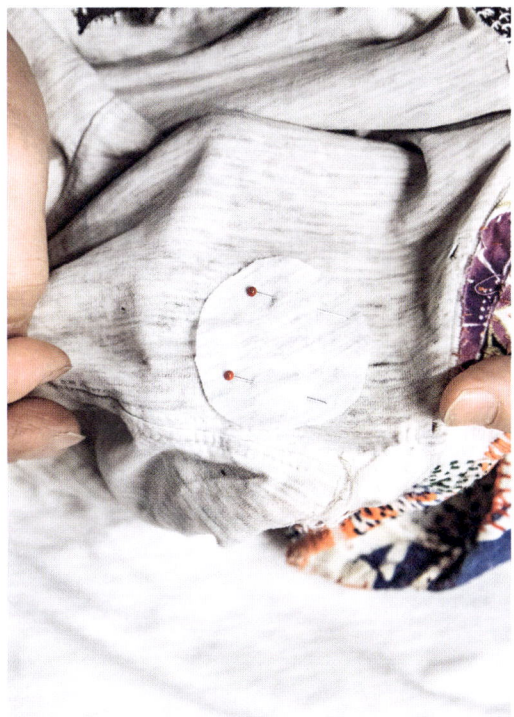

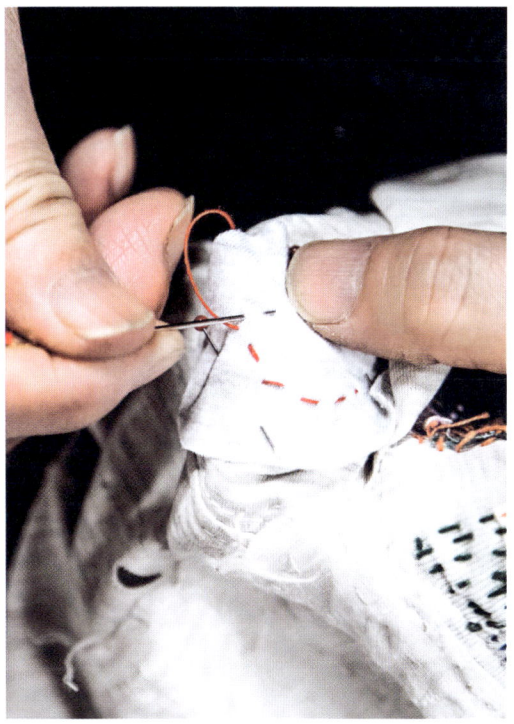

CHOOSING THE PATCH

Cut out a patch to mend with. It's a good idea to mend t-shirts with pieces from other t-shirts. Pin the patch in place and secure the thread with a knot on the inside of the t-shirt.

START SEWING

Start sewing the patch in place with loose stitches. If you sew circles instead of rows of stitches, the stitches have more of a stretch. Start by sewing two circles, one near the edge of the hole and one a few millimetres (¼in or so) away.

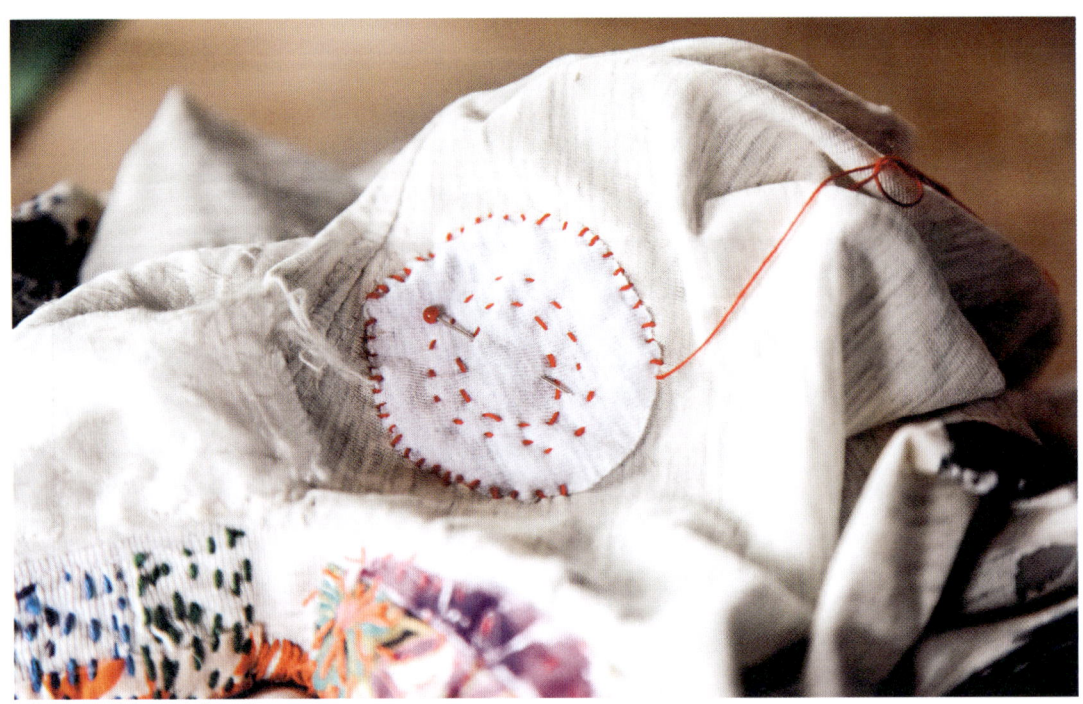

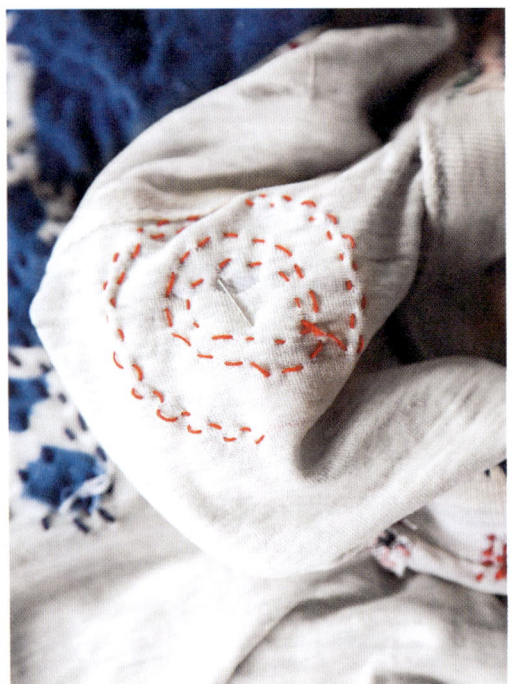

SEWING DOWN THE EDGE

If you want to sew down the edge you can use a type of flat whipstitch, worked like a ladder stitch, that goes straight over the edge at the front of the work and then takes a 90-degree jump at the back to the place at the front where the next stitch starts.

THE BACK

At the back of the mend, you'll be able to see that the stitches are very loose. This makes the mend stretchy, just like the rest of the garment.

FLAT WHIPSTITCH

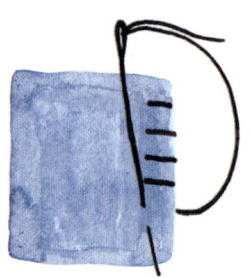
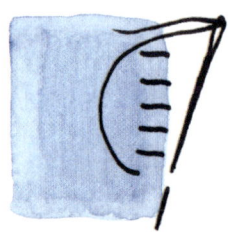

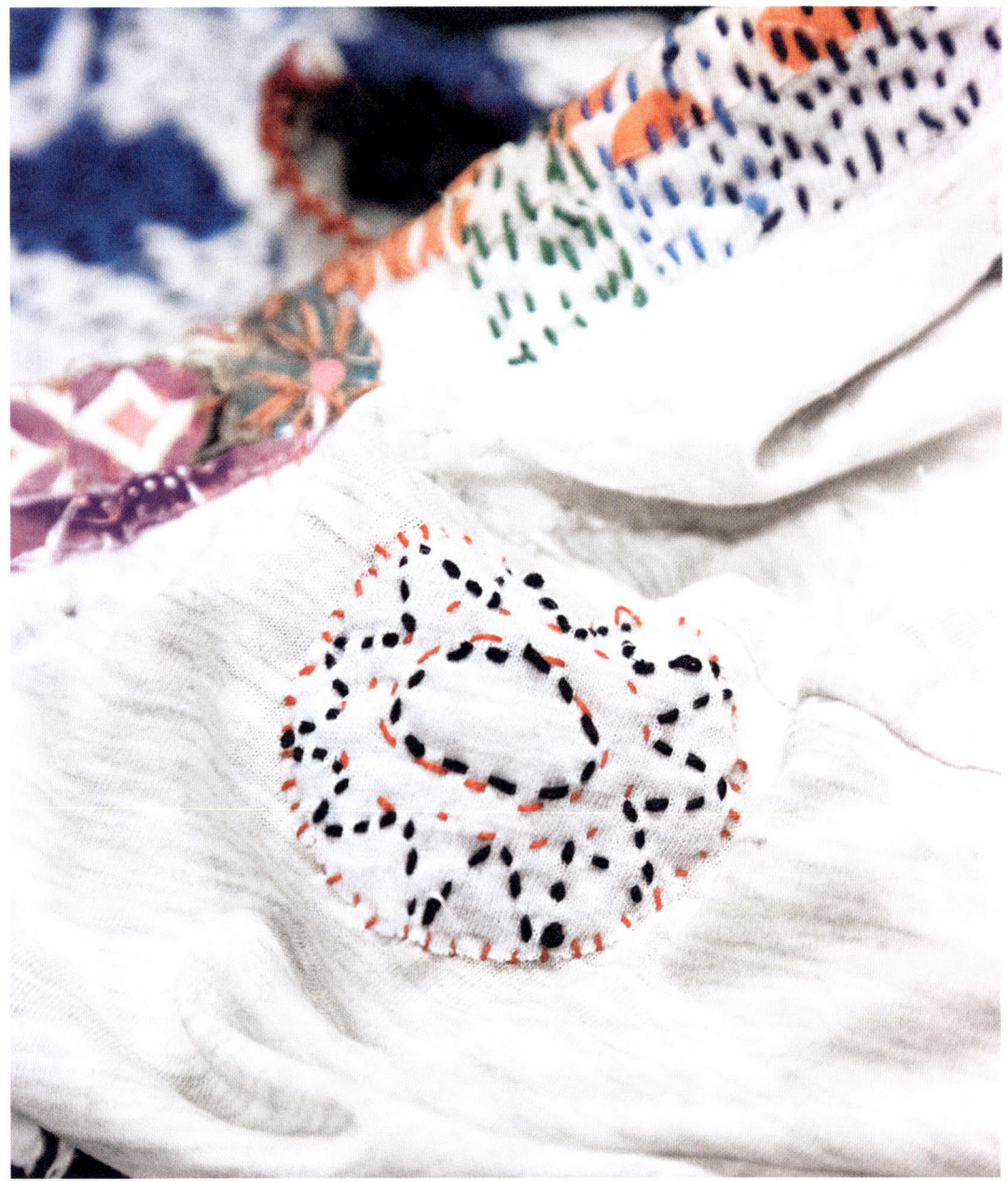

CREATING PATTERNS

When the edge is sewn into place you can add a few stitches in a different colour if you want to create a patten. These will also make the mend stronger.

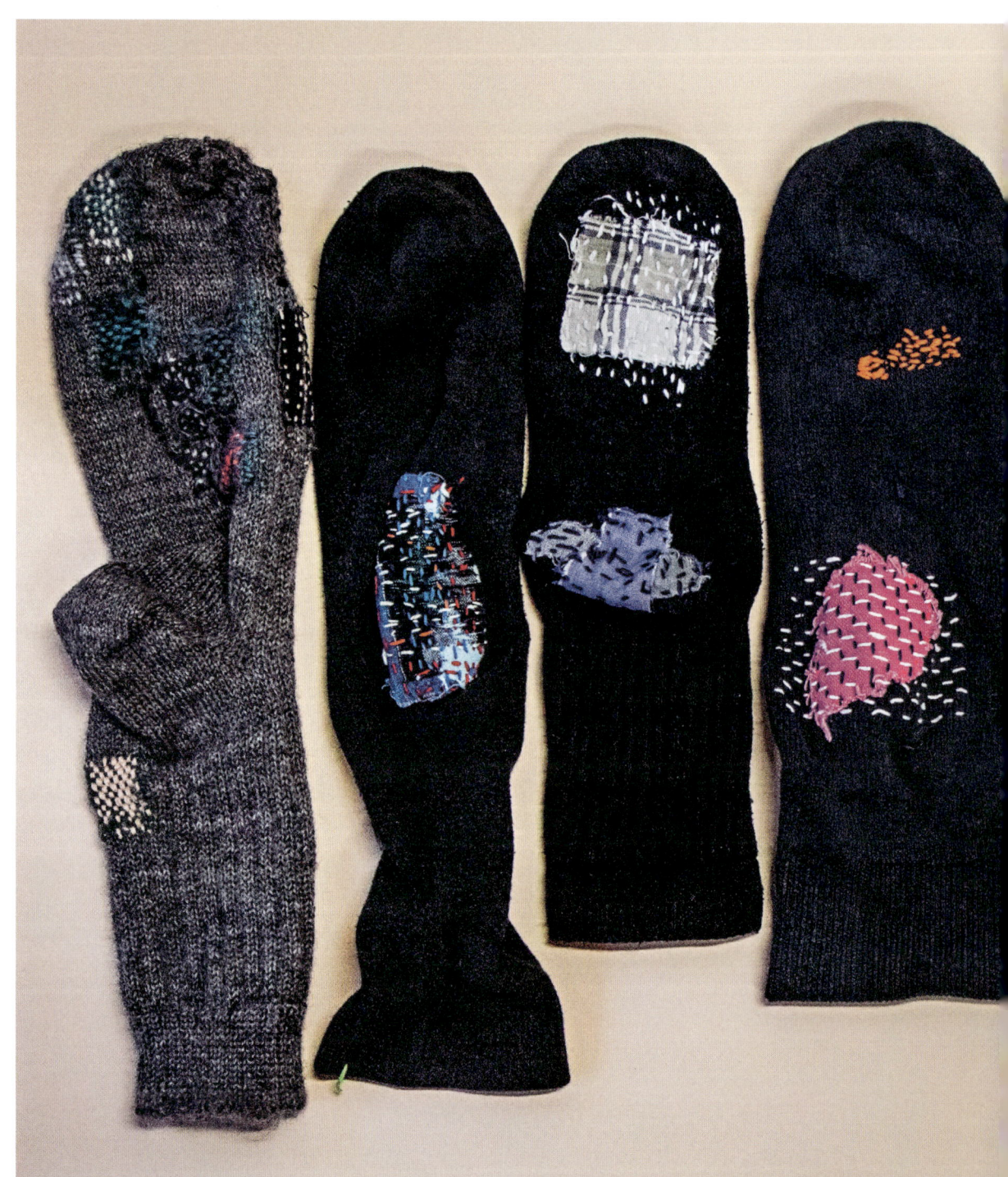

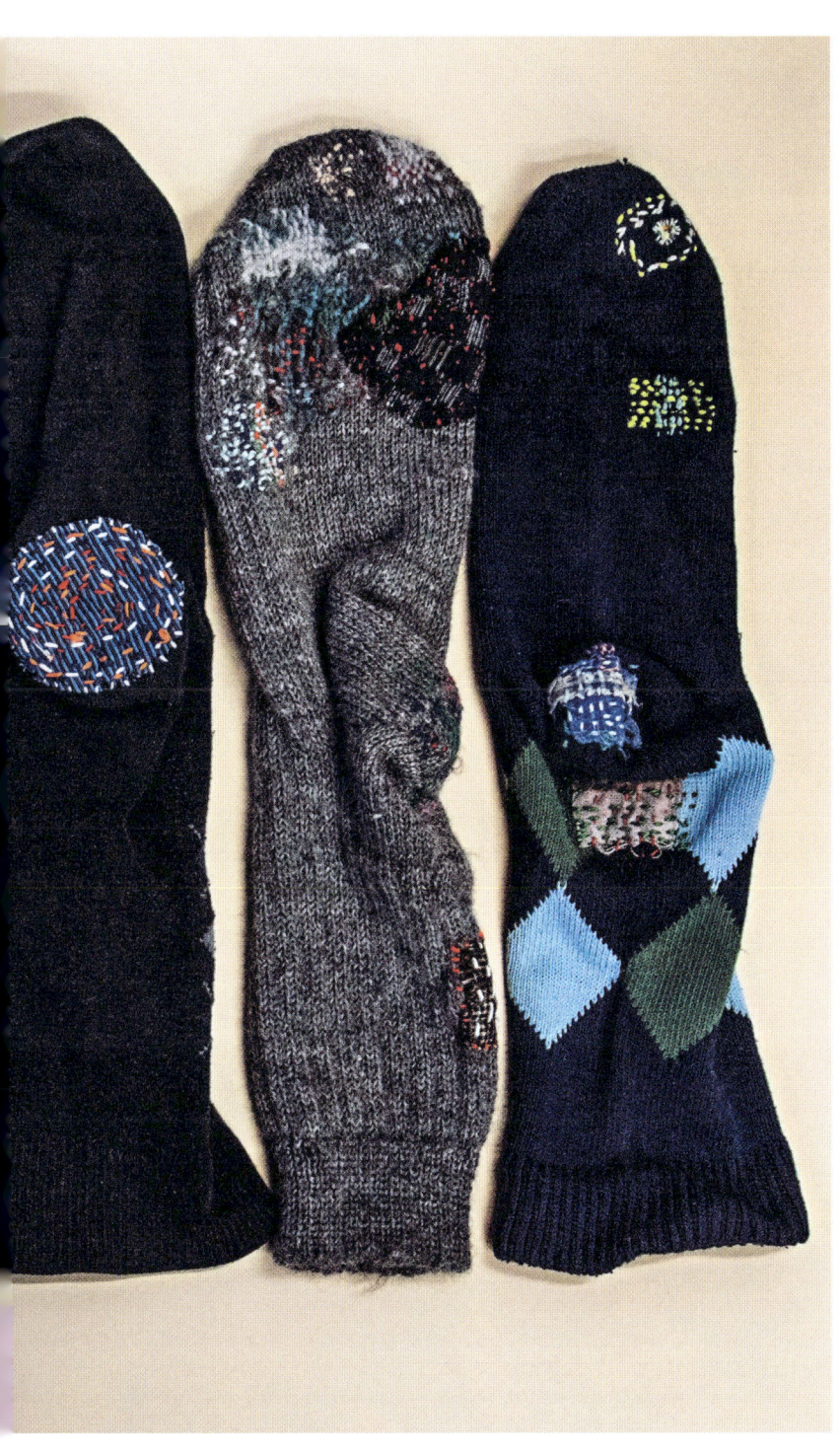

MENDING SOCKS

If you want to mend socks, you can do it the same way as you mend a t-shirt. Here it's important that the mend is as thin and flexible as possible, otherwise the socks won't be comfortable to wear. Properly washed-out t-shirts become nice and thin mending patches.

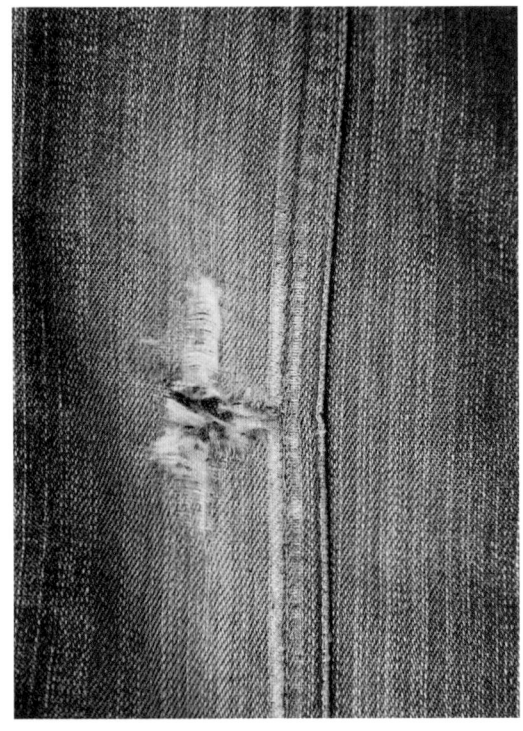

MENDING JEANS

Jeans are often worn down a lot more in the upper parts than the lower. No matter how damaged they might be at the crotch, the fabric below the knees is usually fresh! For those who want to use denim for patches, you could therefore say that the supply of mending material is infinite.

If you are adding a patch to the crotch of a pair of jeans it's important that you try to make the mend as flexible as possible, otherwise wearing the jeans will become uncomfortable. Use a thin fabric, for example from a shirt, for those kinds of mends.

CUTTING OUT A MENDING PATCH

Start by deciding on how large an area you need/want to mend.

What should your mend look like? On the knee or thigh, it might be nice to have a visible mend where the patch sits on the outside of the garment and is sewn on with a thread in a contrasting colour, but if you are mending the jeans at the crotch it's good to think about whether you want an attention-grabbing patch in that particular spot or not. It's your call!

Cut out your mending patch and attach it with pins or basting stitches. Then you can start sewing.

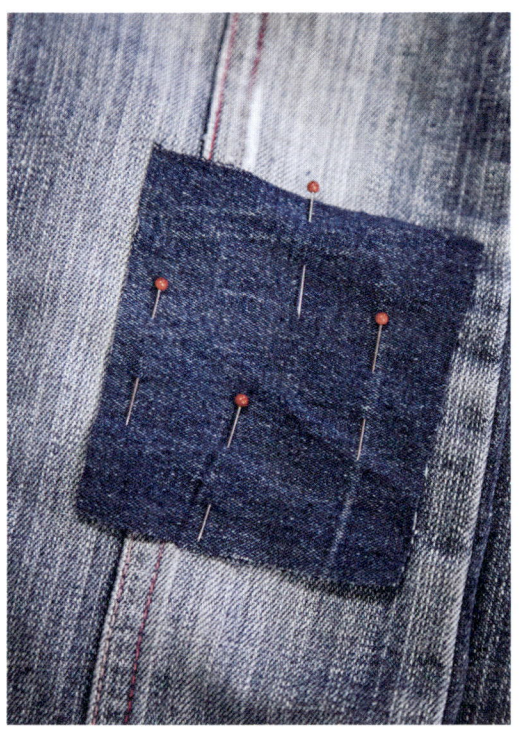

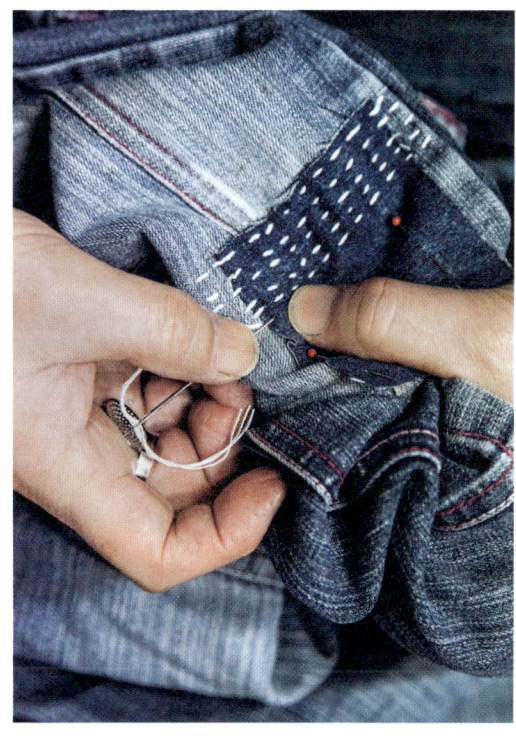

LEAVE THE EDGES RAW

If you fold the edges on a denim patch they will usually form a thick and hard edge. We prefer to keep them raw; they won't fray much anyway when you sew them down.

SEW HORIZONTAL ROWS

You can choose whether you want to make a standard 'patch-covered-in-stitches mend' or a more advanced pattern. Momi starts by sewing the patch in place with a layer of stitches that are approximately 3–5mm (⅛–¼in) long. He tries to sew them so that they sit parallel with the stitches of the previous row. This way the stitches he sews in horizontal rows also form vertical columns. Let the stitches run over the patch by approximately 1–2cm (⅜–¾in), and they will reinforce the fabric around the patch and secure the raw edges in place.

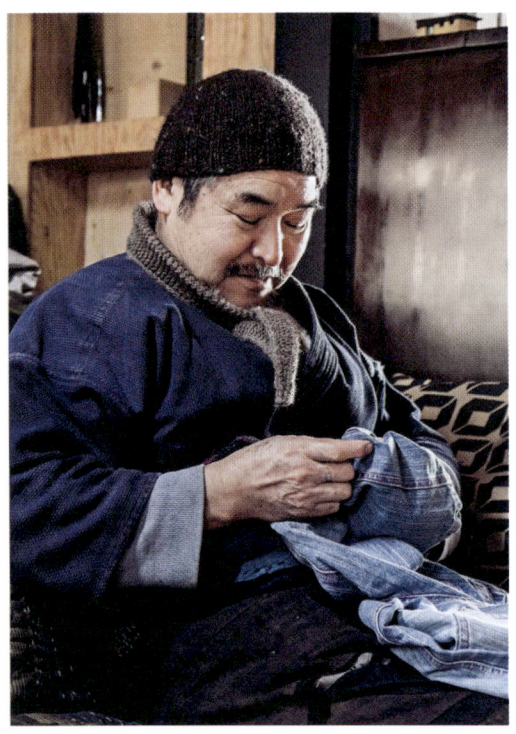

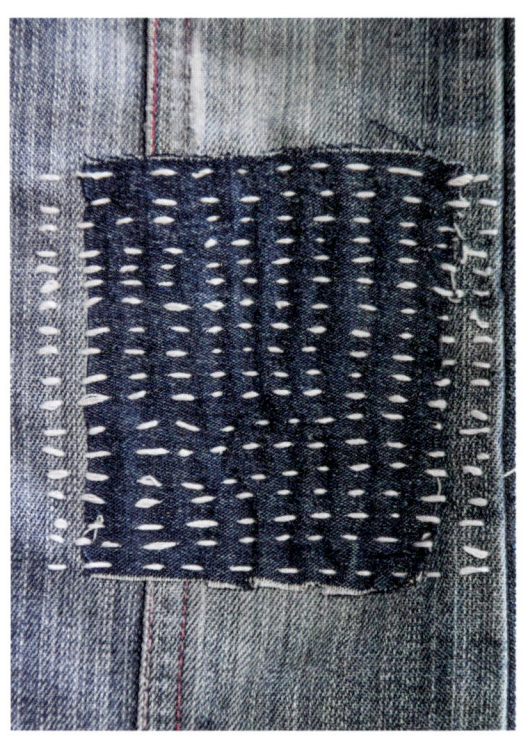

TIP FROM MOMI

When Momi mends jeans he inserts his left hand into the leg of the trousers to make sure that he doesn't accidentally sew through the back of the trousers. You could also insert something else into the trouser leg, as Momi does when mending smaller items such as tabi (see page 108).

DEVELOPING THE PATTERN

When the patch is covered in horizontal stitches you can decide that you're finished with the mend or you can sew another layer, for example vertical stitches between the vertical columns to reinforce the mending patch further. Besides, additional stitches will look lovely!

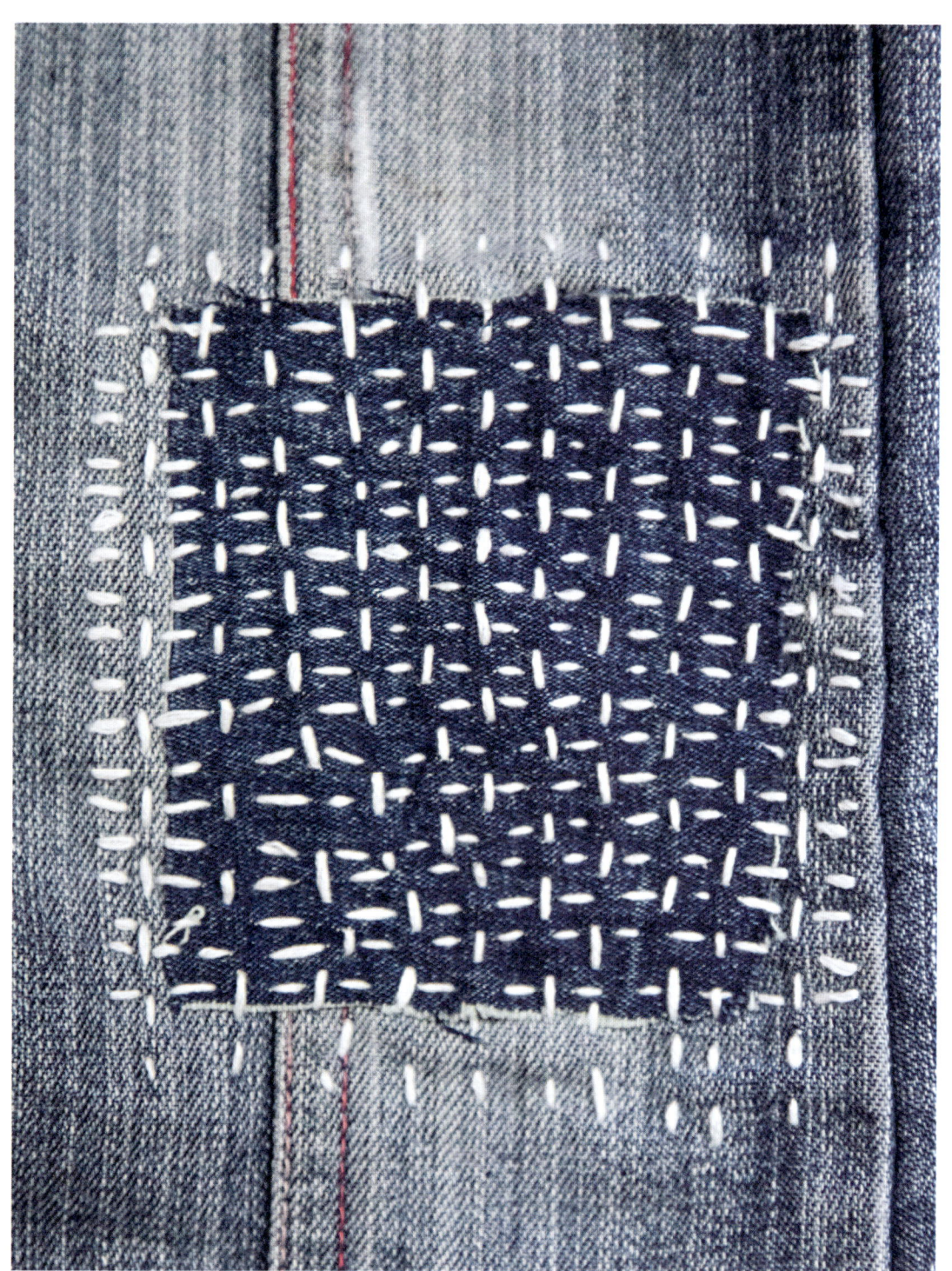

MENDING JEANS WITH HITOMEZASHI

Mending jeans with advanced hitomezashi patterns is very appealing, but it's difficult to count the threads in denim due to how it's woven. Kerstin's trick to get a nice result is to use a mending patch with squares drawn onto it.

METHOD

Start by deciding which pattern you want to sew. How long should the stitches be? Draw up a grid with the required stitch length, here approximately 4 x 4mm (³⁄₁₆ x ³⁄₁₆in) large squares, with a standard biro pen over the whole patch, and then baste it into place on the inside of your jeans. Now you can start sewing the horizontal stitches from the inside of the garment, where you can follow the grid. Here it's important to remember that you can't use unshin stitches; instead you'll have to make the stitches one by one and try to insert the needle straight through the mending patch and the jeans, otherwise it's easy for the stitch to just form a small dot on the outside of the garment.

The next step is to sew the vertical stitch rows from the outside of the fabric – but more on that later (see page 27).

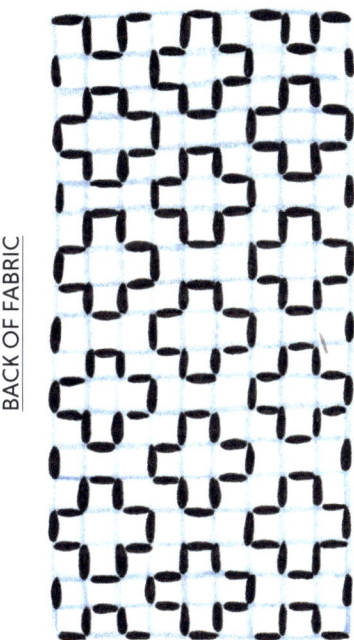

WHAT DOES THE BACK OF THE FABRIC LOOK LIKE?

Advanced hitomezashi patterns look different on the front and the back. You need to keep this in mind when you, as in this case, sew one layer of stitches from one side and the other layer from the other side. The best option is to keep two sketches in front of you before you start sewing: one of how the pattern should look from the front and one of how it should look from the back.

But how do you know which is which? Well, the stitches that aren't on the front should be on the back. Therefore, you can draw out the front pattern and then tape the paper to a window, take another piece of paper and hold it over the sketch. Now it's easy to draw the back stitches 'in between' the stitches that form the pattern on the front on the new paper since the window will act like a light box and both papers will become a bit see-through from the daylight.

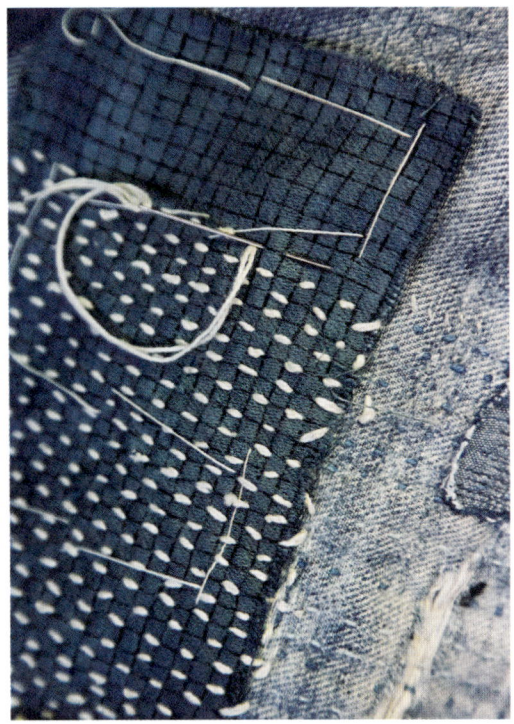

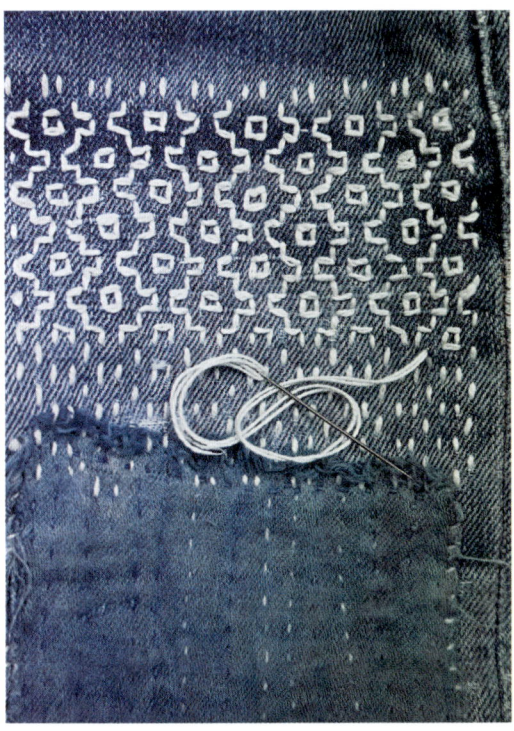

SEW THE FIRST LAYER FROM THE BACK

Start by sewing stitch rows following the pattern sketch for the back. Follow the square pattern and take care to insert the needle as straight as possible through the layers of fabric; this will make the stitches the same length on both the front and the back.

SEW THE SECOND LAYER FROM THE FRONT

When you have covered the mending patch with stitches on the inside you can turn the jeans right-side out and sew the other stitches from the front. Here you won't see the grid but it's not necessary since the horizontal stitches run between the vertical ones. Now sew following the front pattern sketch to get the correct pattern.

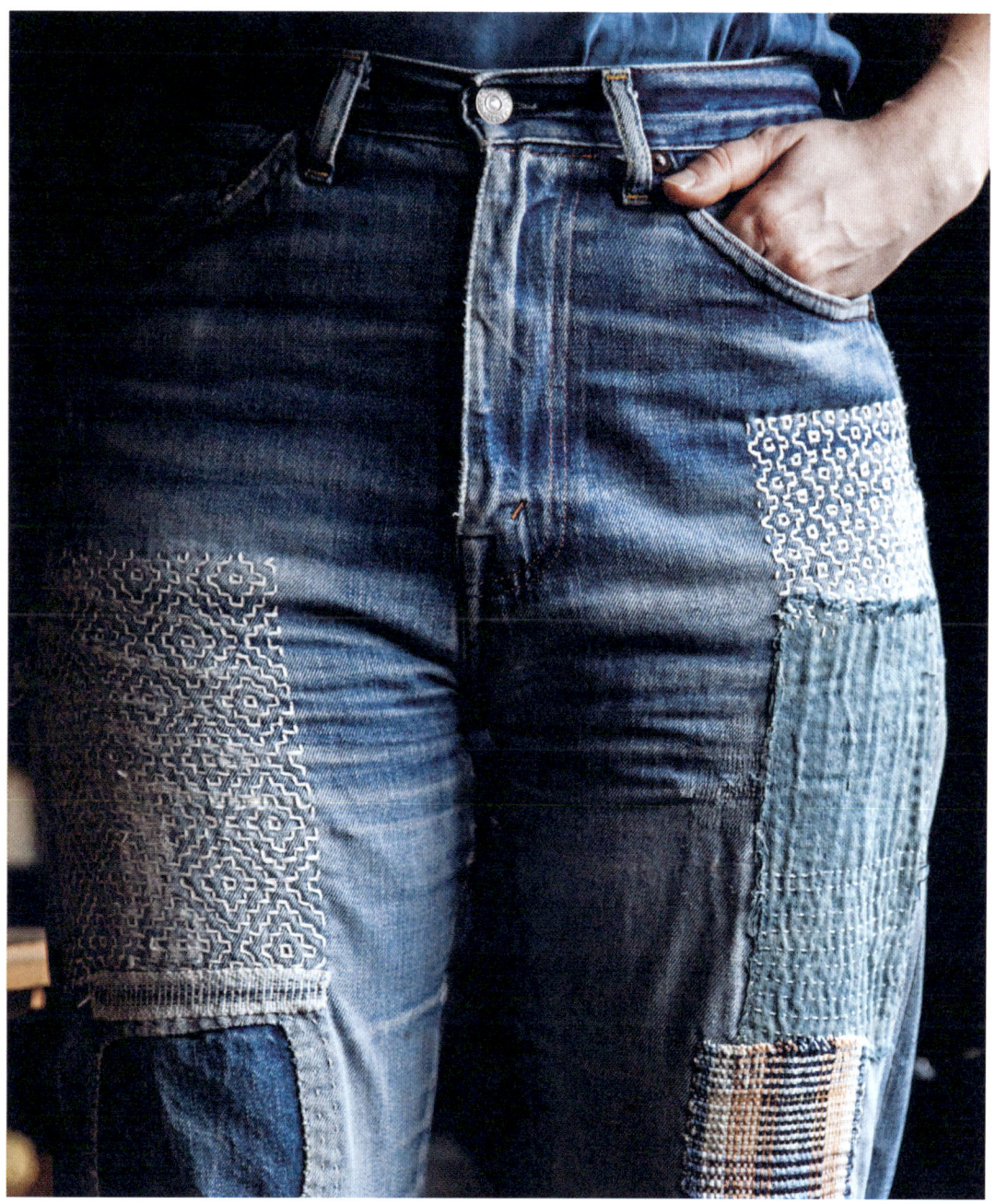

DONE!

This type of mending is suitable for large, worn-down areas that need reinforcing before they tear.

MENDING A TORN JEANS HEM

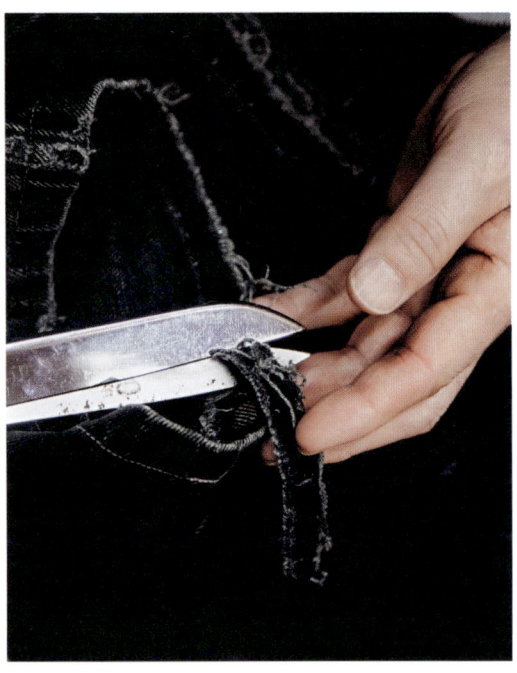

It's fairly common that the bottom hem of a pair of jeans gets so worn down that it tears when you have used the trousers for some time. This is how Momi solves the problem, with a patch that is folded over the damaged edge and then reinforced with hitomezashi.

CUT OFF THE DAMAGED HEM

Start by looking on the inside of the trouser leg's bottom edge. There, the fabric is folded and sewn in place with a seam. Unpick the seam over the area where the hem is torn and cut off the piece of fabric that hangs loose. Also make sure to check the part of the hem that isn't completely torn yet! Is it on its way to tearing? Then you might as well cut that off too.

The point of cutting off material here is to avoid the mend becoming thick and bulky later. You don't have to cut off any fabric that belongs to the outside of the trousers, only what hangs loose once the seam is unpicked.

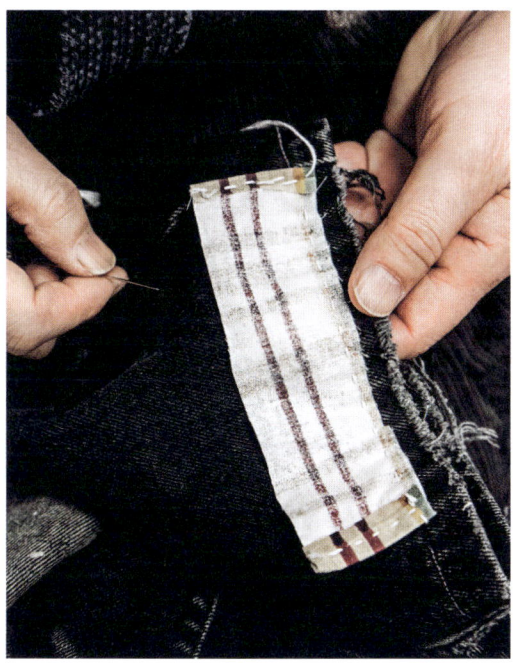

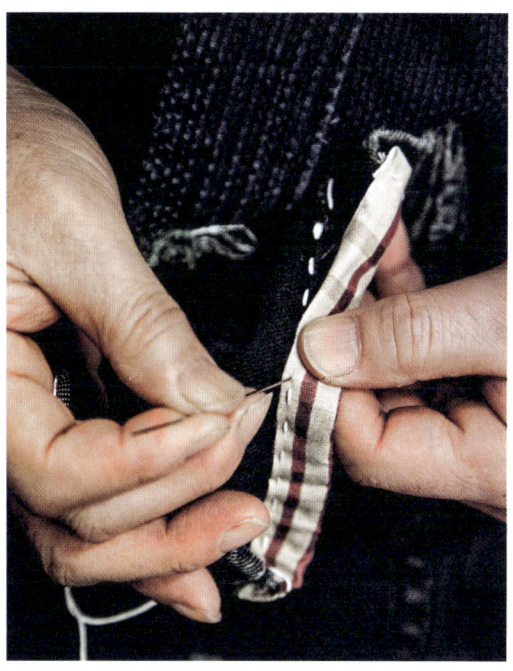

CUTTING OUT AND ATTACHING THE PATCH

Cut out a strip of the fabric you are using for mending. It should be slightly larger than where the hem is torn. You can use the strip that you cut off from the trousers to measure. Add 4cm (1½ in) to the length to be able to fold in the strip's edges later. The height of the mending patch should be twice the height of the hem (you can measure from just above the hem's stitch line to the bottom of the leg for the hem height), plus 2cm (¾in) seam allowance. Does that sound confusing? Take a strip measuring 5.5cm (2⅛in) in height – that should be enough.

Fold over 1cm (⅜in) of the edge at both ends of the mending patch and sew them in place against the wrong side of the patch with a few stitches. Then place the patch over the trouser leg's outside, with the edge approximately midway between the damaged edge and the old hem seam. Sew the mending patch to the trousers in line with the old hem stitching. This way it will start in line with the old hem, which gives a harmonious expression.

ATTACH THE PATCH TO THE INSIDE

Now you can fold the mending patch around the edge of the hem and against the inside of the trousers where it is to be sewn in place. For a neat result, Momi folds in the remaining raw edge of the patch so that it doesn't get longer than just covering the row of stitches that were created when he sewed the patch in place on the front. You don't need to measure it; it's enough to fold the patch around the edge of the hem and up against the inside of the trousers, and you will see how much needs folding. Sew the mending patch in place with stitches that go through all layers of fabric at the same time.

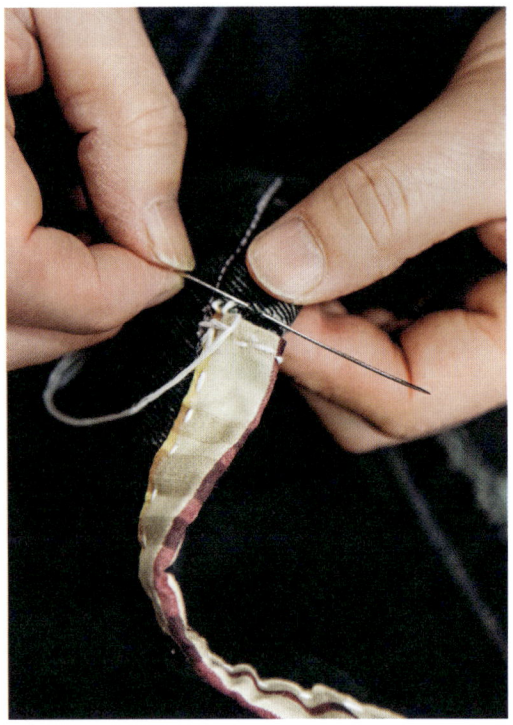

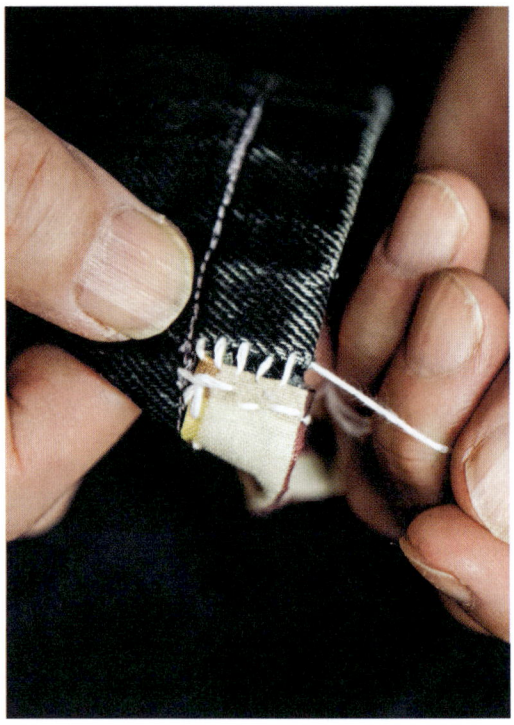

SEW DOWN THE EDGES OF THE PATCH

You can sew down the short edges of the patch to the jeans fabric with standard sashiko stitches, but Momi uses a clever stitch to secure the edge of the mending patch closely against the trousers' side seam. This is called a 'ladder stitch' and it actually looks like a ladder! The stitch is sewn from side to side, with completely straight 'jumps' in between. Sew it by inserting the needle through the jeans fabric's outer layer and then bring it up again after a few millimetres (⅛in or so) . Then move the needle straight over to the edge of the mending patch, as if making the middle line in the letter 'H', and insert the needle there. The needle will run straight ahead for a few millimetres (⅛in or so) in between the mending patch's two fabric layers before you bring it up again and pull the needle and the thread back over to the jeans side again. (This is the same stitch as in the illustration on page 62.)

PULL THE STITCHES TIGHT

When you have covered the whole area you want to sew down with stitches, you can pull the thread tight, and behold! When the stitches are pulled tight the two fabric edges are fixed together and sit flat against each other (see the photographs opposite).

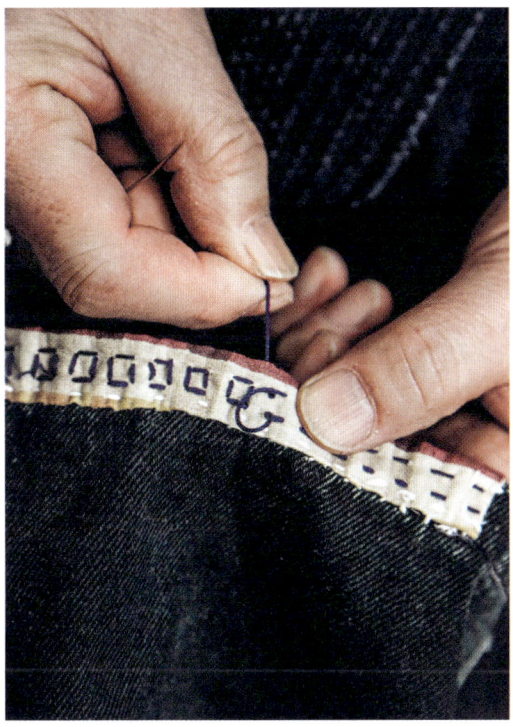

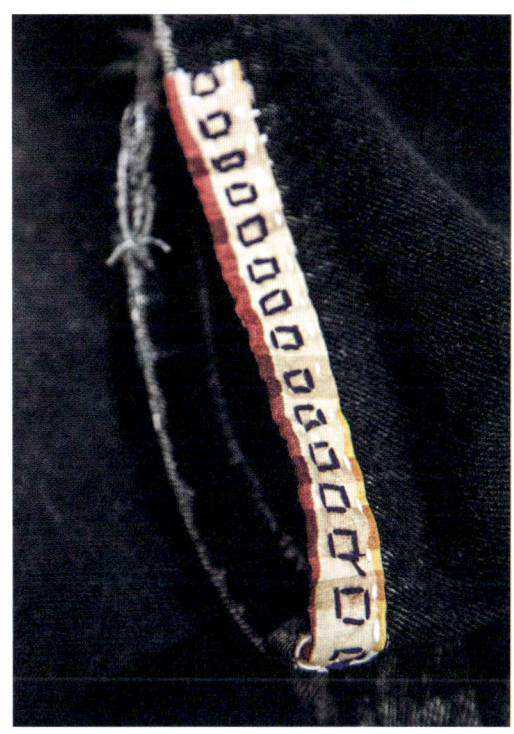

REINFORCE THE HEM

Now the torn hem is finished, and to give it further strength, Momi sews a layer of hitomezashi over it. With a thick blue thread, he first sews two rows of parallel stitches along the length of the patch, and then he joins them by sewing stitches in the other direction so that a pattern of squares is formed.

DONE!

MENDING A JEANS POCKET

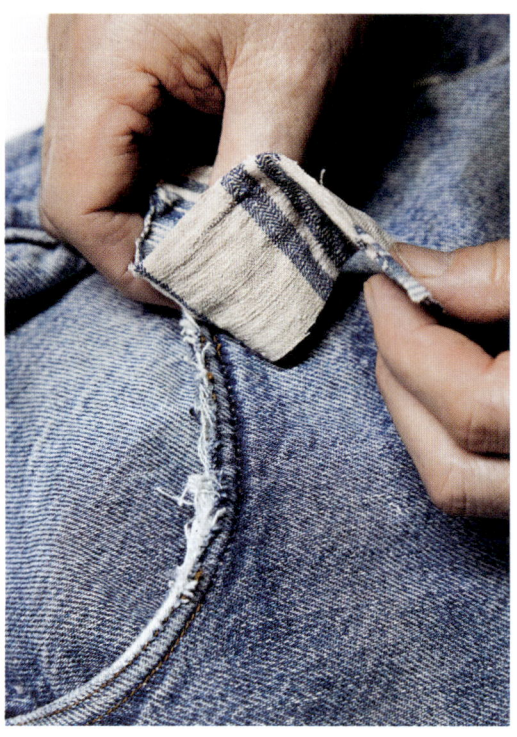

The edge of a jeans pocket can easily get worn down, and it's common that the pocket becomes loose along the seam at the inside of the opening. Momi sews a protective patch along the edge of the pocket, and the jeans are ready for new adventures.

METHOD

Cut a strip of mending fabric that is slightly longer than the damaged area and approximately 3cm (1¼in) wide. Fold it over the pocket edge and pin into place so that you have about the same amount of mending patch on both the outside and the inside of the pocket edge.

Don't fold over the mending patch's edges; leave them raw so that the patch doesn't get bulky and annoying.

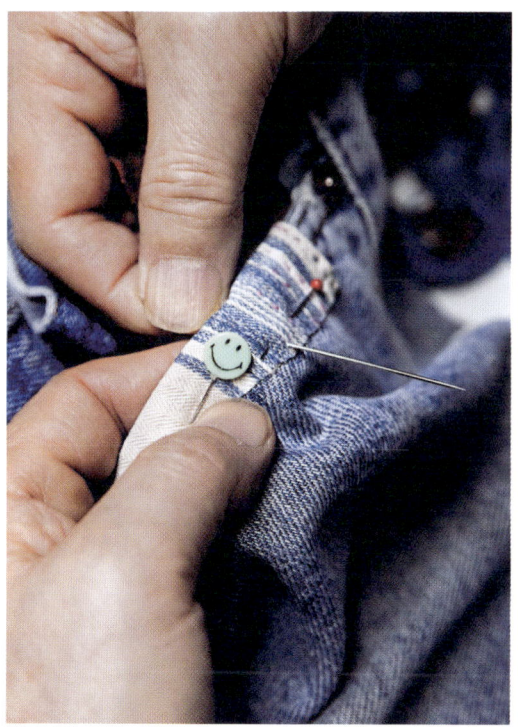

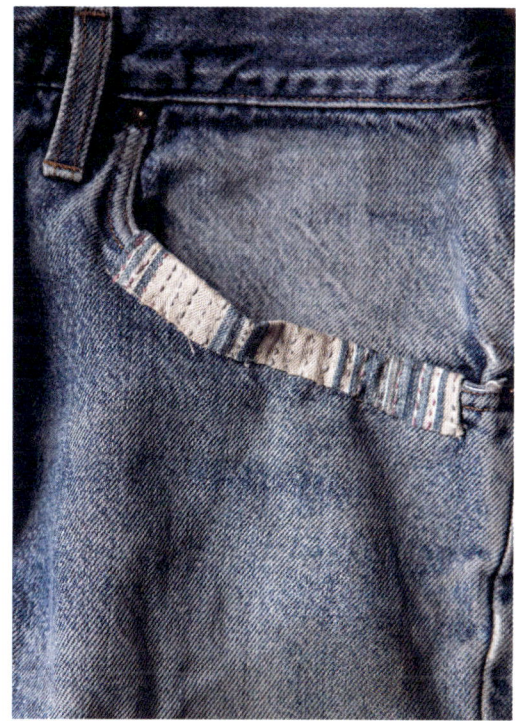

ATTACH THE MENDING PATCH

Now you can start sewing the patch in place. Momi attaches it with small rows of stitches that go through all fabric layers at the same time. When you come to the edge of the mending patch it's good if the last stitch runs over the edge to secure it in place and to prevent the fabric from fraying.

DONE!

The fabric is fairly thick at the pocket edge, so it's not possible to use unshin stitches here. When you have sewn the whole strip in place with small stitches you're done!

MENDING STRETCH JEANS

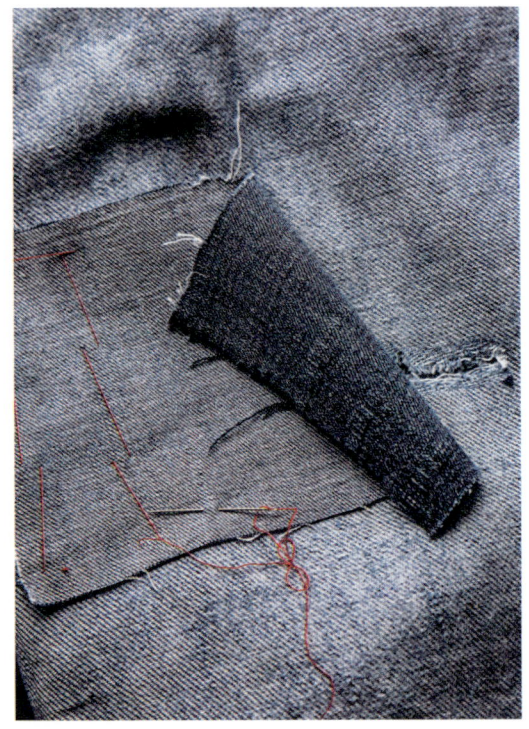

Mending stretch jeans can be difficult since you don't want to ruin the stretchiness in them. Sashiko stitch rows are rigid, so Kerstin's tip is to not sew any straight rows in the direction where you want to keep the stretchiness, and in most cases it's the width of the trousers that needs to be stretchy. Therefore, don't sew any horizontal stitches.

Also, keep in mind to mend with a stretchy fabric too!

ATTACH THE PATCH

Start by cutting out a mending patch and basting it into place over the hole. If it's a large hole it's a good idea to iron the trouser fabric flat first, but be careful to set the iron to a low temperature because otherwise the stretchy elastane threads in the fabric will melt.

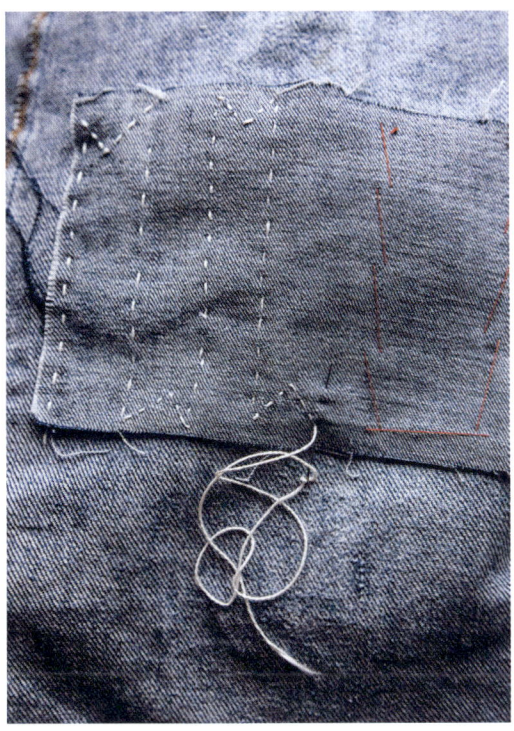

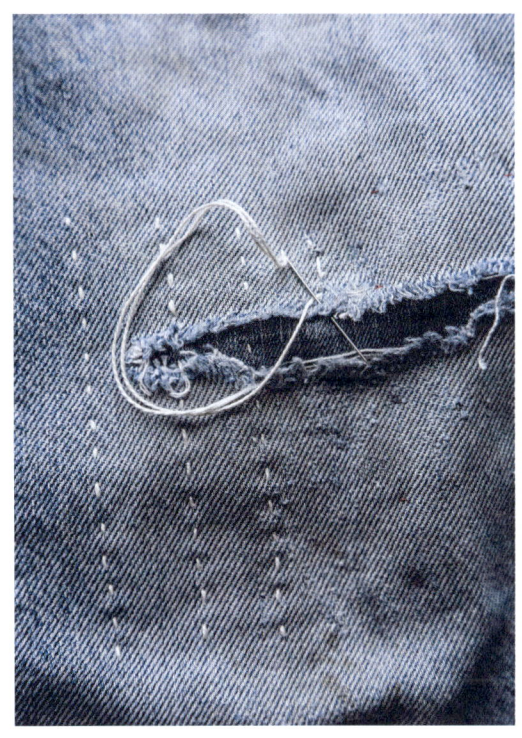

START SEWING

Sew the patch in place with straight, vertical stitches that are placed with a wide gap in between. You will need at least 1cm (³⁄₈in) in between the rows of stitches to allow the fabric to stretch a little, but a wider gap is better. When you have finished one row and are about to start the next you can secure the thread at the end of the previous row and at the beginning of the new row if you want, but if you think that's tedious and takes up too much time you can instead sew your way to the start of the next row. The rule about not making any horizontal stitches still applies however, so instead of sewing straight across you can sew a V-shape to get to the start of the next row – the diagonal stitches in the V won't become rigid.

V-SHAPE ON THE OUTSIDE?

If you don't want these V-shaped stitches that join the previous row with the next one to become visible from the outside of the jeans, you can sew them with small stitches that only go through the fabric of the mending patch, not the trousers. You can leave the basting stitches in place as you work and remove them when you're finished, or remove them in stages as you sew.

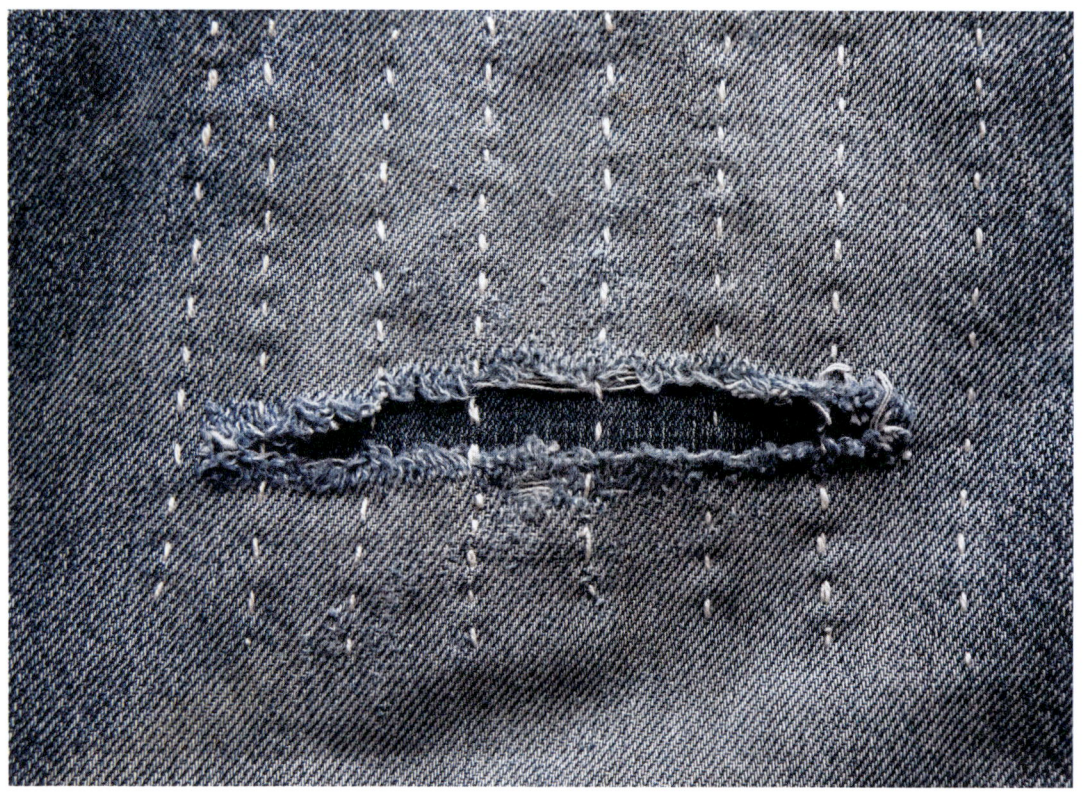

STRETCHINESS OR STRENGTH?

Since the stitch rows are sparsely placed, this kind of mending doesn't become as strong as the jeans mending on page 66, but the benefit is that you get to keep some of the stretchiness in the trousers. You'll have to weigh up what is the most important, strength or stretchiness, and place your stitches closer together if strength is the most important and further apart if you want to prioritize stretchiness.

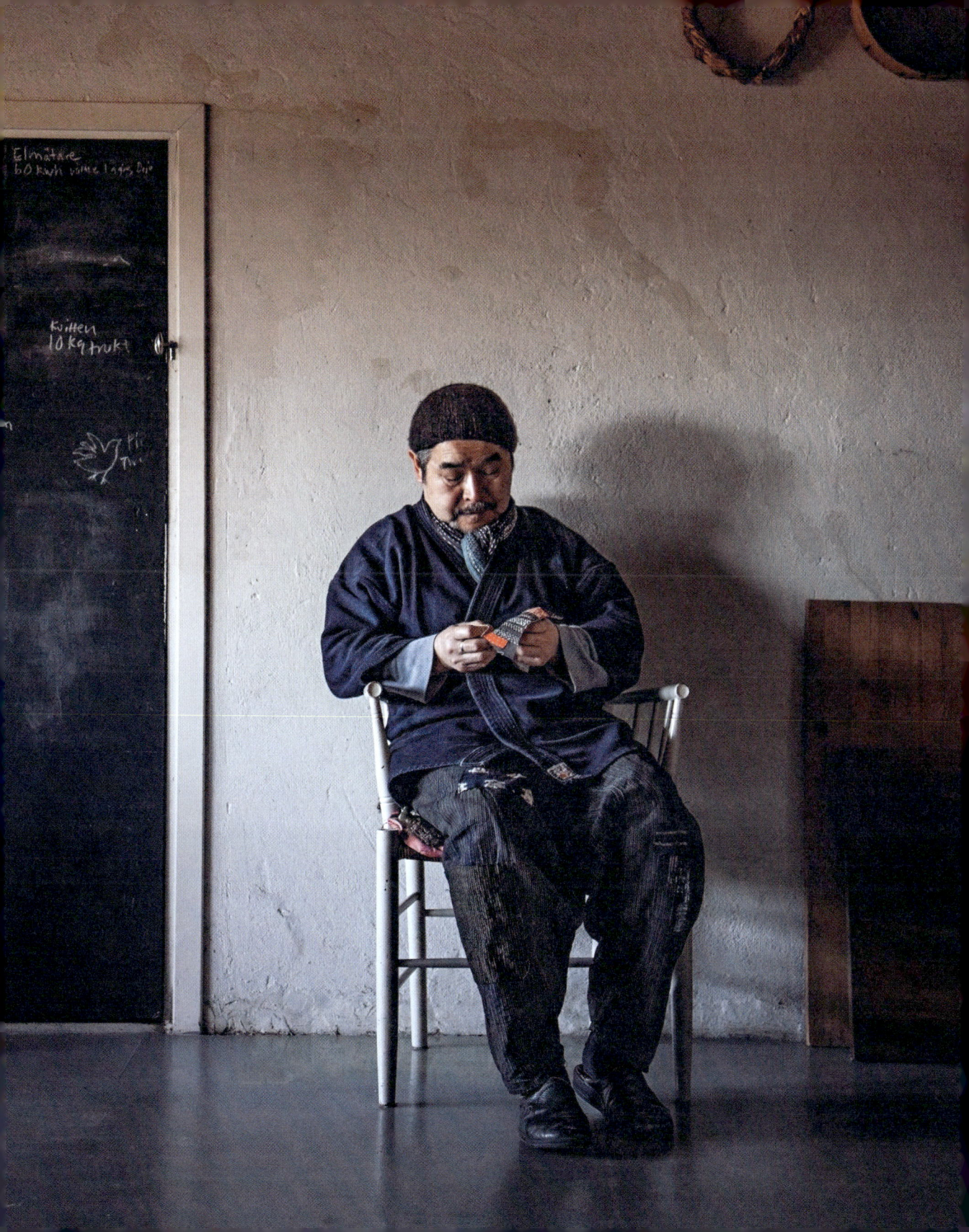

MENDING A HANDKERCHIEF WITH FUROSHIKI

In the past it was common in Japan to use large pieces of fabric to carry things in. They were called furoshiki and were tied with all four corners into something that we in Sweden would recognize as a 'bindle'. Today the furoshiki tradition lives on in Japanese society in the form of small cloths for wrapping gifts in.

The old furoshiki cloths were exposed to a lot of wear, which gave rise to the tradition of sewing sashiko in the corners of the cloth to reinforce it even before it became worn down.

Kerstin's best handkerchief started to get damaged in the corners because that's where she usually ties it, so she decided to make mending patches and secure them with moyozashi in the chrysanthemum flower pattern.

METHOD

Start by checking how large the area is that needs mending. Take out the fabric you're intending to use for the mend and draw out the shape of the mending patch(es) on the fabric. These patches have a rounded edge (see opposite) so that they follow the pattern of the sashiko. It can be difficult to fold in the edge nicely on a rounded patch, but here is a good trick: sew two rows of basting stitches – one where you want the finished edge to be and the other closer to the fabric edge. Now you can carefully pull in the outer basting thread so that the fabric gathers, making it easier to fold in the edge in a curve! You will get a few little folds, but it doesn't matter, as these won't be visible later.

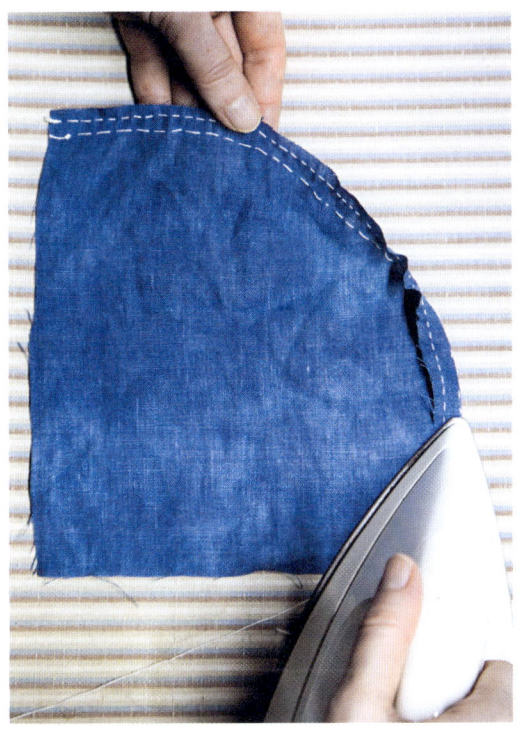

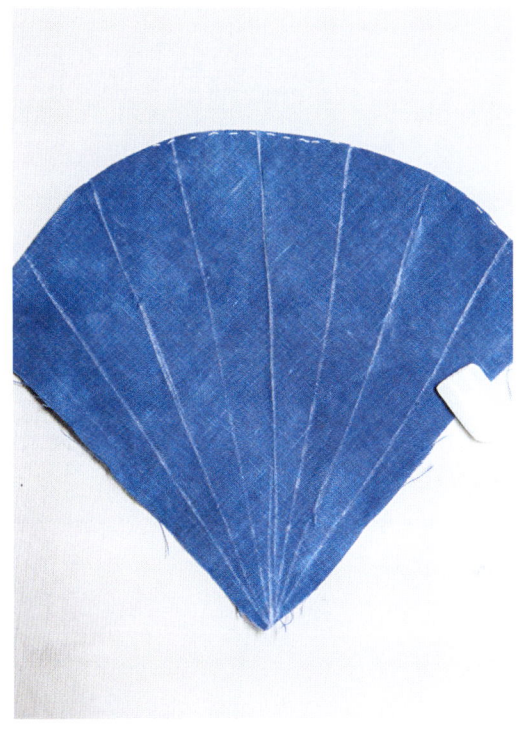

IRON THE EDGE FLAT

When you iron the curved edge flat you can see the first row of basting stitches that you worked – the one that marks where the edge should be – and fold the fabric along this. If you want, you can baste the folded edge after ironing it to keep it in place.

DRAW OUT THE PATTERN

To make it easier to draw out the pattern you can make guide lines by folding the fabric and running your nail over the fold. Then it's easy to draw out the shape of the petals with a piece of chalk.

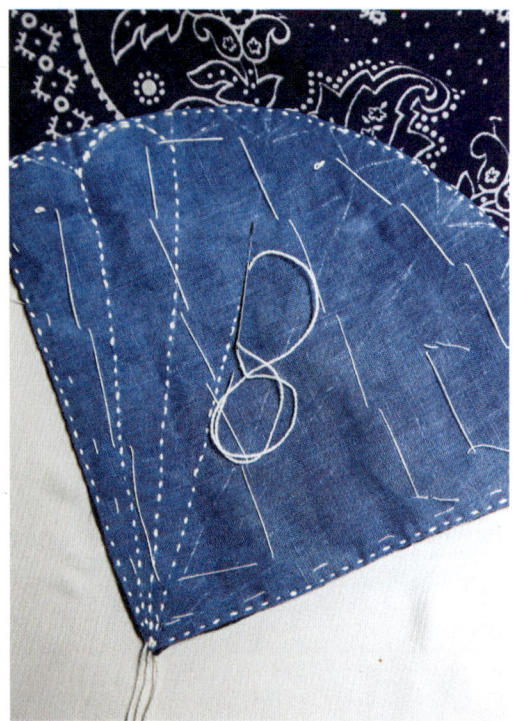

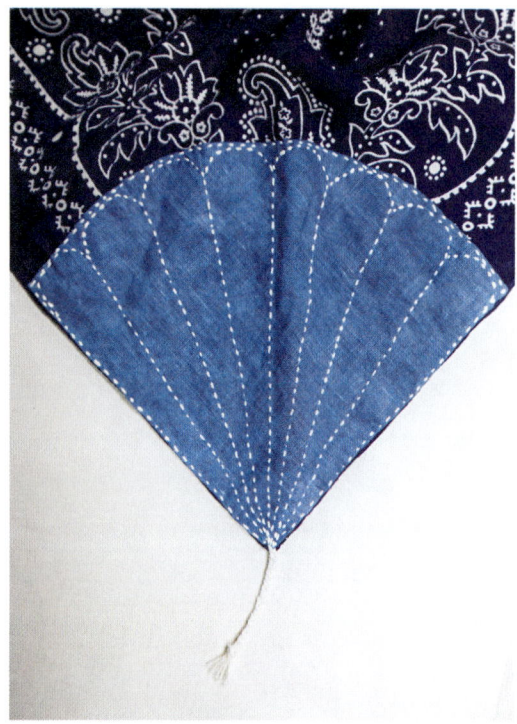

ATTACHING THE PATCH

When the pattern is drawn out it's time to sew. Fold in the straight edges, iron flat and baste the patch to the handkerchief. Sew the patch in place with small stitches a few millimetres (⅛in or so) from the edge, and then start the petals. When you have finished the sashiko, remove all basting stitches.

BRAIDED CORNERS

On old furoshiki you can sometimes see a braid at the corners of the cloth. If you want to make one you can skip securing the thread at the corner and instead leave 7–8cm (2¾in–3⅛in) long ends. Braid these threads together and finish off with a standard overhand knot.

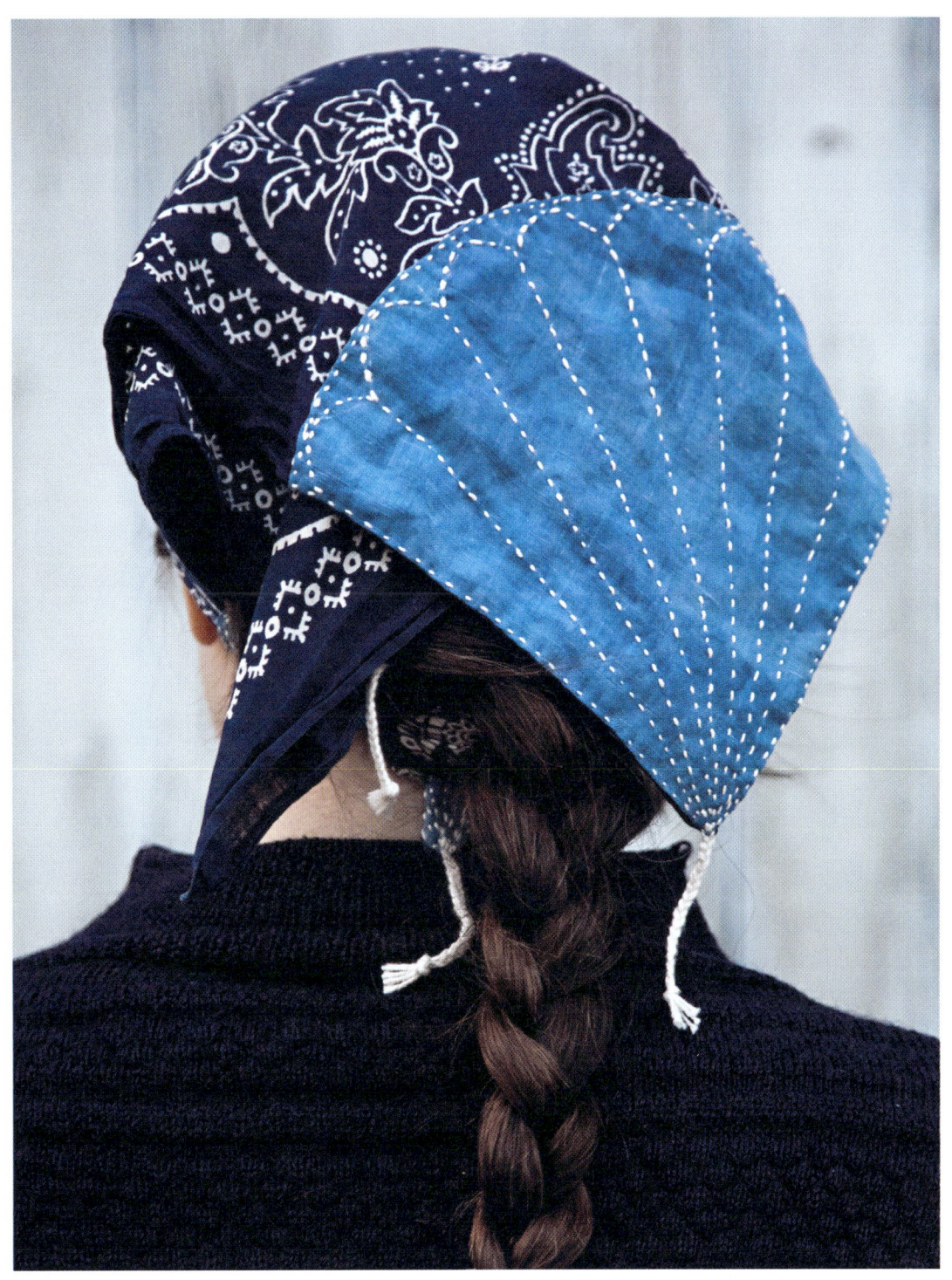

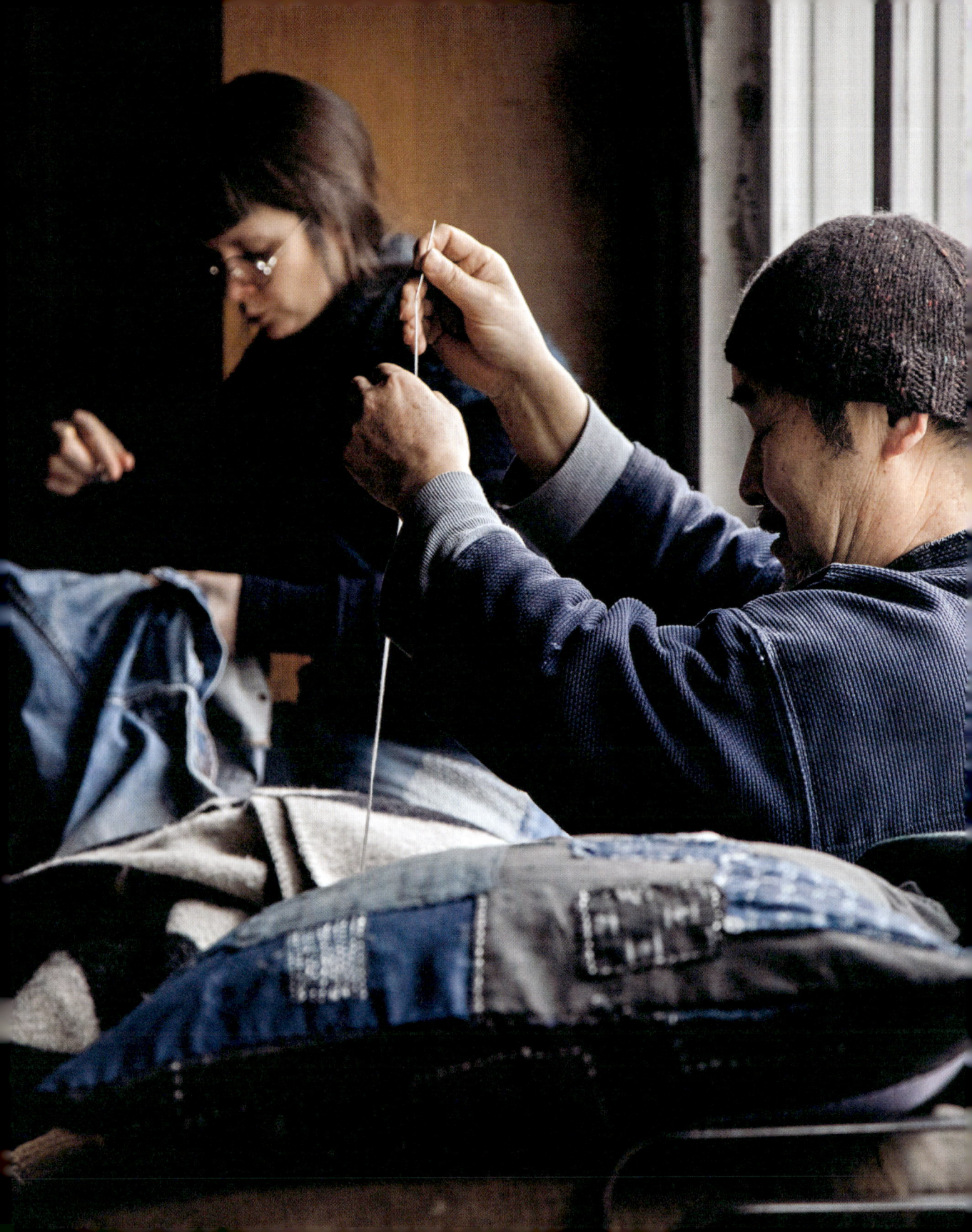

MENDING
A CUSHION
COVER

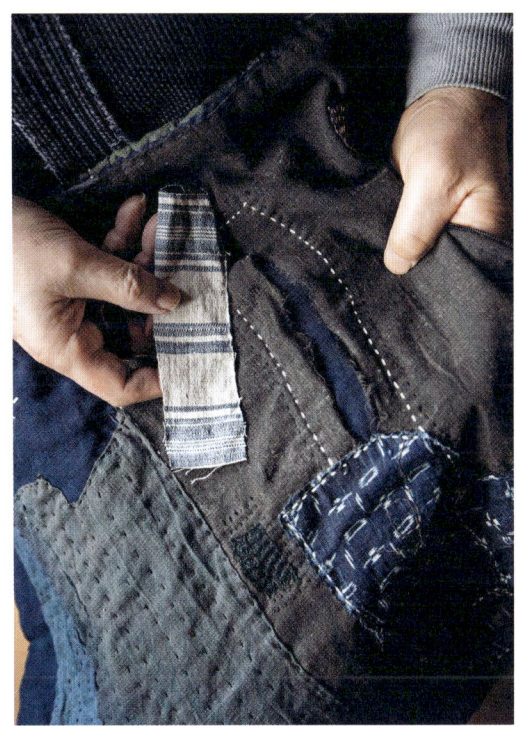

A cushion cover made from already fragile old Japanese fabrics needed mending once more. Momi made an extra-durable mend using two fabric patches.

METHOD

Start by attaching a patch to the inside of the cushion cover. You can sew the stitches from the inside or the outside, it doesn't matter, but here they are sewn from the outside. The seam needs to be placed at least 2cm (¾in) from the edge of the hole, so the patch needs to be slightly larger than that!

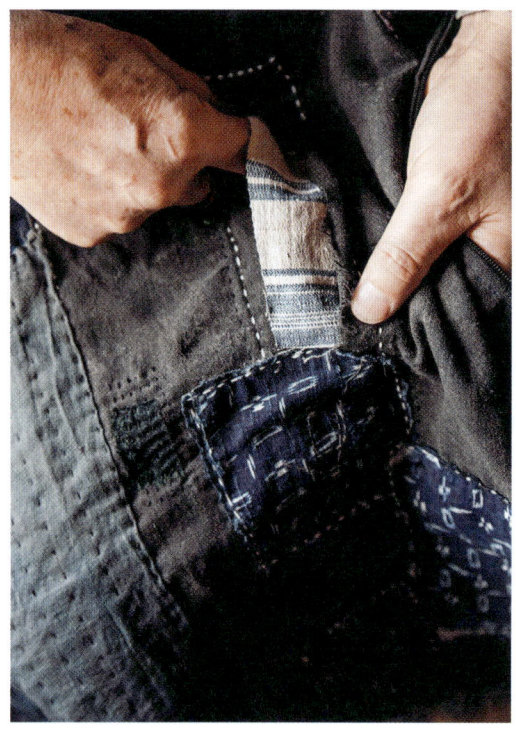 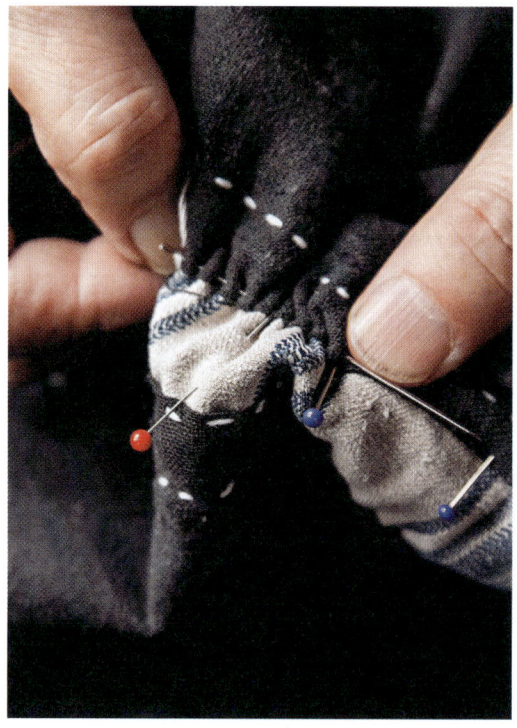

PATCH NUMBER TWO

Cut out another patch that is large enough to insert between the fabric of the cushion and the first patch (see the previous photograph). Position it so that it sits in the pocket created by the first patch behind the hole. Fold in the edges of the hole and secure in place with pins (or basting stitches).

SEW ALONG THE EDGES

Now you can sew along the edges of the hole to the fabric of both patches. Momi uses unshin stitches, but yokogushi will work just as well.

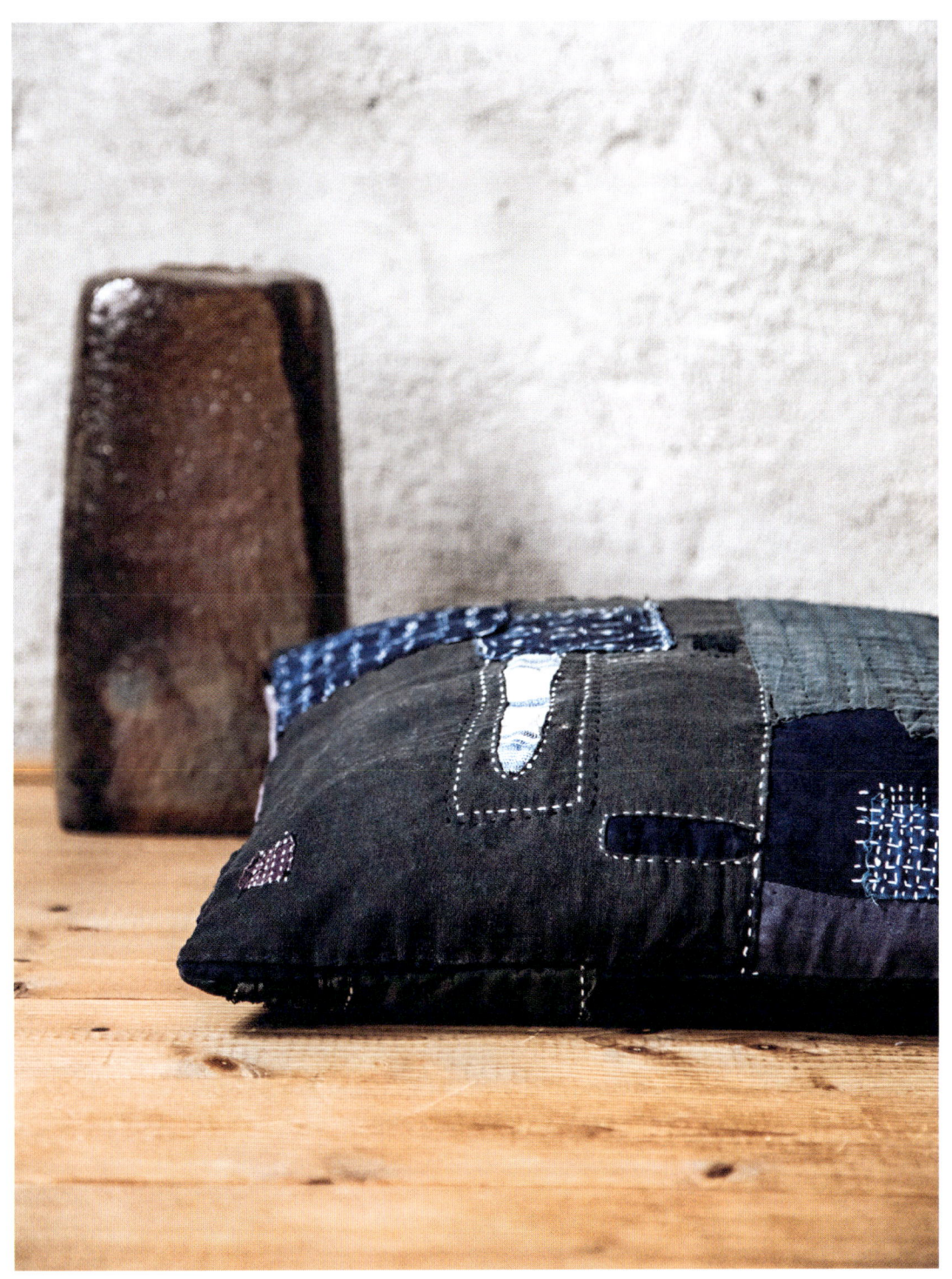

MENDING A SHIRT COLLAR

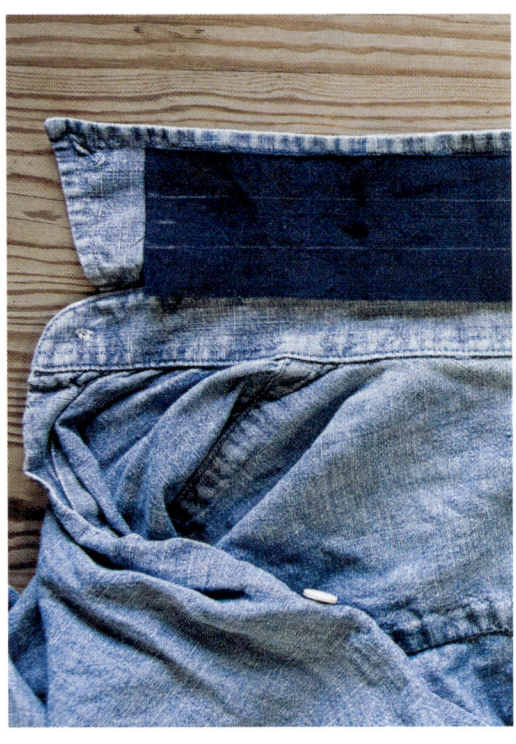

Shirt collars often wear down at the neck. Kerstin mends them by sewing on patches where needed. Here the patch uses a pattern that gives extra strength to the collar.

CHOOSING YOUR PATCH

Cut out a patch that is large enough to cover the damaged area with some excess. When you mend shirts, which are often made from thin fabrics, it's extra important not to mend with thick fabric patches as this will make the mended area bulky. If you want guidelines on your patch you can draw them out with chalk before you attach the patch to the collar.

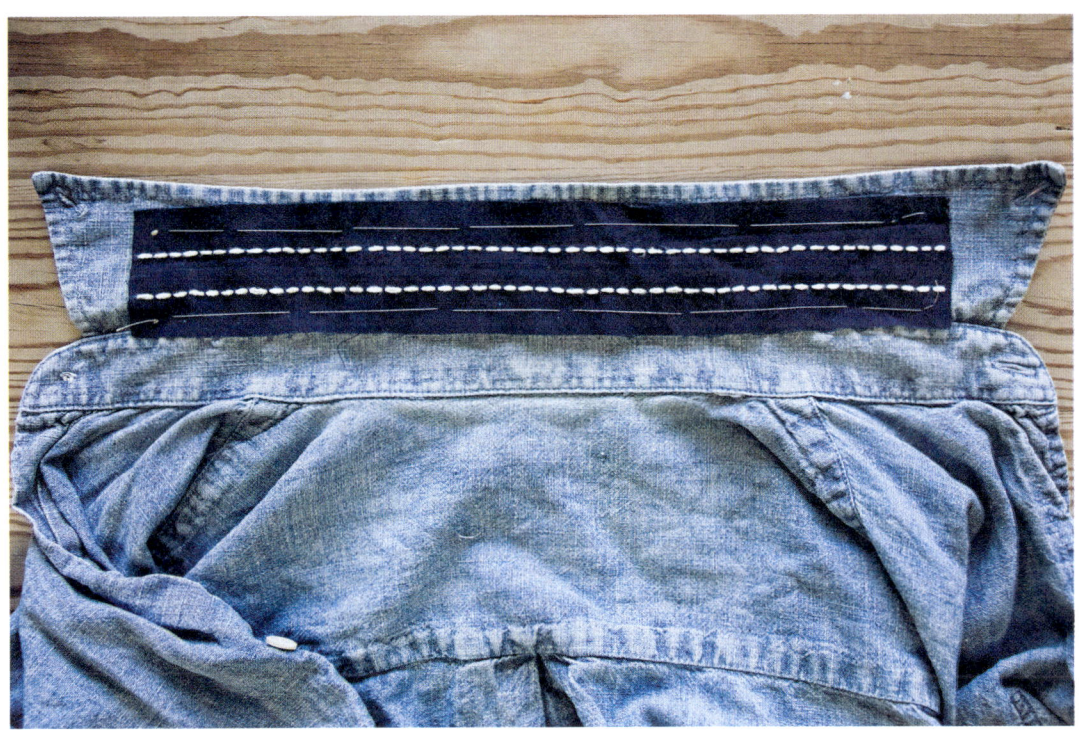

POSITION THE PATCH

Place the patch so that it just overlaps the seam of the collar stand to avoid sewing the patch to the collar's damaged and fragile fabric.

START SEWING

Baste the patch in place and then sew two rows of sashiko stitches that are a lot longer on the front of the fabric (the side that will be visible when the shirt is worn) than on the back.

Kerstin's stitches measure approximately 5mm (¼in) and they are sewn with double cotton thread for a bolder result. It's a bit tricky to get the stitch rows parallel, but if you succeed you can use them as a guide for the next step.

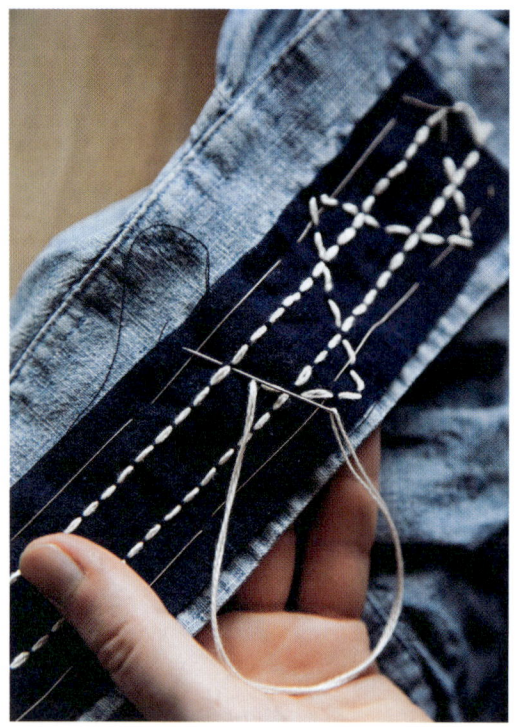

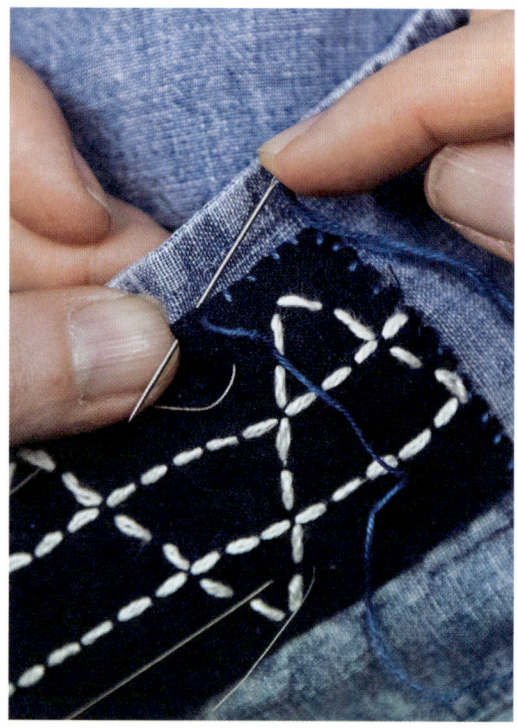

MAKE IT MORE DURABLE

You can reinforce the collar further by sewing a row of stitches between the parallel lines. The diagonal stitches here are made so that the row continues two stitches above the parallel lines before it turns back down again, then it goes down three stitches away (on the nearest of the parallel lines) from the place where it first crossed the line.

SEW DOWN THE EDGES OF THE PATCH

It's good to sew the edge down properly on a patch that sits on a collar. Kerstin uses blue thread that doesn't interrupt the visual presentation of the sashiko and sews with straight whipstitch that runs around the edge of the patch to keep it in place.

STRAIGHT WHIPSTITCH

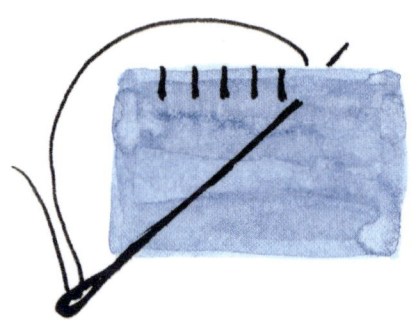

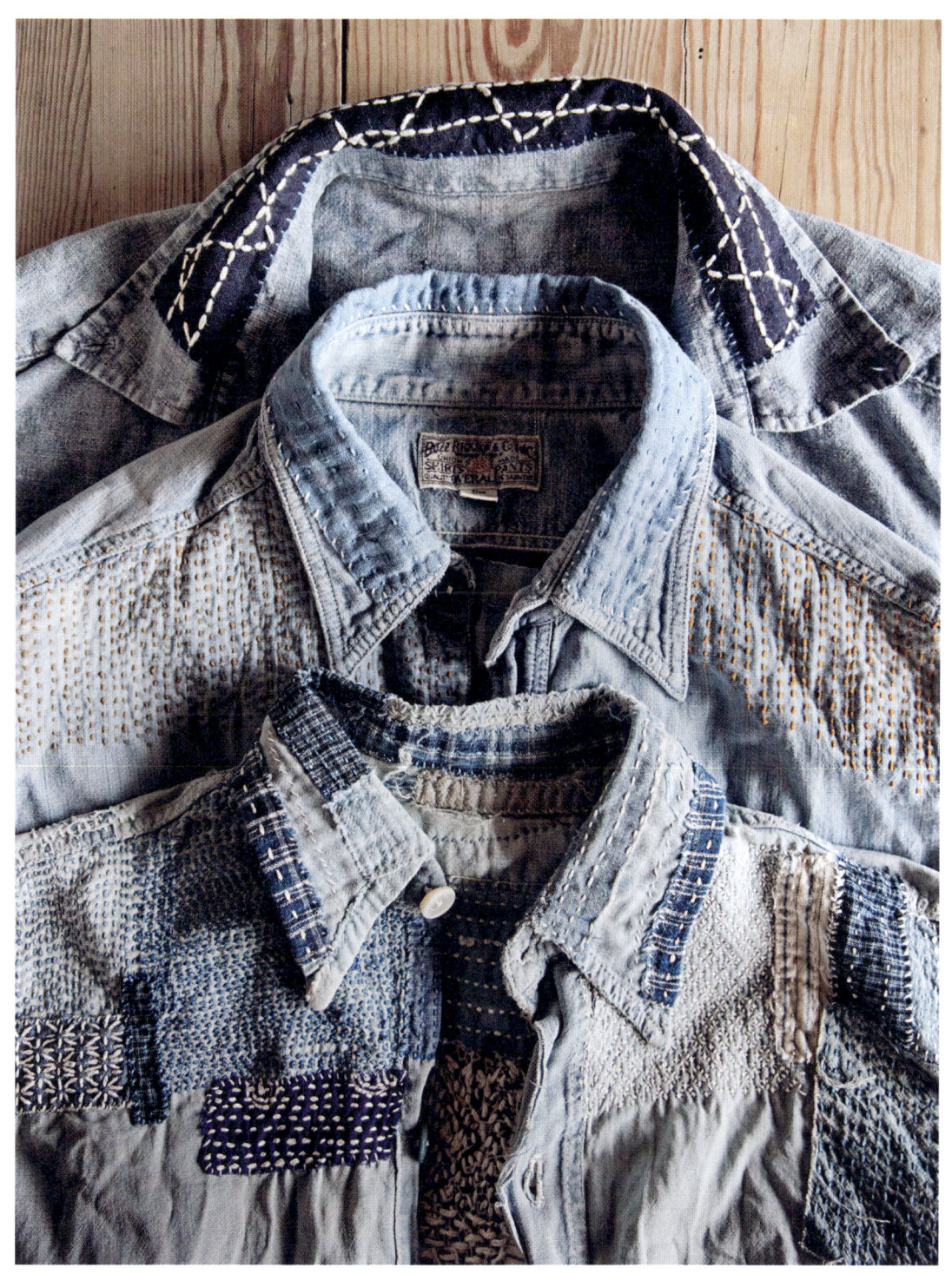

95

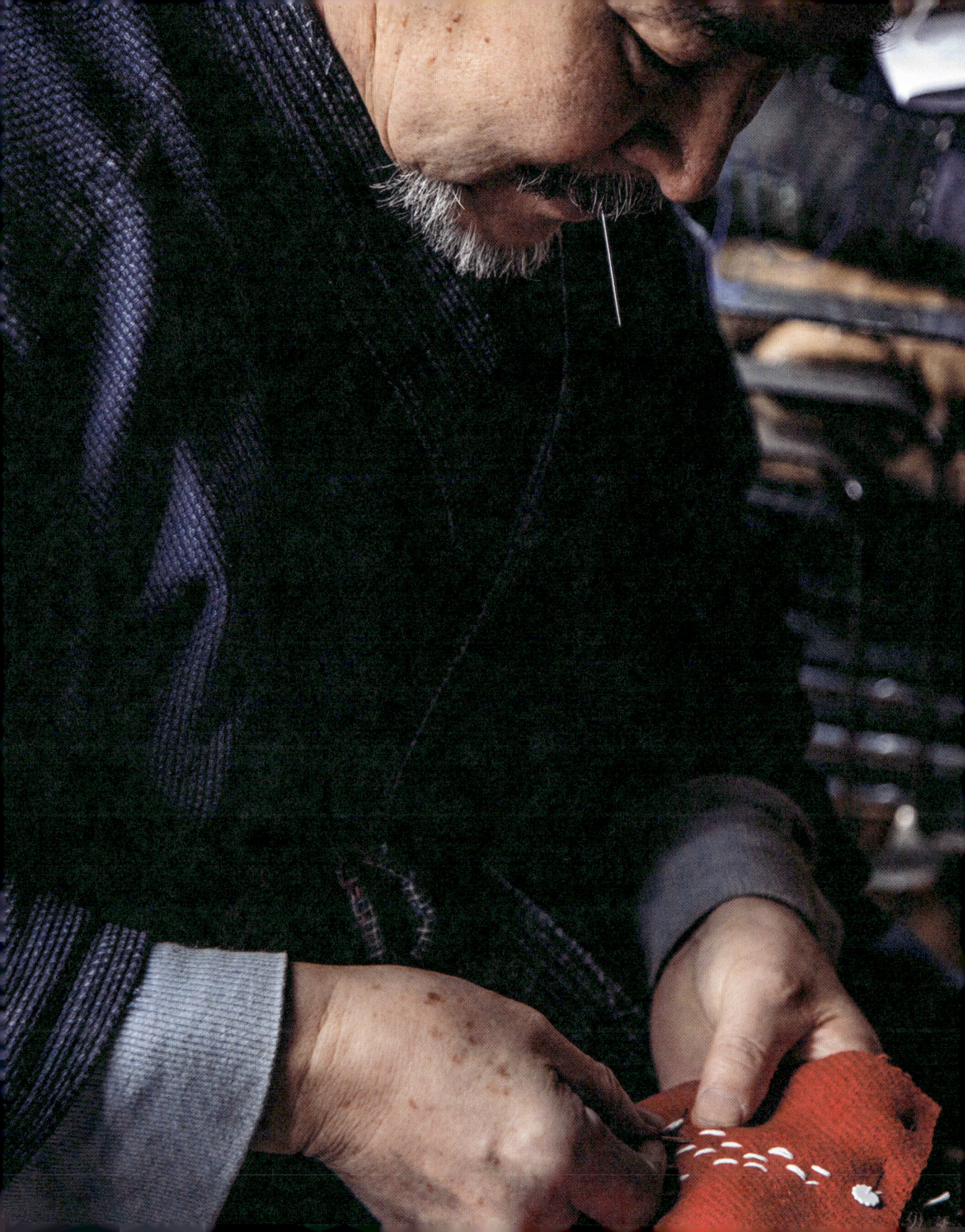

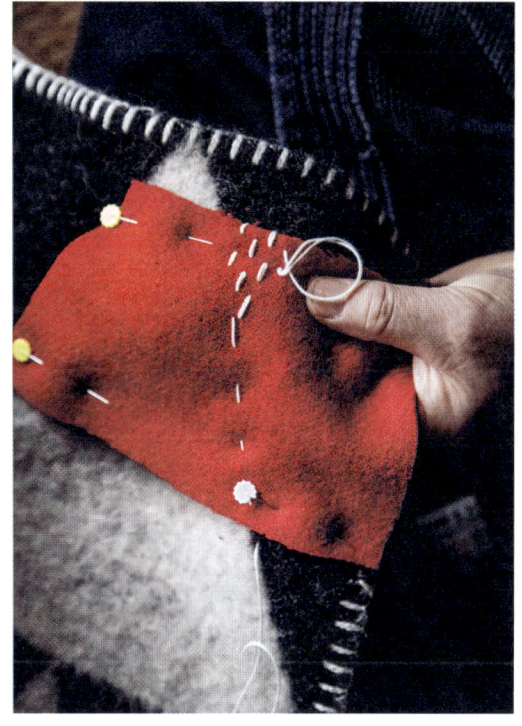

MENDING A BLANKET

When one of the blankets Momi designed became torn, he decided to mend it with a wool patch using a pattern of threaded/woven stitches. This makes the mend very durable and it also looks interesting! This technique with threaded stitches is called kugurizashi and comes from the Shonai region. By dividing the patch into two areas with a line that follows the design of the blanket, Momi had enough space to sew two different pattern variations.

CHOOSE YOUR PATCH

Start by choosing your mending patch and pin it in place. If the blanket is made from wool it is nice to use a piece of wool to mend with, but you can use other materials if you want. Avoid fabrics that are tightly woven however, such as denim, since this will make the mend hard and thick which makes the blanket uncomfortable.

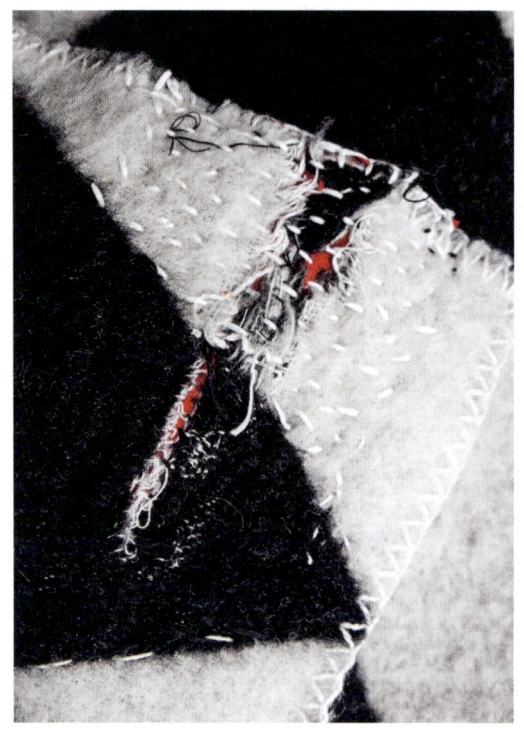
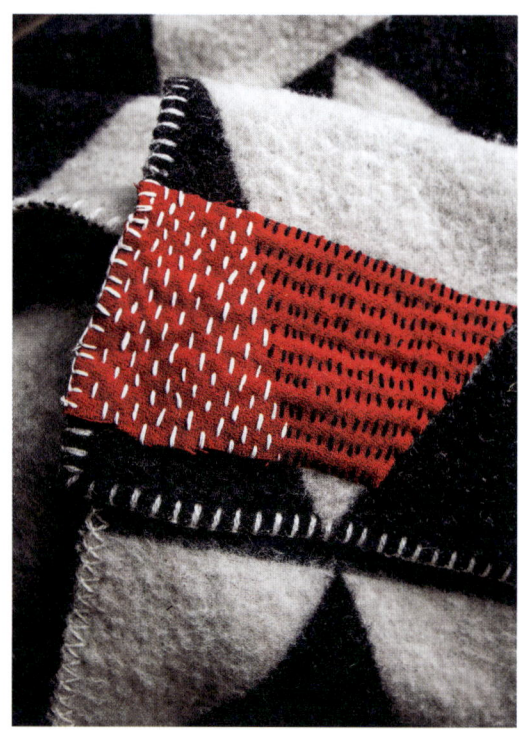

SECTION ONE

Choose a thick white thread and start sewing with offset lines of stitches that are approximately 8–10mm(⁵⁄₁₆–³⁄₈in) long with approximately 7mm (⁵⁄₁₆in) gaps between the rows, working over the first section (see page 26 for an illustration of offset stitches). When you come to the place where the blanket is damaged under the patch it's good to feel with your fingers so that the torn edges lie flat at the back and don't fold in any direction. Continue to sew your offset rows over the whole area, including the place where the tear is; it should just hang at the back.

SECTION TWO

On the part of the patch that covers the white triangle, Momi has sewn black stitches in parallel lines. These stitches are slightly shorter, approximately 5mm (¼in), and are also a bit denser: about 4-5mm (³⁄₁₆–¼in) in between the rows is good. If the edge of the blanket is finished with blanket stitch, it's nice to finish the edge of the patch the same way. Blanket stitch is fairly easy to sew: you sew around the edge of the fabric but before you pull the thread tight you insert the needle through the loop that the stitch forms.

BLANKET STITCH

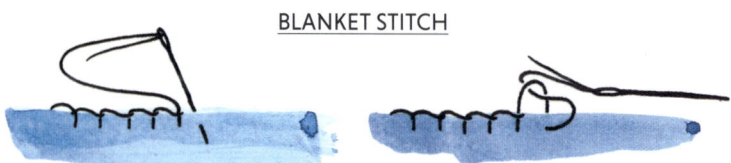

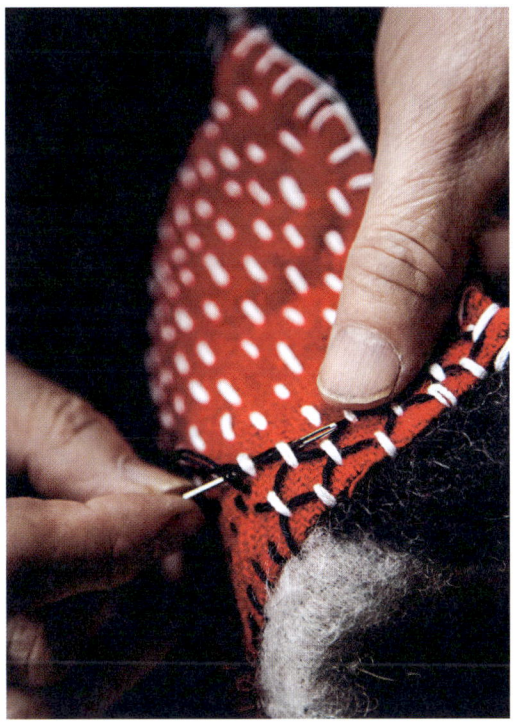

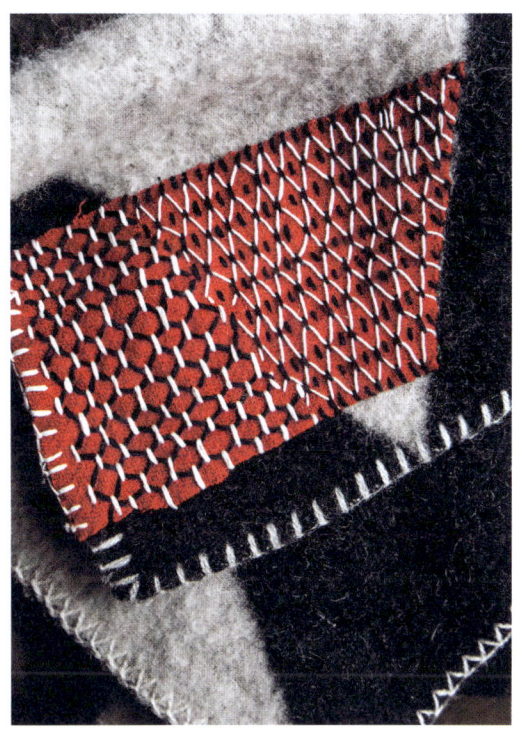

ADD BLACK THREADING

Now the mending could be complete at this point if you wish, but Momi makes the pattern more exciting by threading through the already sewn stitches. On the area with offset white stitches he weaves black thread through the stitches in rows (a stitch also used for crewel embroidery under the name of cloud filling stitch). A tip is to use a blunt needle or, as here, the eye end of the needle for threading.

ADD WHITE THREADING

On the area with black stitches Momi weaves a white thread that zigzags through every other black stitch. This way the stitches that he doesn't sew through become little framed dots!

MAKING A
POTHOLDER

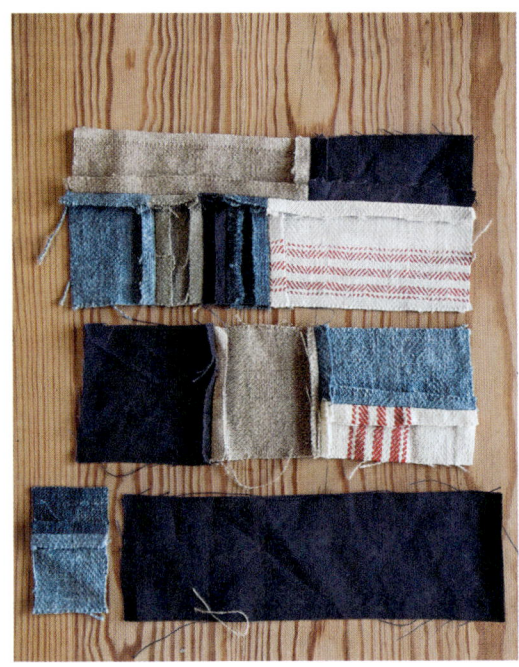

Potholders are perfect projects to make use of little leftover fabric pieces. Even pieces that are only large enough for wrapping three beans (remember mottainai?) can be used here (that is approximately 3 x 3cm (1¼ x 1¼in)). Kerstin sews her potholder with a sewing machine, but you can sew by hand if you'd prefer! This potholder is made from three layers of fabric: a front in patchwork technique, a fluffy filling and a plain back.

CHOOSING YOUR PATCHES

Choose which fabrics you'd like to use. Potholders get a lot of wear, so use slightly heavier fabrics and make sure to avoid synthetic fabrics since they risk melting when they come into contact with heat.

The front of the potholder is made from fabric pieces that are sewn into strips that are the same length but different widths and these strips can be made out of one or several patches. A nice way to work is to decide on a length for the strips and then join patches without measuring too carefully! As long as you stick to the same length, the width of the individual patches doesn't matter too much. When you have reached the required length, you can just trim off the end to make it the required size for the potholder.

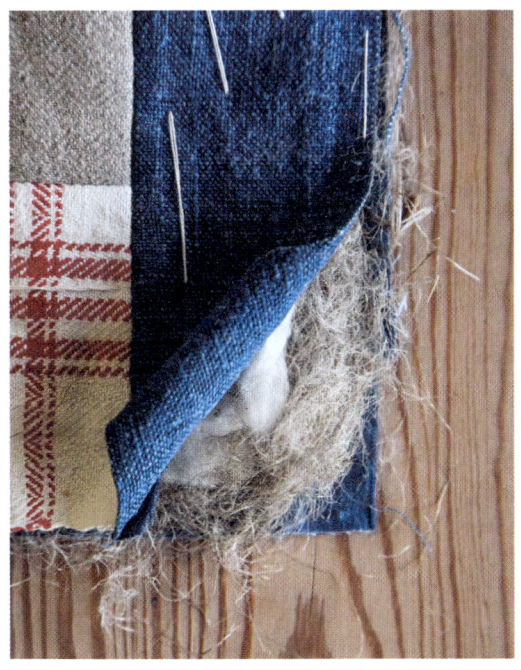

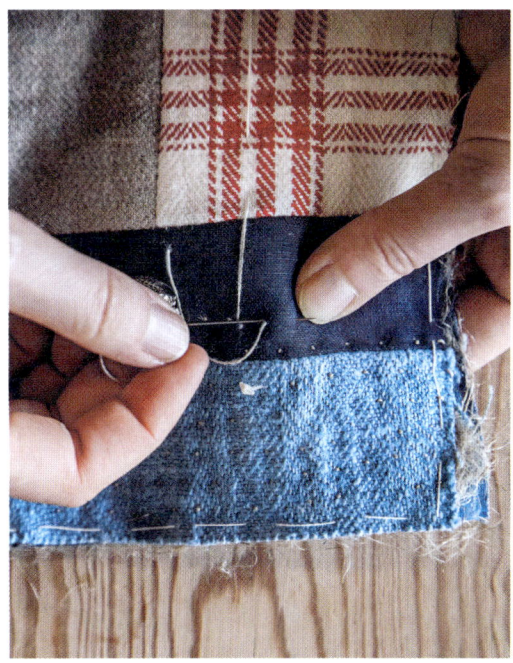

SEWING THE FRONT TOGETHER

Place the strips right sides facing and sew together with a 1cm (⅜in) seam allowance. You don't need to zigzag any edges as they will be enclosed inside the potholder when you're finished and and so are unlikely to fray. Each new seam is pressed open once sewn, meaning you iron the back of the seam and open up the seam allowance.

When the front is done, you can cut out a piece of fabric the same size for the back. Now you need something for the filling. You can take an old wool blanket, or like here, leftover cotton wadding and linen fibres. Baste together all three layers to keep the filling in place.

SEWING TOGETHER ALL THREE LAYERS

Now all three layers need to be sewn together. You can use sashiko stitches or, like here, spaced backstitches. Regardless of which, it will be more comfortable if you use a thimble when inserting the needle through the layers. Here the stitch rows are fairly dense, approximately 2cm (¾in) apart, but you can place them more sparsely if you want – up to a 5cm (2in) gap will work fine.

SPACED BACKSTITCH

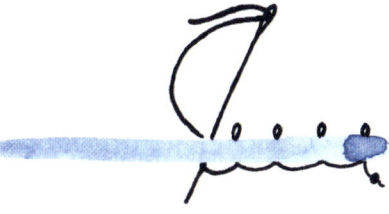

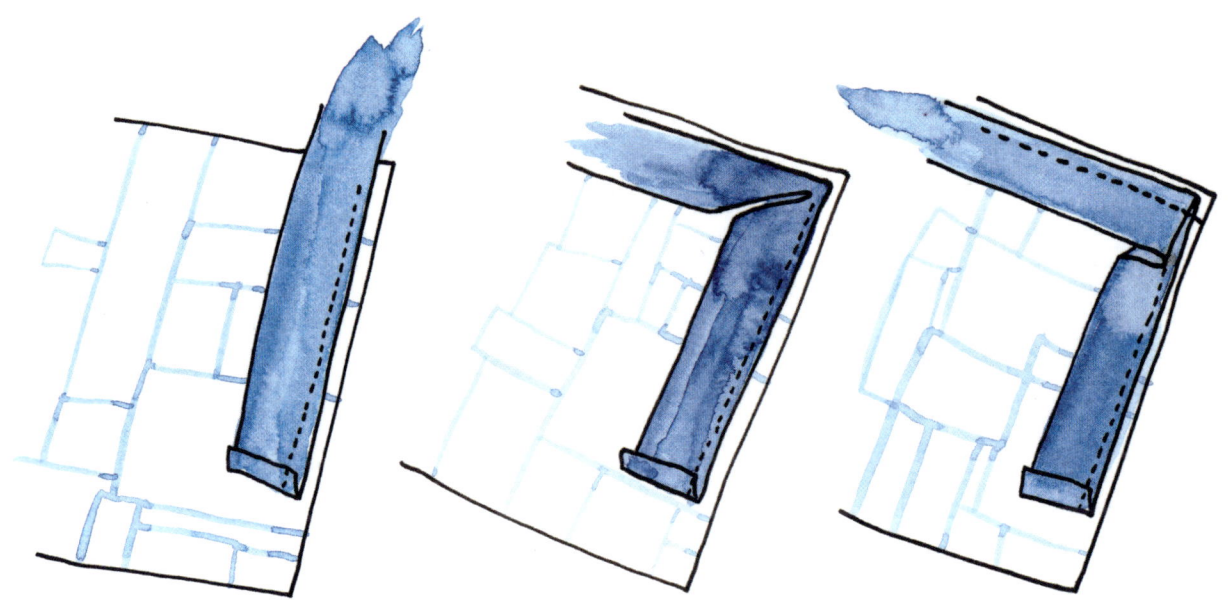

SEWING ON THE BINDING

When the potholder is covered in stitches it's time to sew on a binding. It should be long enough to go around all four edges of the potholder and wide enough that it's enough to cover the edges of the front and back plus seam allowances. If you want the binding to be 1cm (⅜in) wide, the strip needs to be 4cm (1½in) wide.

Start by sewing along one of the potholder's long sides. Position the binding over the potholder, right sides together. Fold over the last centimetre (⅜in) of the short edge before you start sewing, and it will be easy to get a nice join when you're finished.

Don't sew all the way to the next corner. Stop and secure the seam 1cm away from the edge of the corner, and fold the binding so that it follows the next side of the potholder.

A large fold will appear on the binding at the corner. Fold it so that it sits flush with the first edge, and then sew the binding in place along the next side.

FINISHING

When the binding is sewn into place around the whole potholder, sew it to the start of the binding so that it overlaps a little, this way no raw edges will be visible at the front later.

To finish, you fold the binding over to the back of the potholder and sew it in place there. You'll get a nice result if you sew by hand with small stitches that just grab hold of the fabric at the back, so that no stitches are visible from the front.

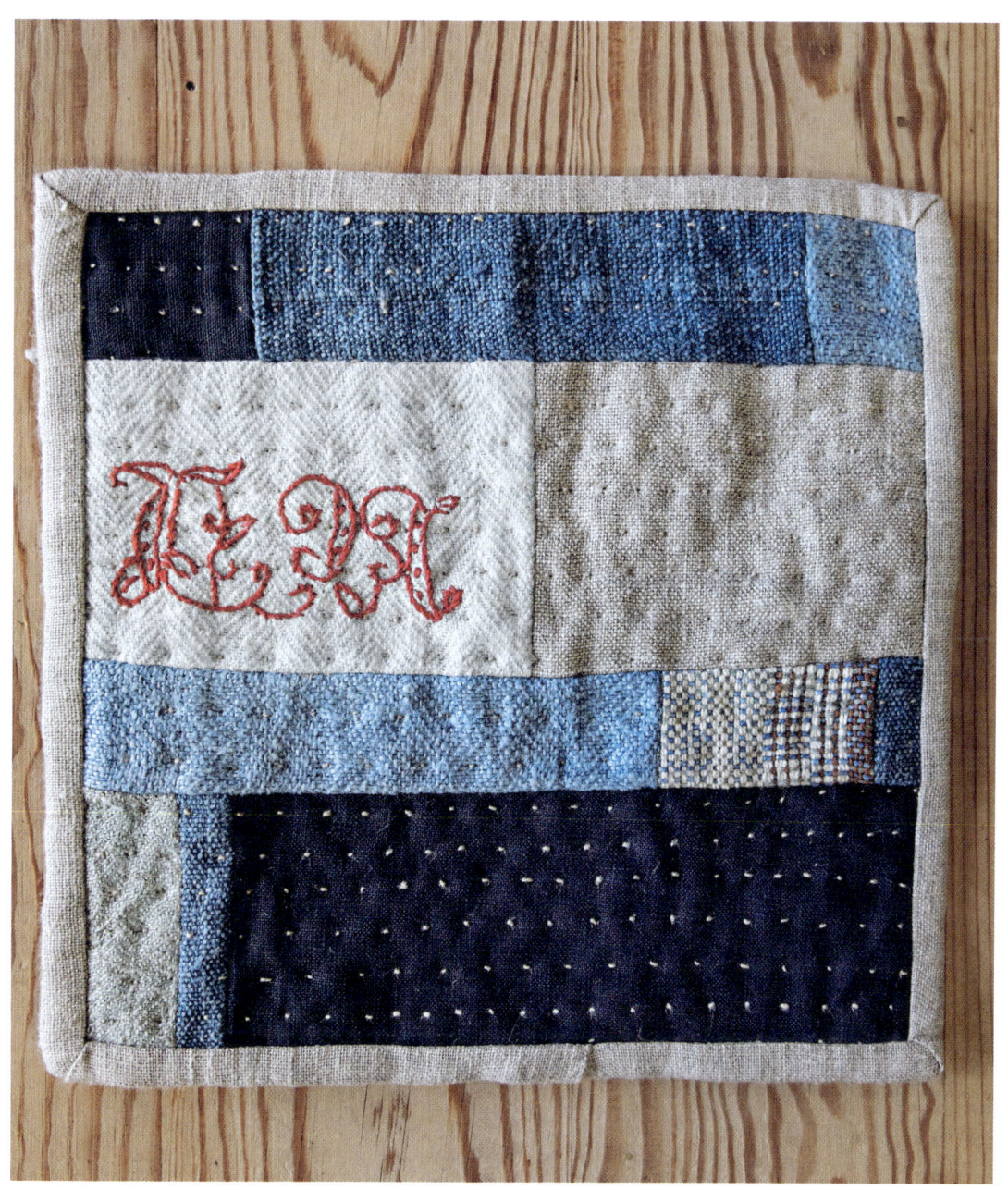

PS

This potholder is constructed just like a patchwork quilt, it's just the scale that sets it apart.
So if you want to make a patchwork quilt you can use the same instructions!

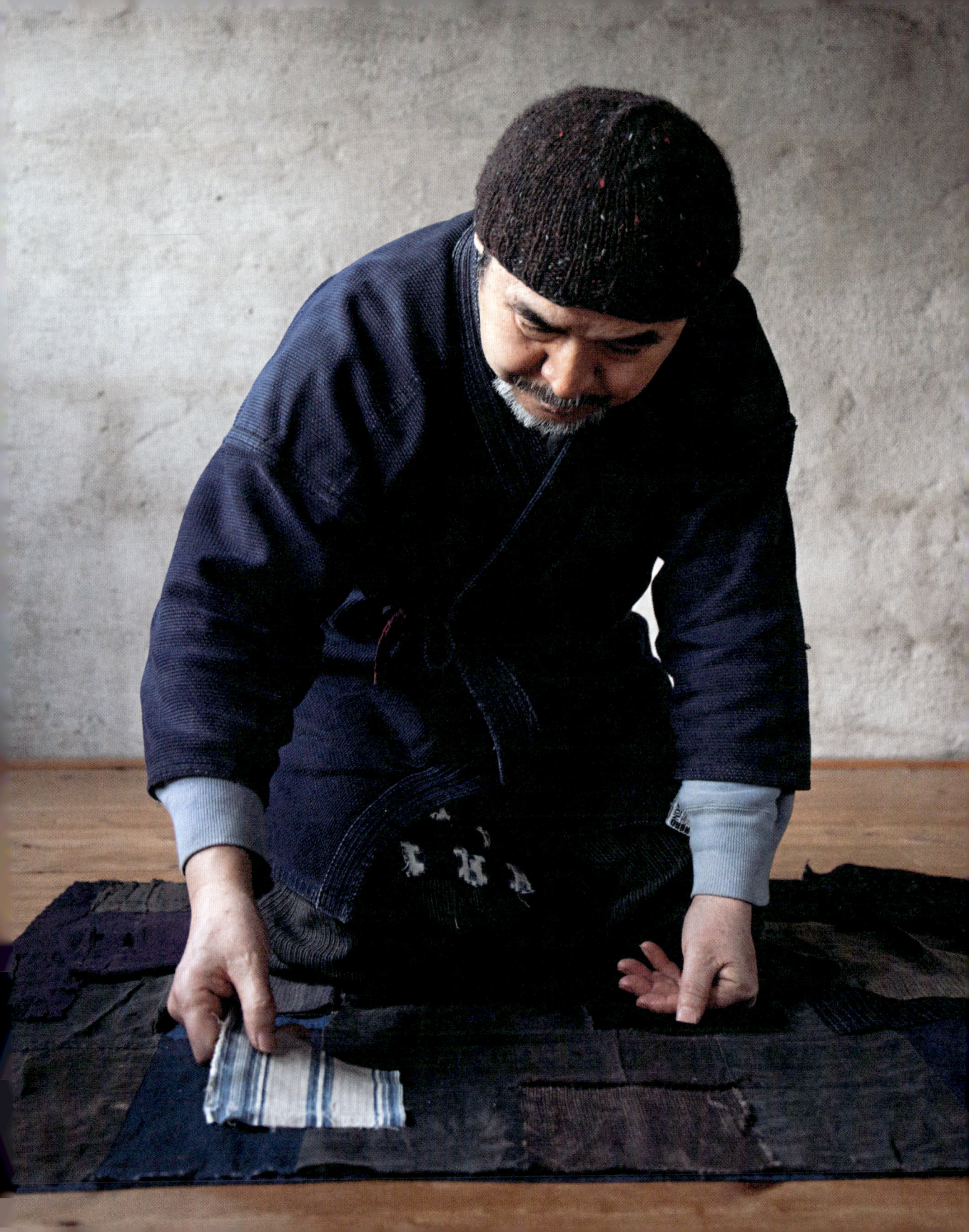

BODOKO – ALMOST A PATCHWORK QUILT

Bodoko is a large piece of fabric that was used for bedding in old Japanese fisher homes. The word is usually translated to 'life cloth' and it's said to have been used as a sheet for childbirth, with the intention that the first thing the baby touches should be a fabric made up of textiles that have been worn by the previous generations. When it became worn, new patches were sewn on, and an old bodoko can be made from dozens of fabric layers!

You could therefore say it's a Japanese version of a patchwork quilt. Momi makes a bodoko to hang on the wall, but you can, of course, use it as a warm blanket instead if you want to.

METHOD

Use a worn-down piece of fabric that needs patching as the starting point. If it's too small you can add a piece of fabric with a 1cm (⅜in) overlap along the edge you want to lengthen and sew it in place with running stitches, so you get the size you had in mind. Take out the patches you'd like to use and place them over the fabric. Here you can achieve a lot by varying the structure and materials of the patches!

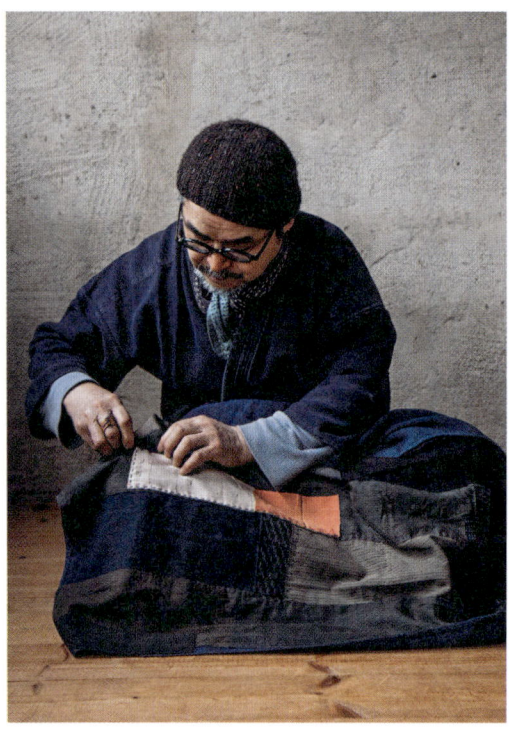

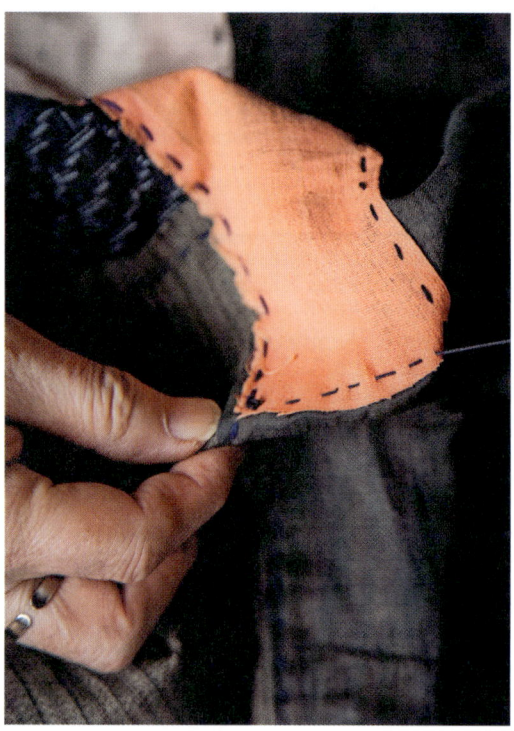

ATTACHING THE EDGES

When you're happy with your composition you can pin or baste all the patches in place so that they don't move around.

START SEWING

Momi sews all patches in place with rows of running stitch around the edges. It would also look nice to sew sashiko stitches over some of the patches and perhaps let them run over the edges of the patch!

A few patches in a contrasting colour can lift a composition. It's a good idea to use complementary colours such as blue and orange.

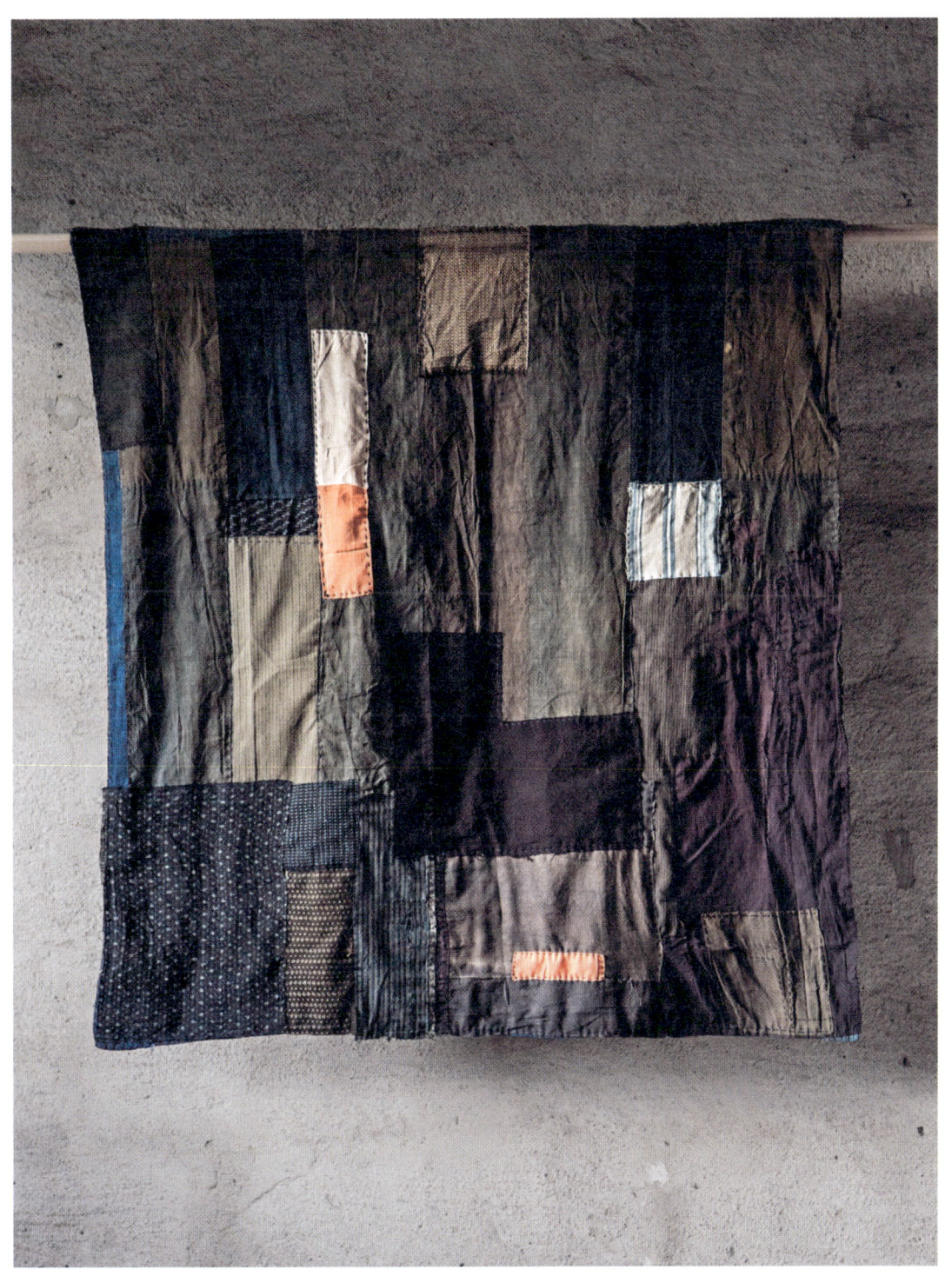

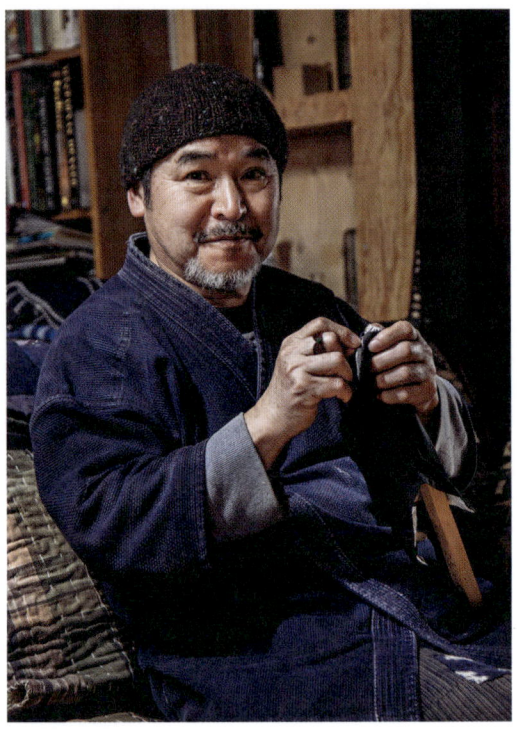

MENDING TABI

Momi's mending journey started with a pair of tabi, traditional Japanese socks that are sewn in a non-stretch fabric and have a special space for the big toe. When mending tabi it's important that all stitches are short and that you sew all loose threads in place properly.

METHOD

Before you start, look for something that is hard and flat to insert into the sock while you're mending. Usually you might try to keep your hand inside the sock, but this is a bit tricky and you don't have anything dividing the sock's front and back so there's a chance you could sew them together. Momi usually uses a piece of wood.

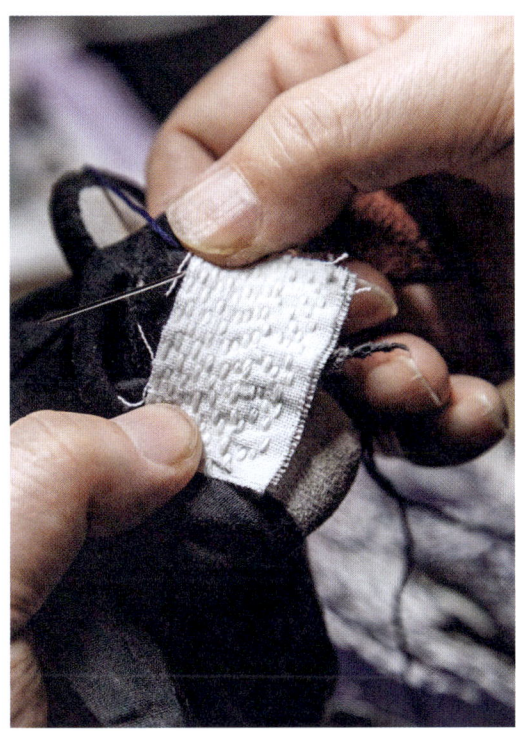

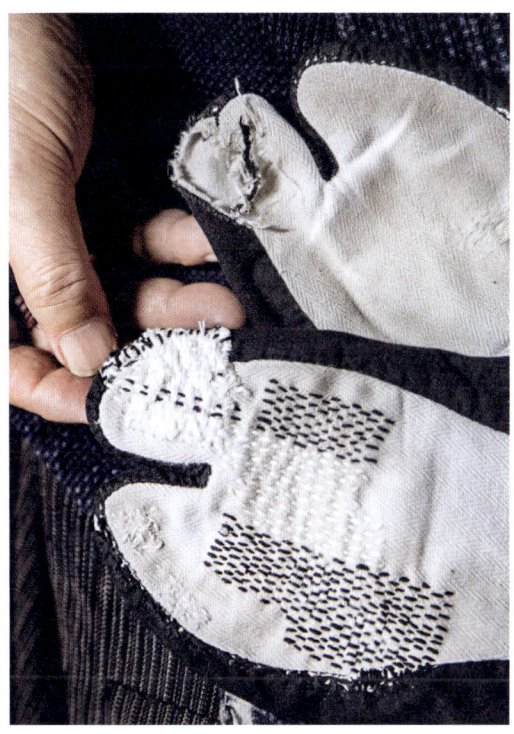

REINFORCE WITH STITCHES

The best time to mend a pair of tabi is before there's a hole in the fabric, when it's just a bit worn down. Then you don't have to sew on a patch, and it's enough to reinforce with stitches that cover the worn-down area.

If you do end up waiting until there's a hole, it's important to choose a mending patch that is thin but strong. A thick patch would feel like a lump underneath your foot and then you can't concentrate on what you're doing – your training, for example!

SEW DENSE STITCHES

Sew the patch in place with many small, dense stitches. When you have finished you can secure the edges of the patch with straight whipstitches (see illustration on page 94).

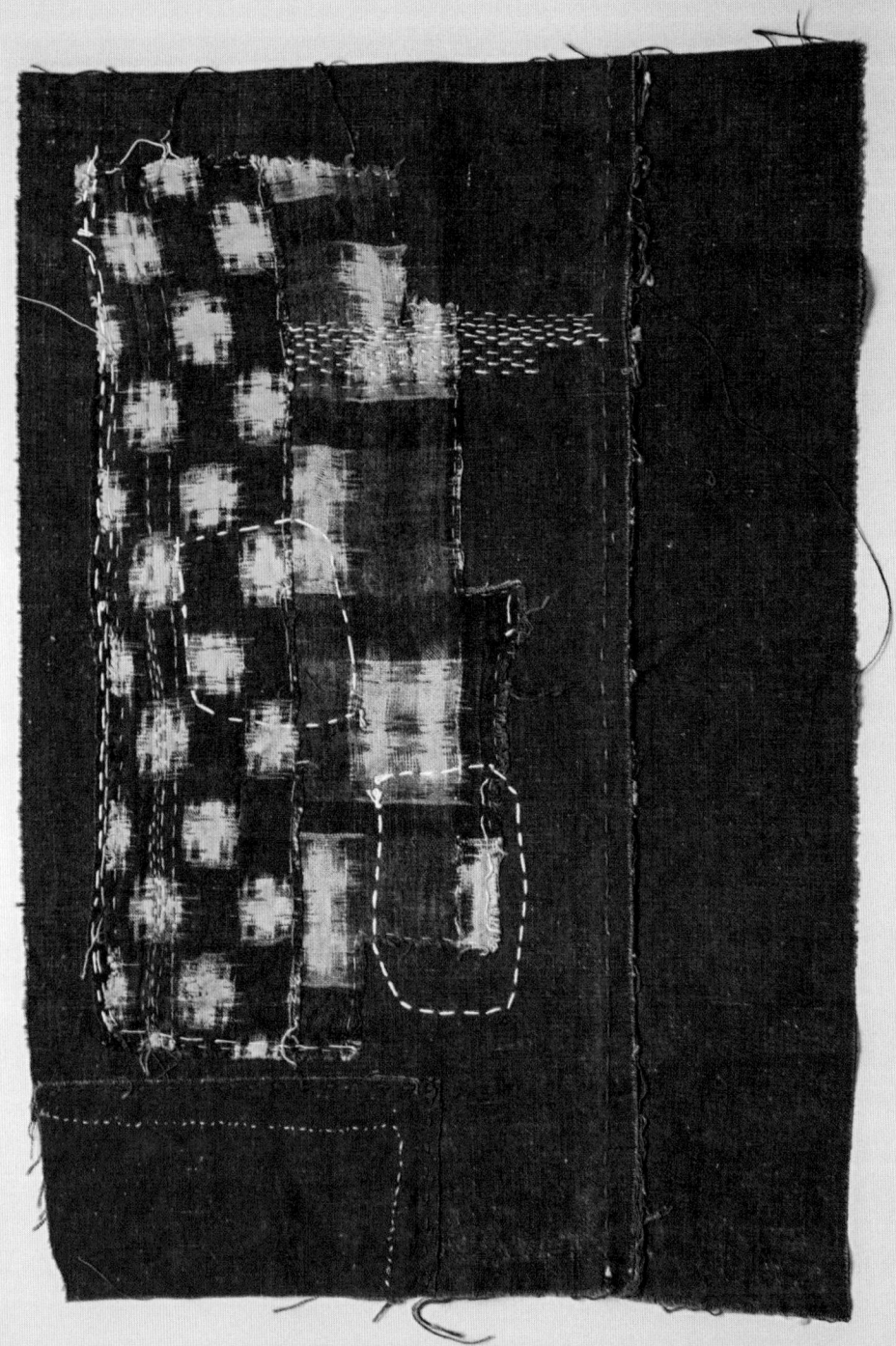

SASHIKO DIARY ENTRY, 08.06.2020
'A field landscape. I'm imagining that the seam between the two blue
fabric pieces creates the tracks from a tractor that has driven past.'

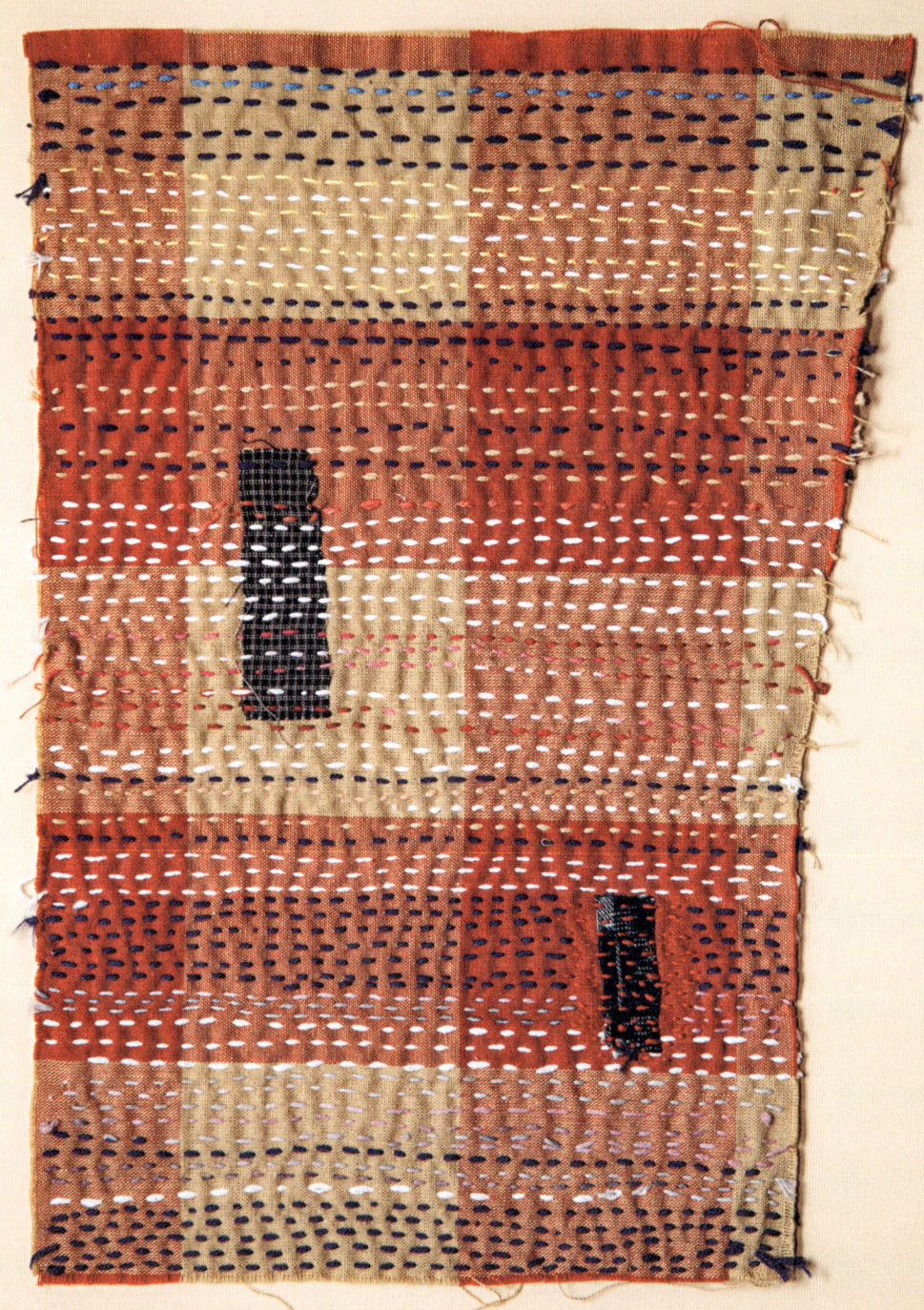

SASHIKO DIARY ENTRY, 05.10.2022
'I'm practicing unshin. Every day I pick a new colour for the thread!'

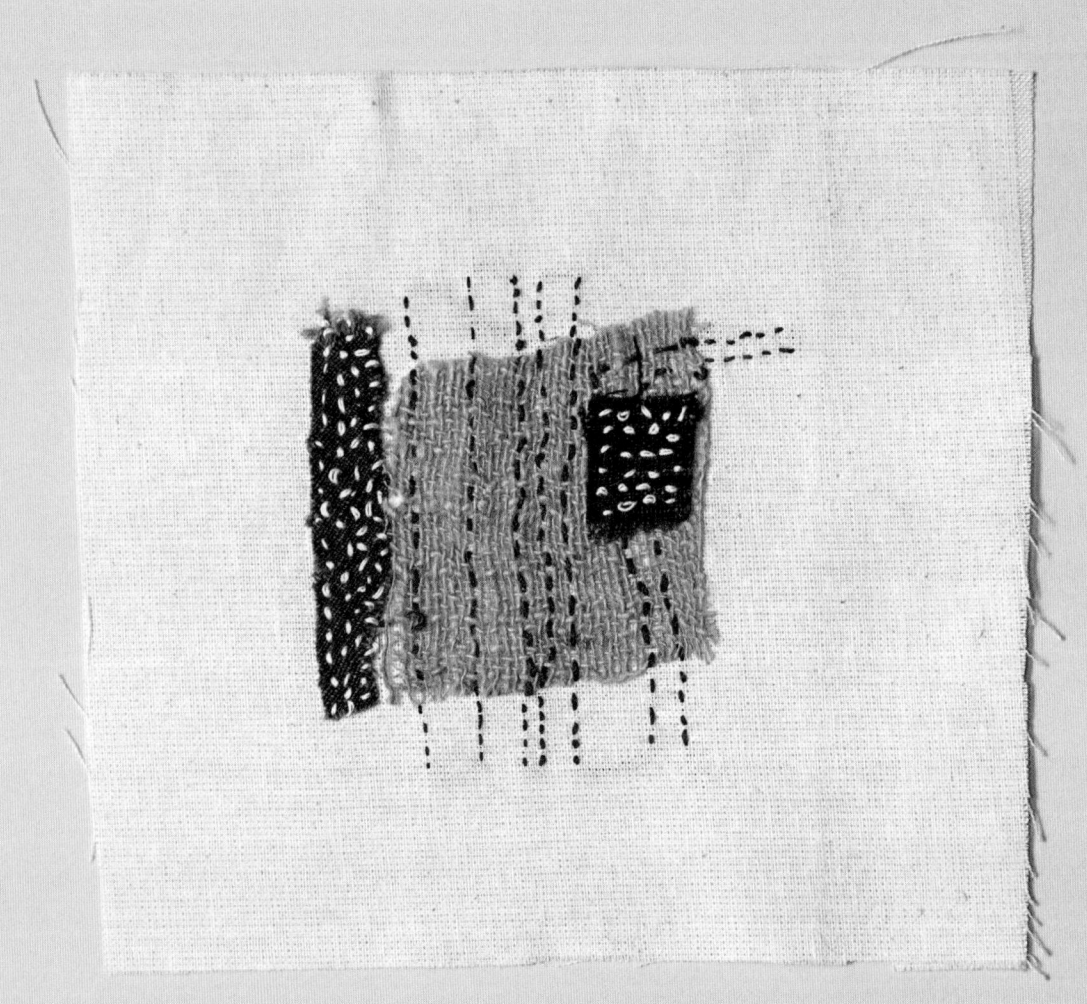

SASHIKO DIARY ENTRY, 10.01.2020
'An attempt at using small pieces. How much does the presentation
change if I vary the stitches?'

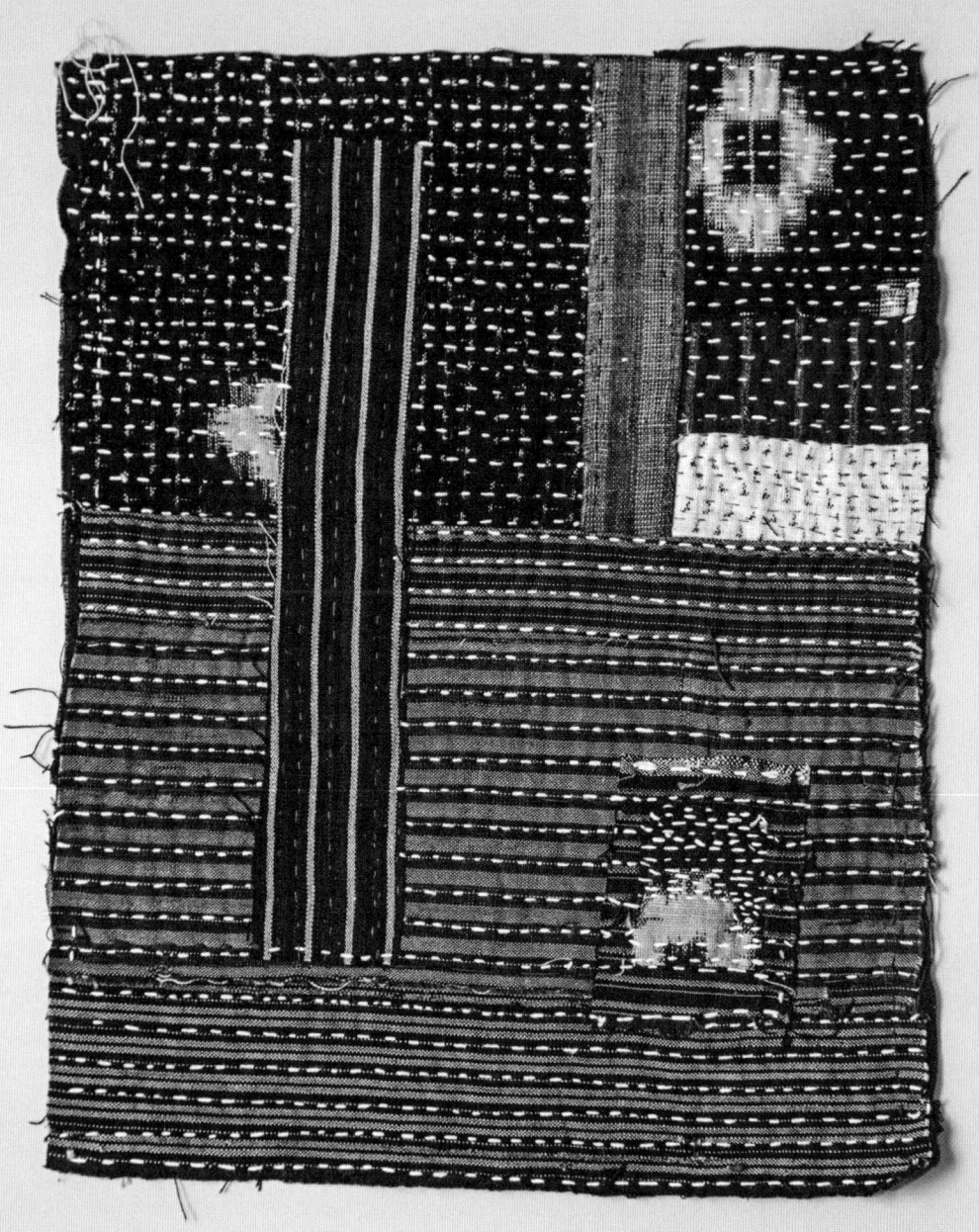

SASHIKO DIARY ENTRY, 17.03.2022
'I'm practicing unshin and composition, but I think an orange or red piece is missing underneath the long and narrow stripy line … I need to add one. Then it's finished!'

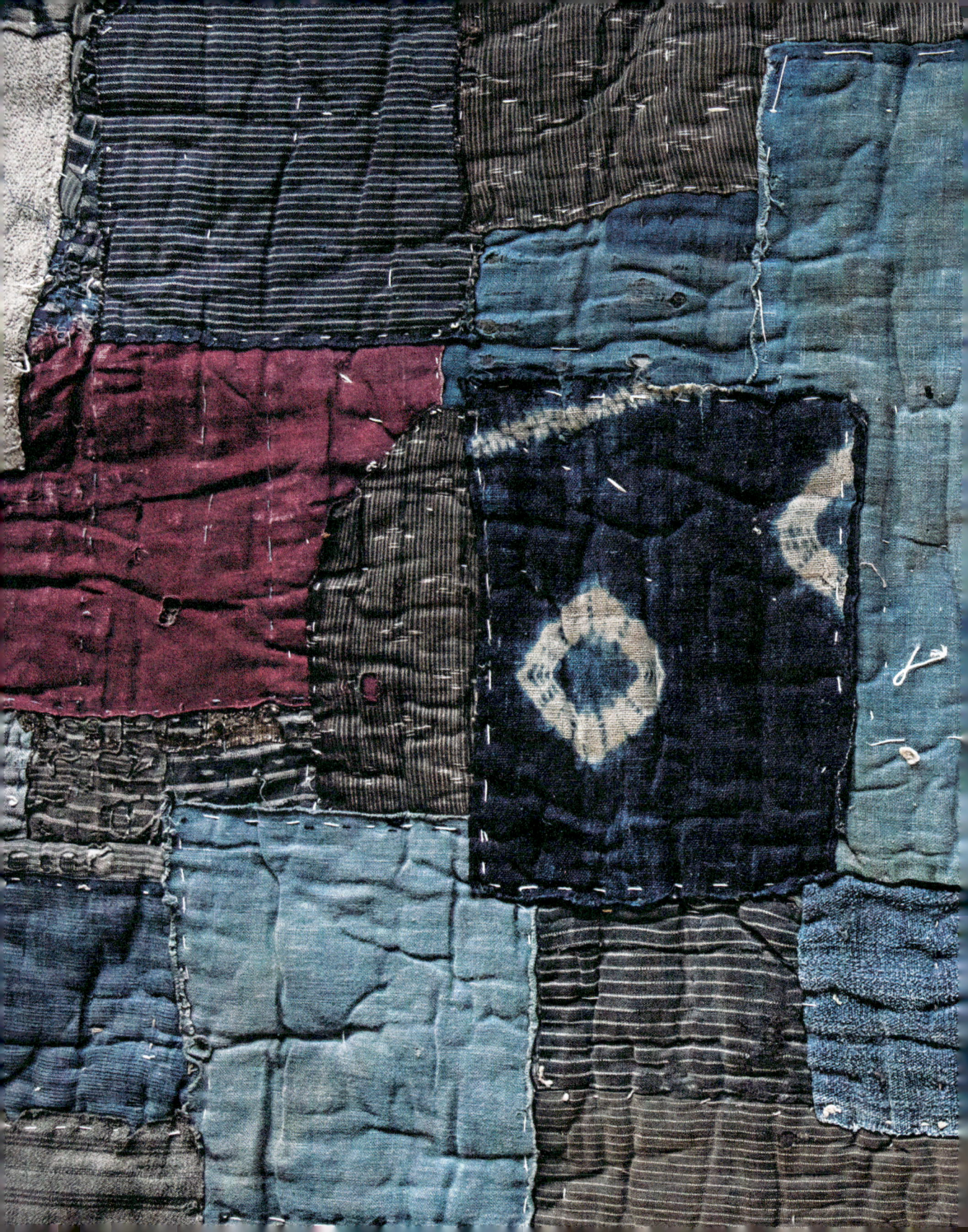

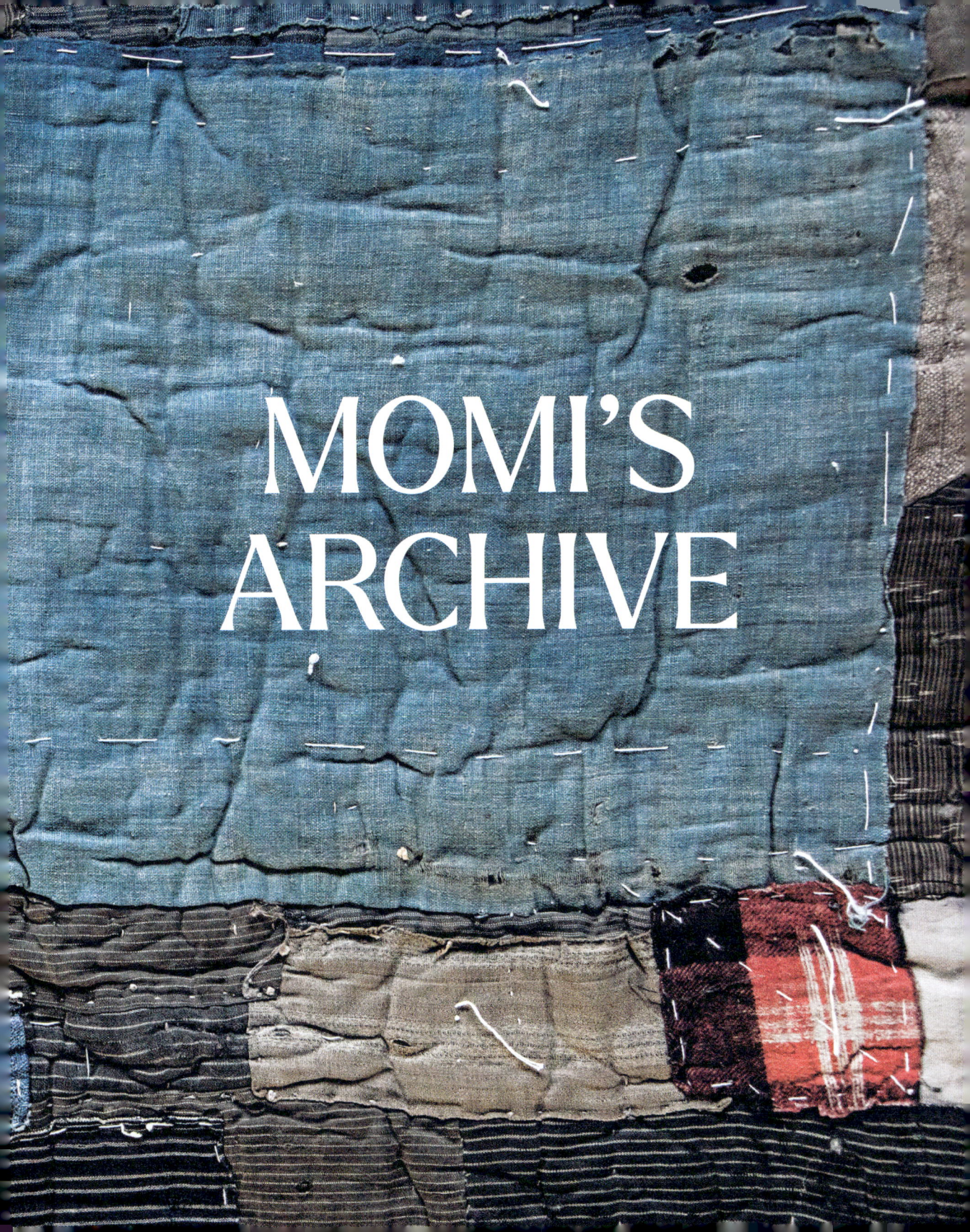

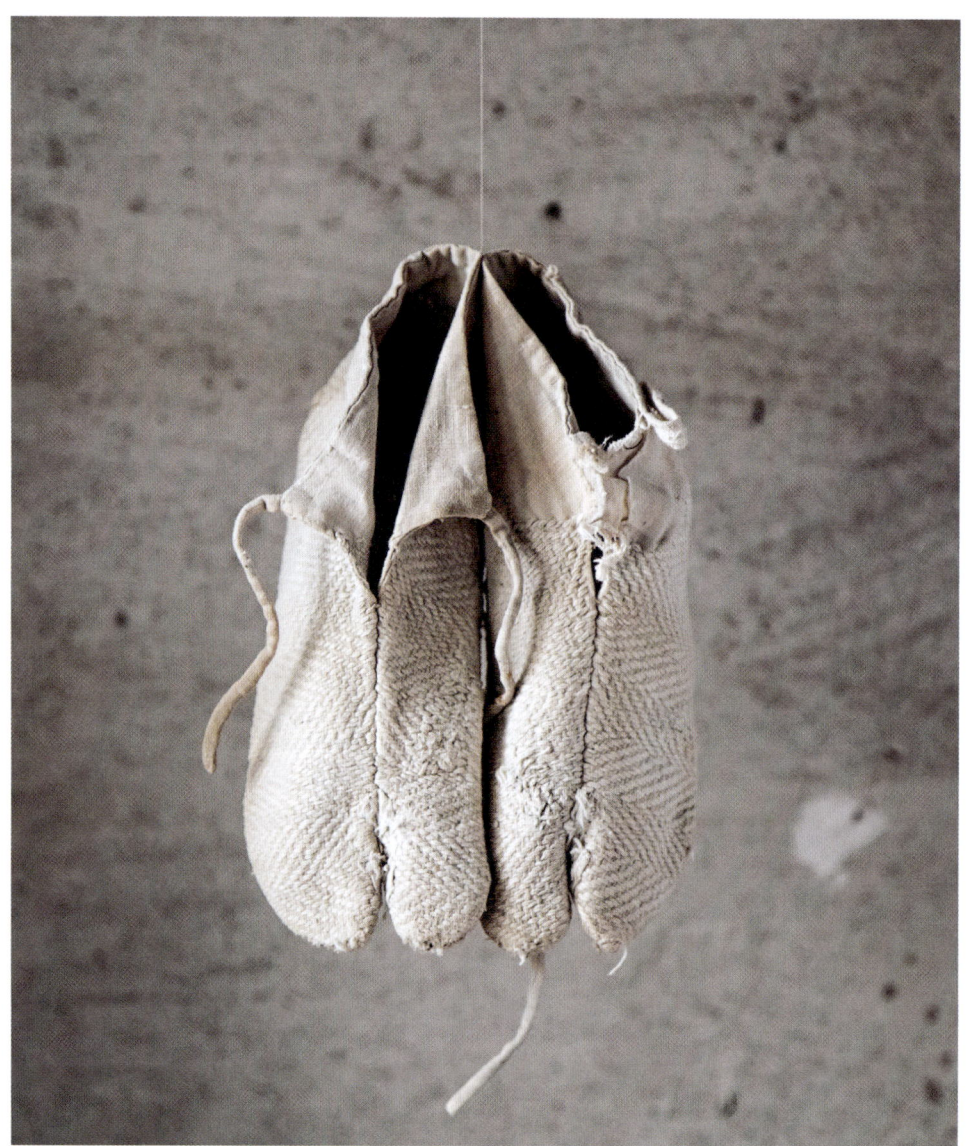

TABI, JAPANESE TRADITIONAL SOCKS

When practicing iaido, you wear tabi, and it can take six months to wear down a pair. Momi has four pairs on rotation that he reinforces with sashiko stitches and mends when needed.

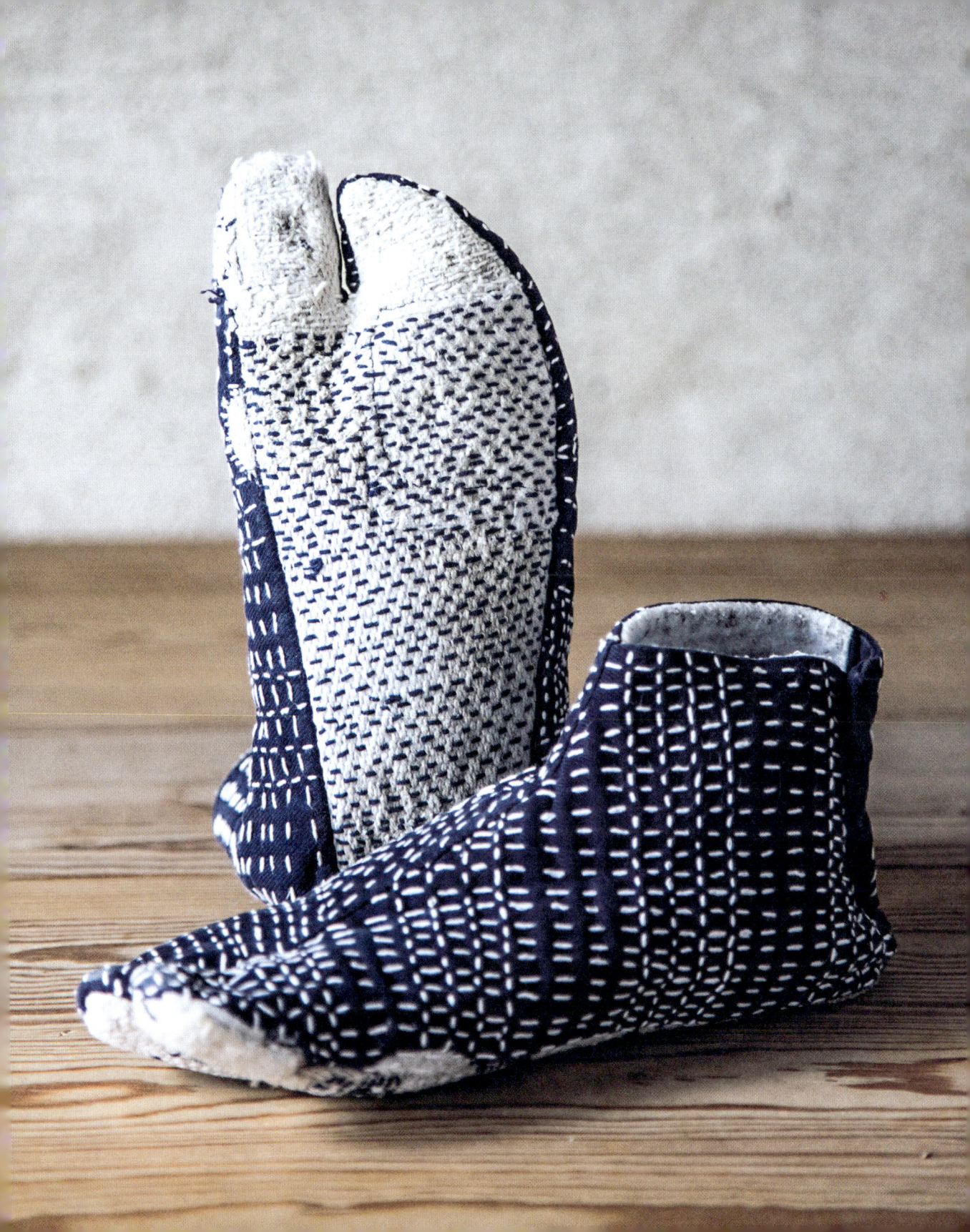

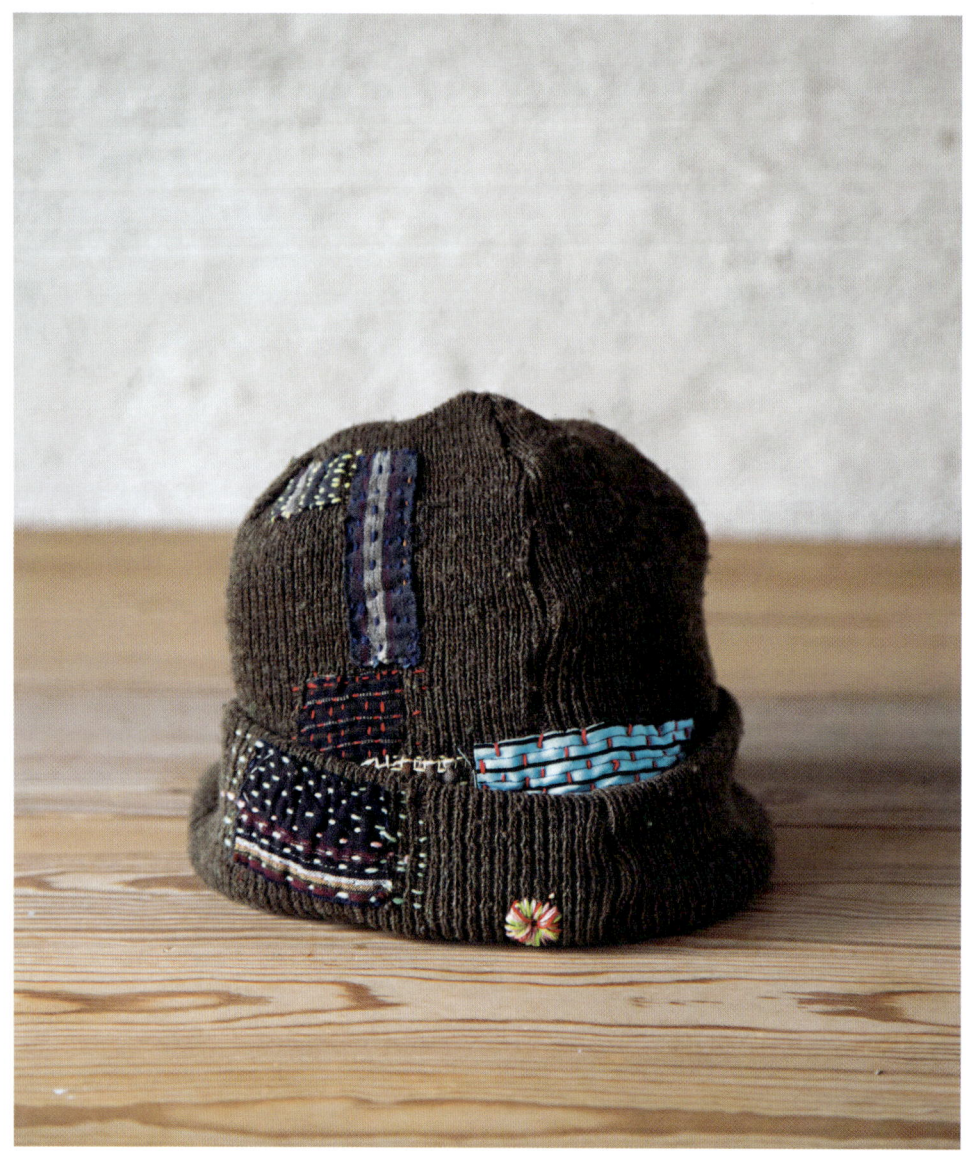

WOOL HAT

This hat fell victim to a moth attack. Momi mended it with a mix of modern and old fabrics, and distrubuted the un-stretchy patches so that there were still stretchy areas between them.

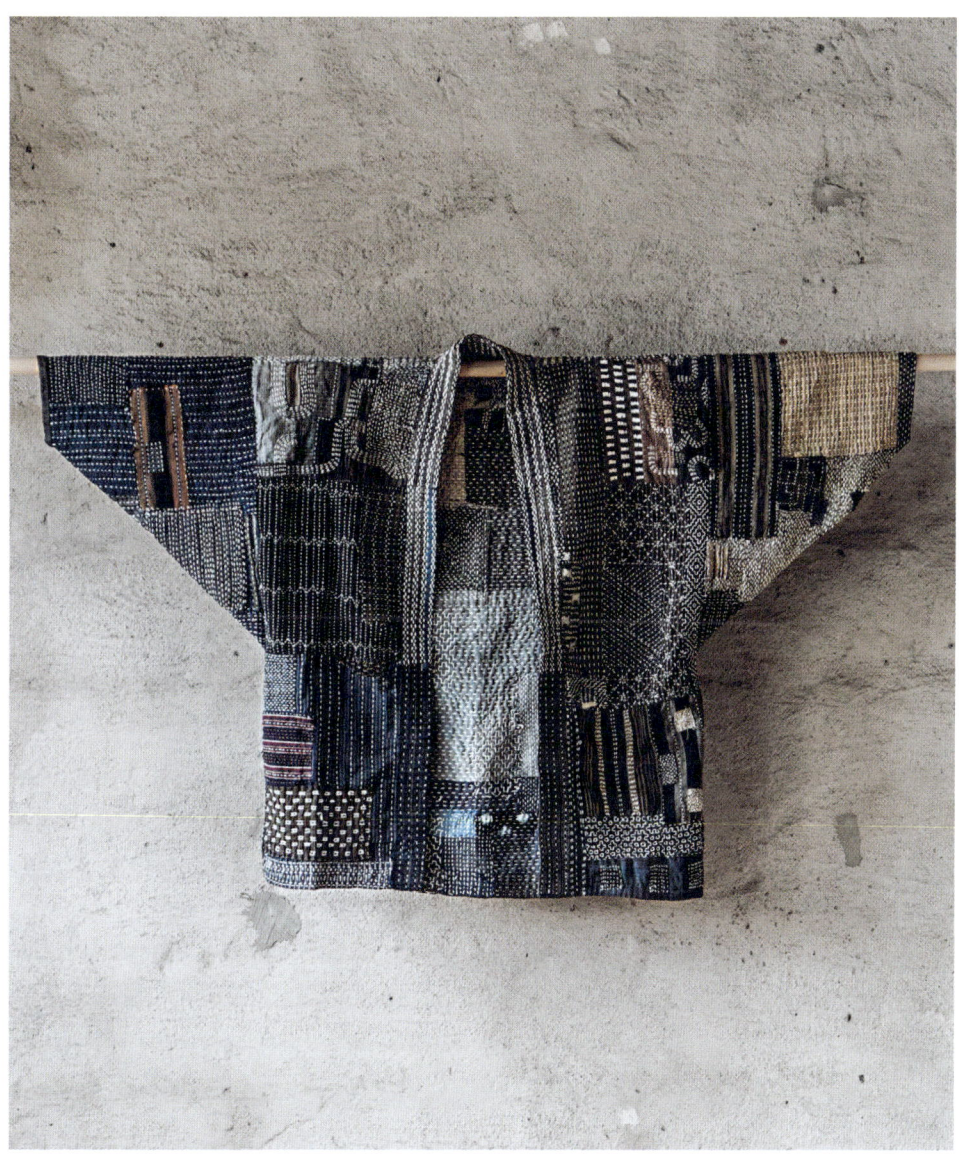

NORAGI, WORK JACKET FROM JAPAN

When Momi bought this jacket only the left-hand side remained – the right-hand side had completely worn off. He reconstructed the right side by looking at how the left was sewn and built up a new fabric with old patches and sashiko.

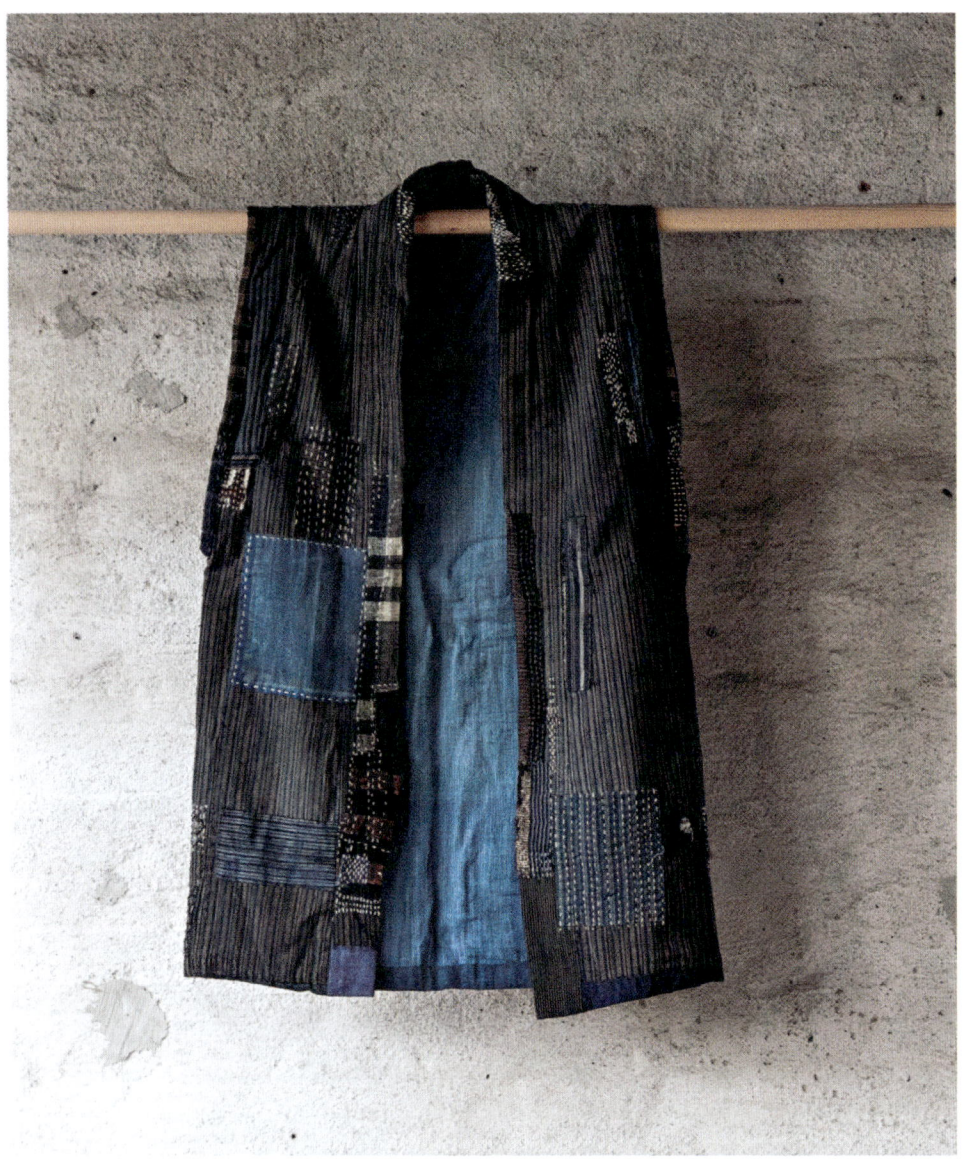

WORK WAISTCOAT FROM JAPAN

This waistcoat was already damaged when it was bought and Momi has patched and mended it with old fabrics. 'I remember my grandad and grandma always wearing this type of workwear. It's a typical work garment for the cold season, and you can wear it over a noragi with sleeves if you want extra warmth over your back when you're out working.'

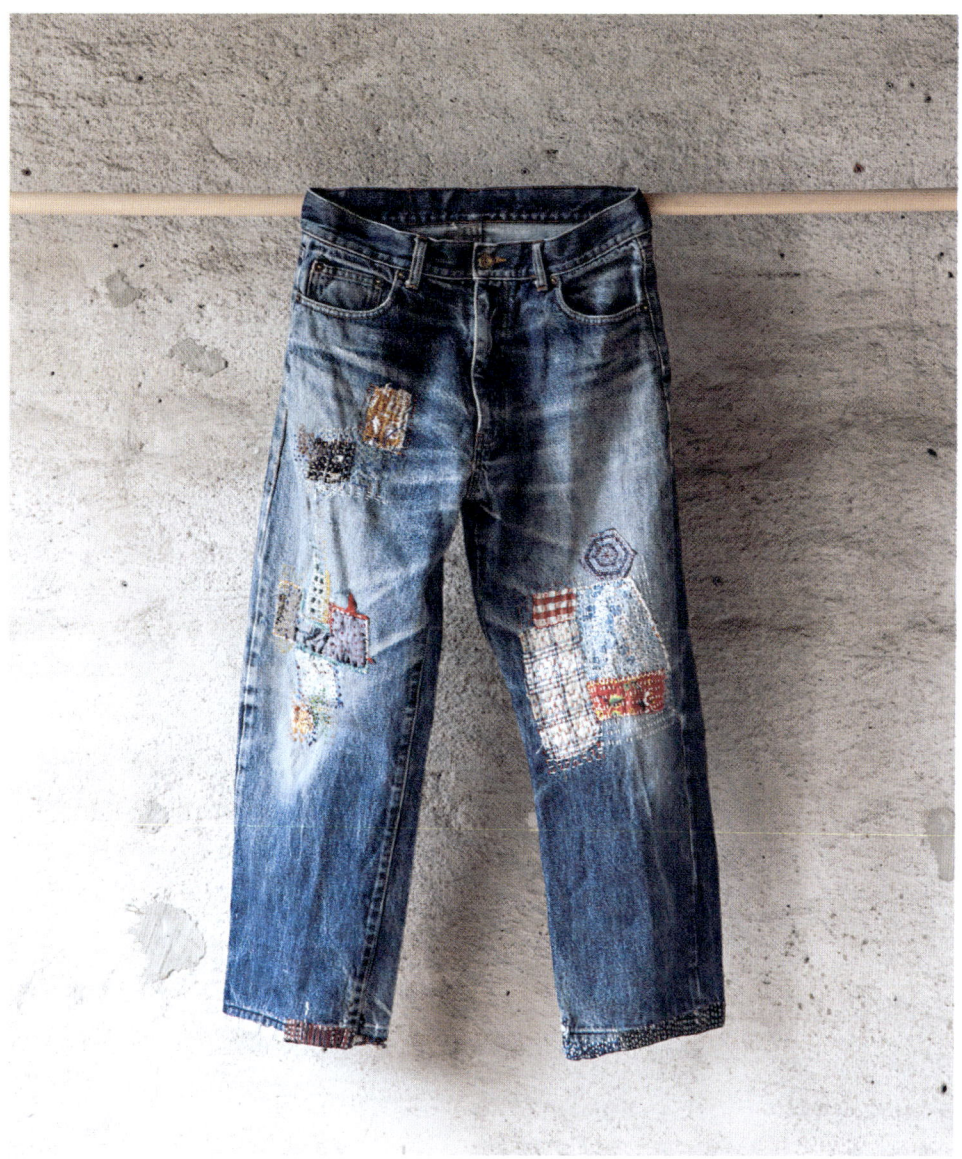

JEANS

First there was a tear on the left knee, so Momi started mending with hitomezashi in a version of the kaki no hana pattern (see page 26). Then, when the other knee also needed mending, he thought he'd try making an image composition for the first time, and it became like a little town with a church!

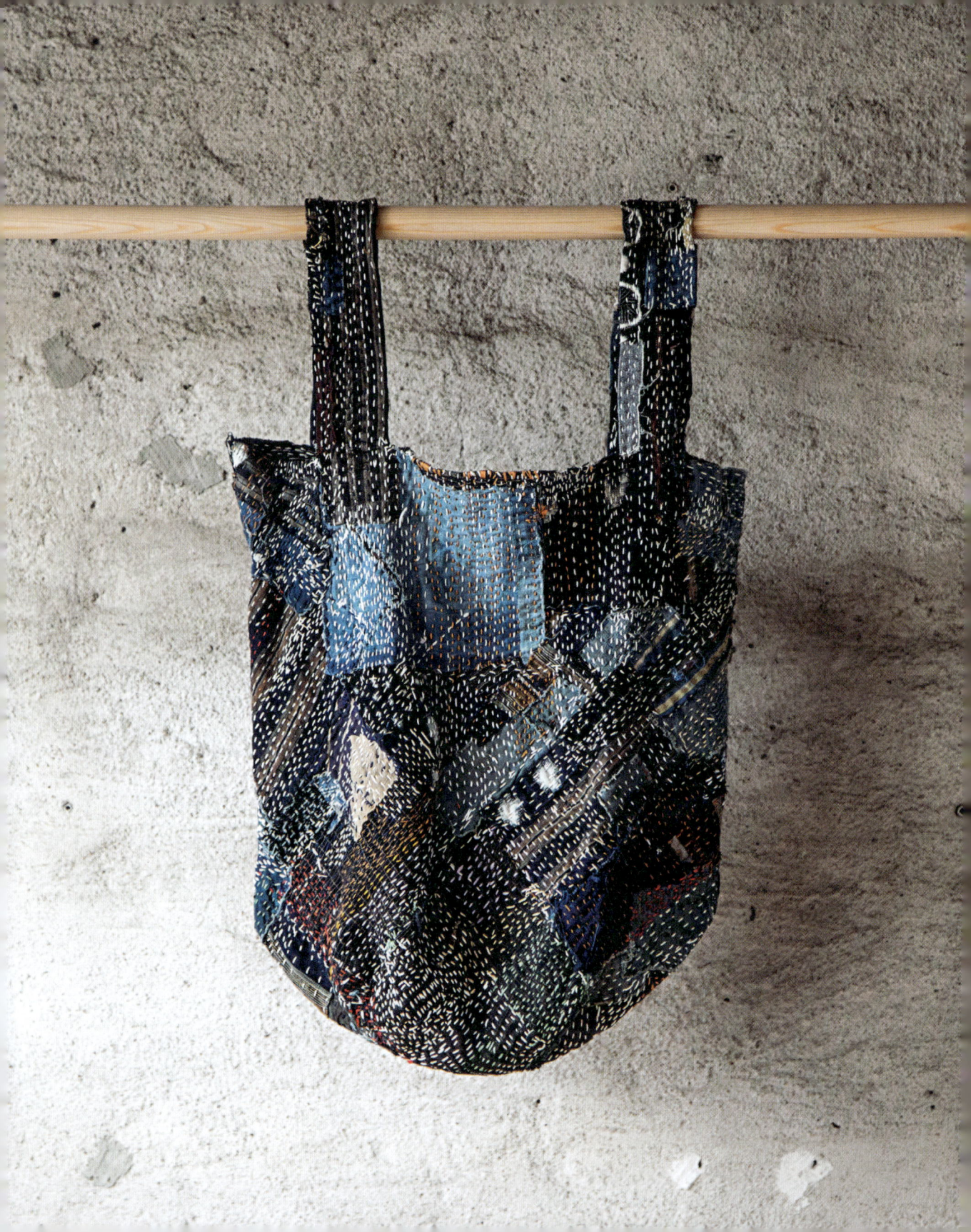

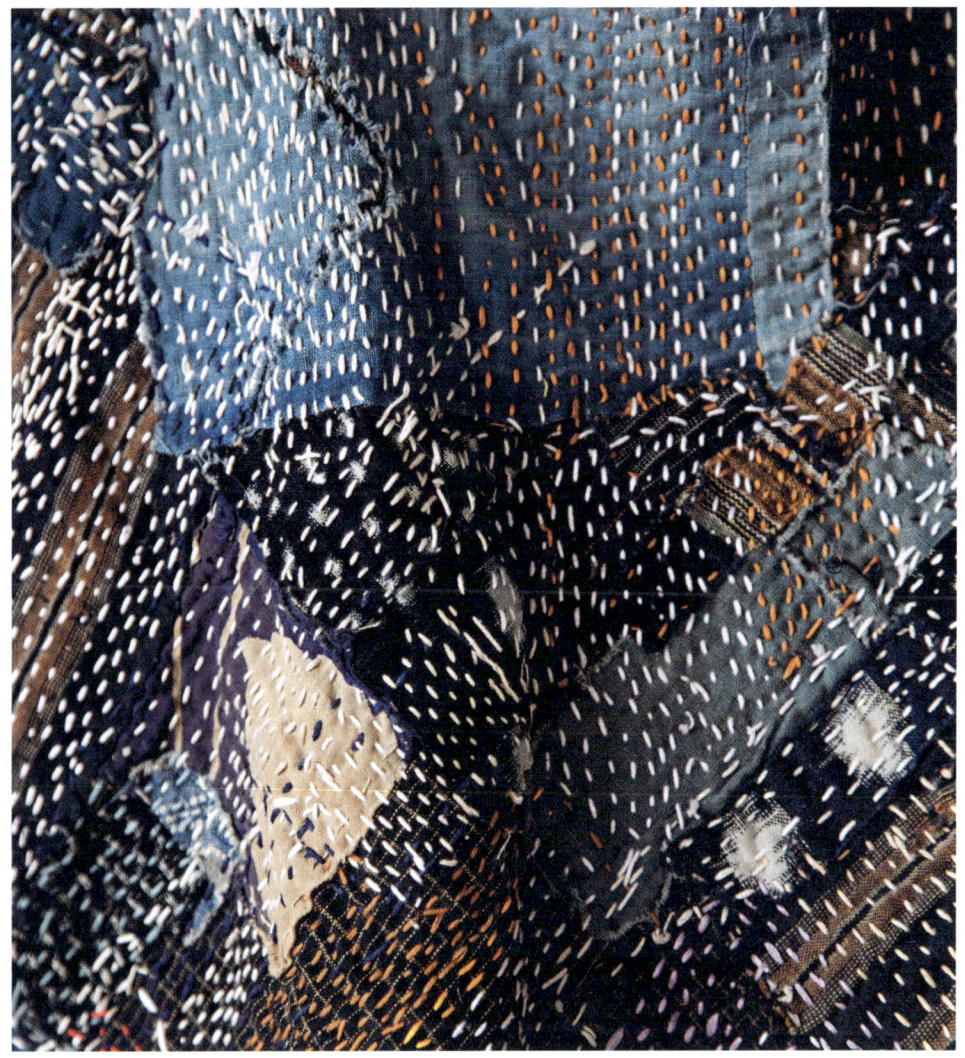

SHOPPING BAG

The bottom part for this bag is a komebukuro, a traditional bag for carrying rice. Momi bought it at a flea market and intended to mend it and finish with the traditional drawstring. But then he thought that it would be more practical if it was a bit bigger! He extended the bag with patches so that it was about double the size and could hold about the same volume as a bag from a supermarket. When he was happy with the size, he added handles.

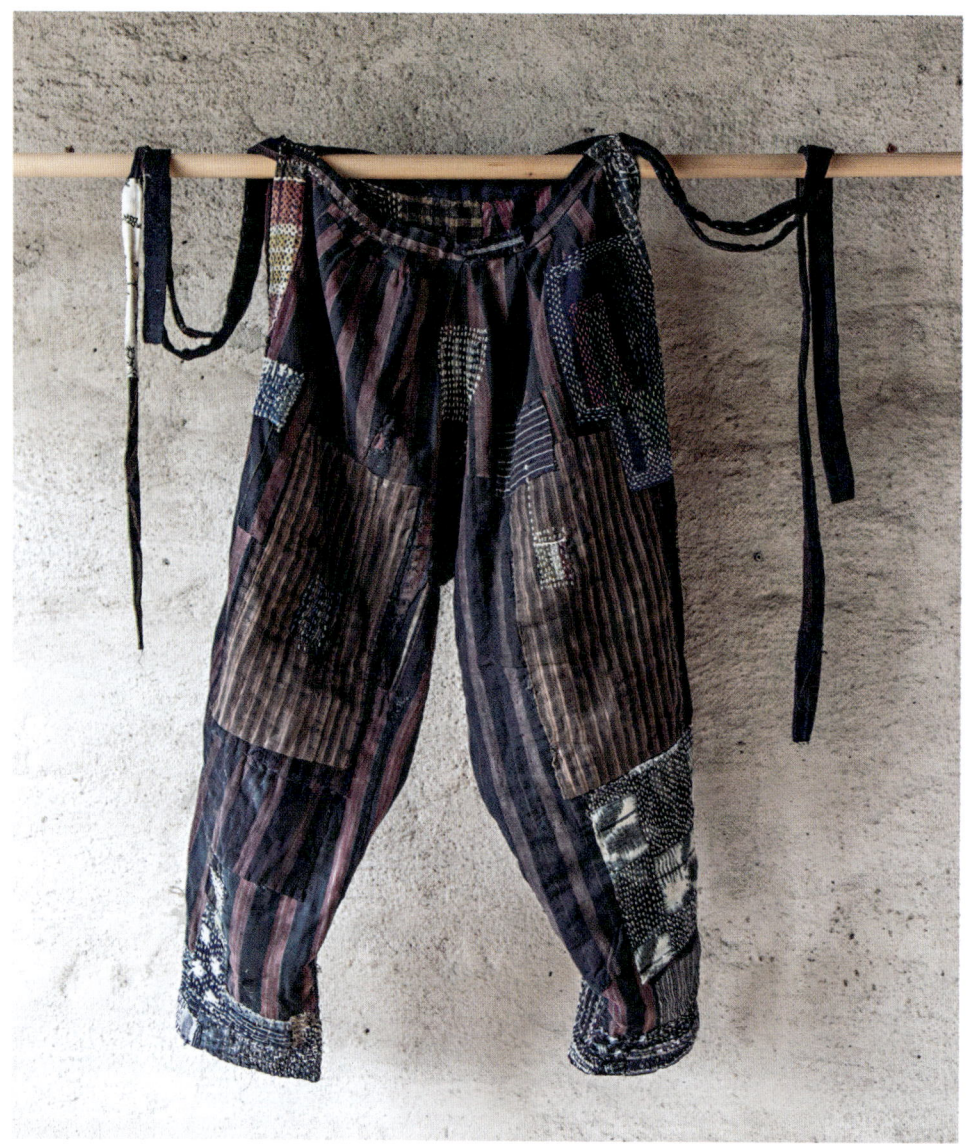

MONPE, WOMEN'S WORK TROUSERS

This type of trousers was traditionally mainly worn by women in Japan. They are wide at the top so that you can tuck in the garment you're wearing on top and narrower at the bottom to make them easier to work in. Momi bought this worn-down and torn pair at a flea market and mended it with old Japanese fabrics.

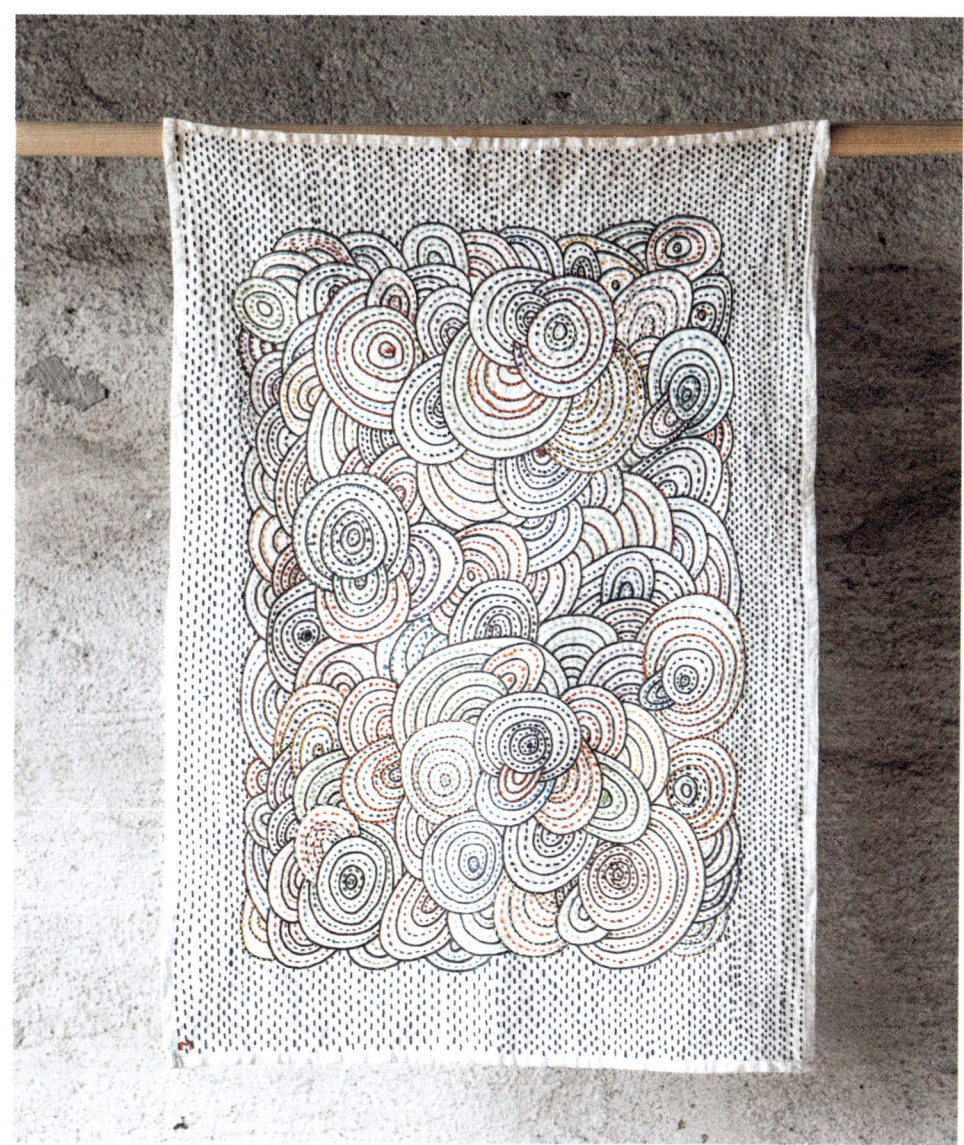

PRINTED TOWEL WITH EMBROIDERY

Momi worked as a textile artist for a long time and created different printed products. For this towel pattern he took inspiration from the traditional pattern seigaiha-mon (see page 27), which resembles the movement of waves on the water's surface. One day Momi started to embroider the towel and by following the printed pattern a completely new piece of textile appeared!

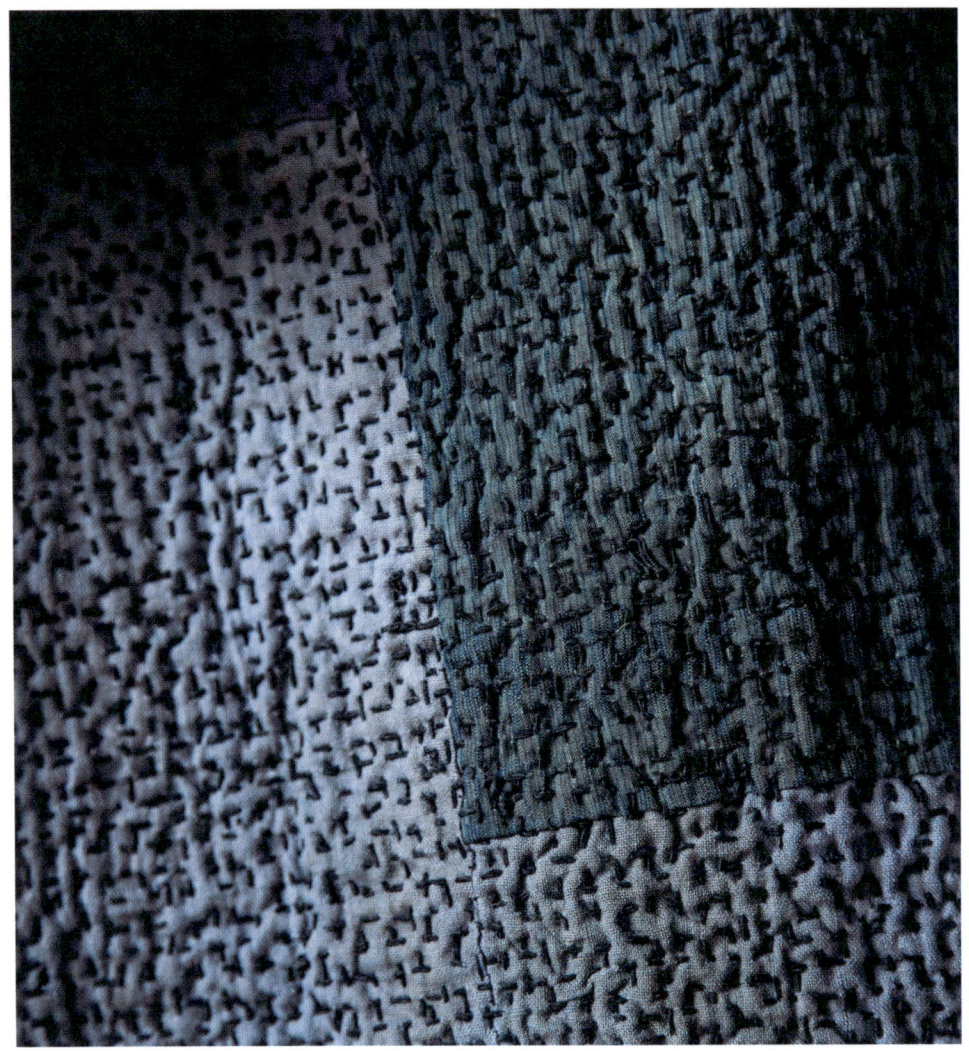

NORAGI, MEN'S WORK JACKET

The cut of garments for men and women doesn't differ much in Japan, but that doesn't mean the clothes look the same. This jacket is photographed inside out since we wanted to show the beautiful indigo-dyed lining, but the right side that can be seen through the garment's opening tells the story of the original wearer: the dark, stripy fabric is mainly associated with men's garments.

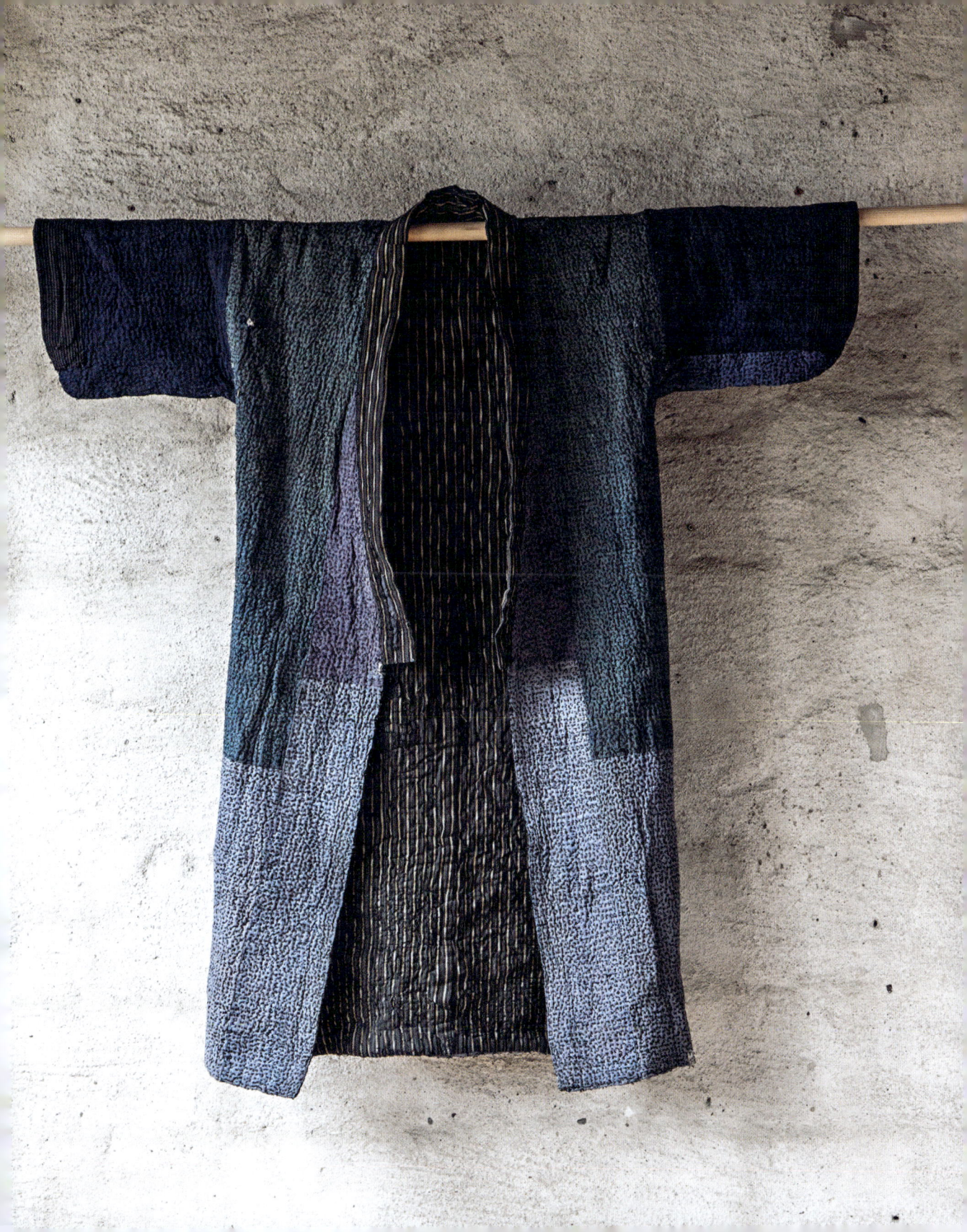

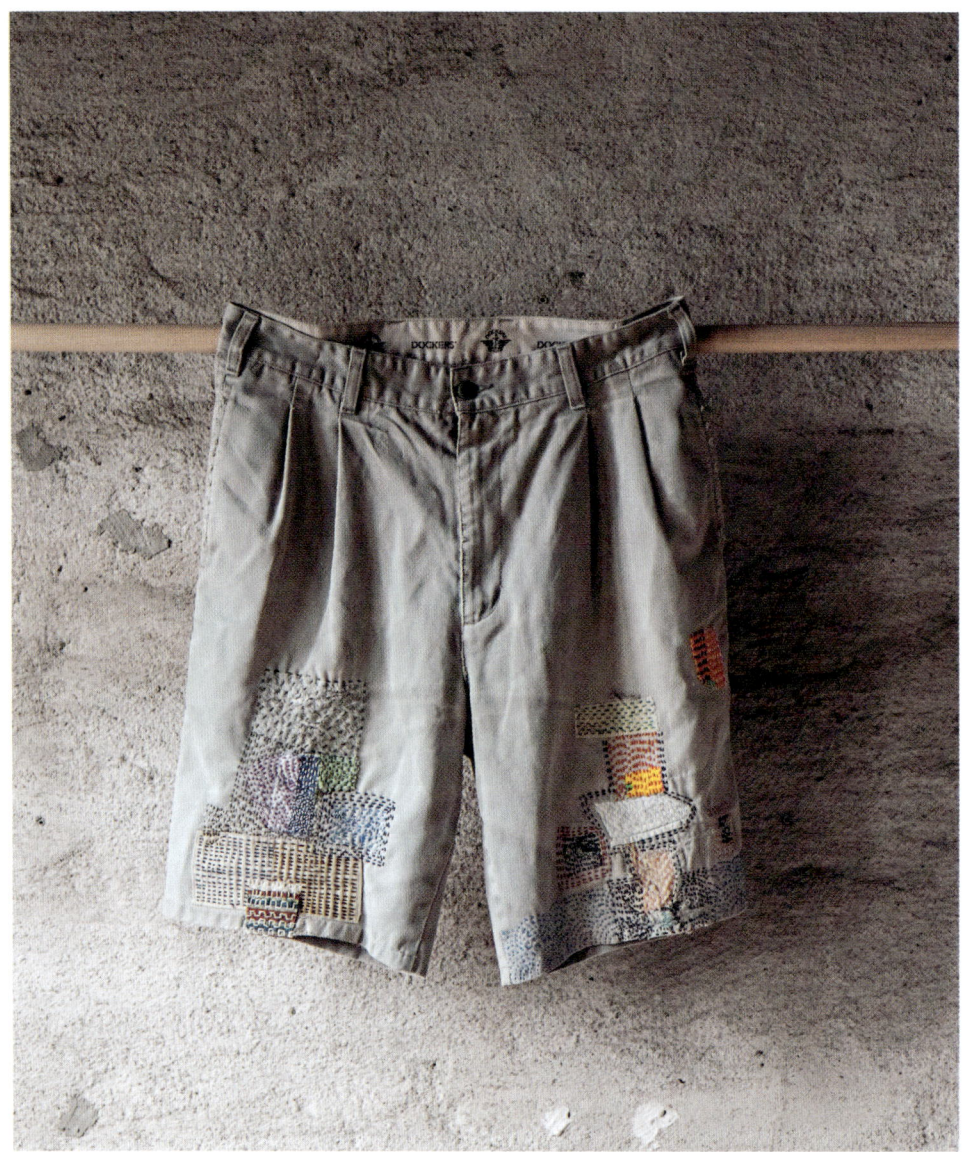

SHORTS

Carrying baskets in the garden has worn down the front of these shorts, where Momi has added patches from old shirts. Here he has experimented with how the stitches work together with the patterned fabrics so that new combinations appear. Using patterned fabrics can also save time and help those who want to sew straight lines of stitches without using a ruler.

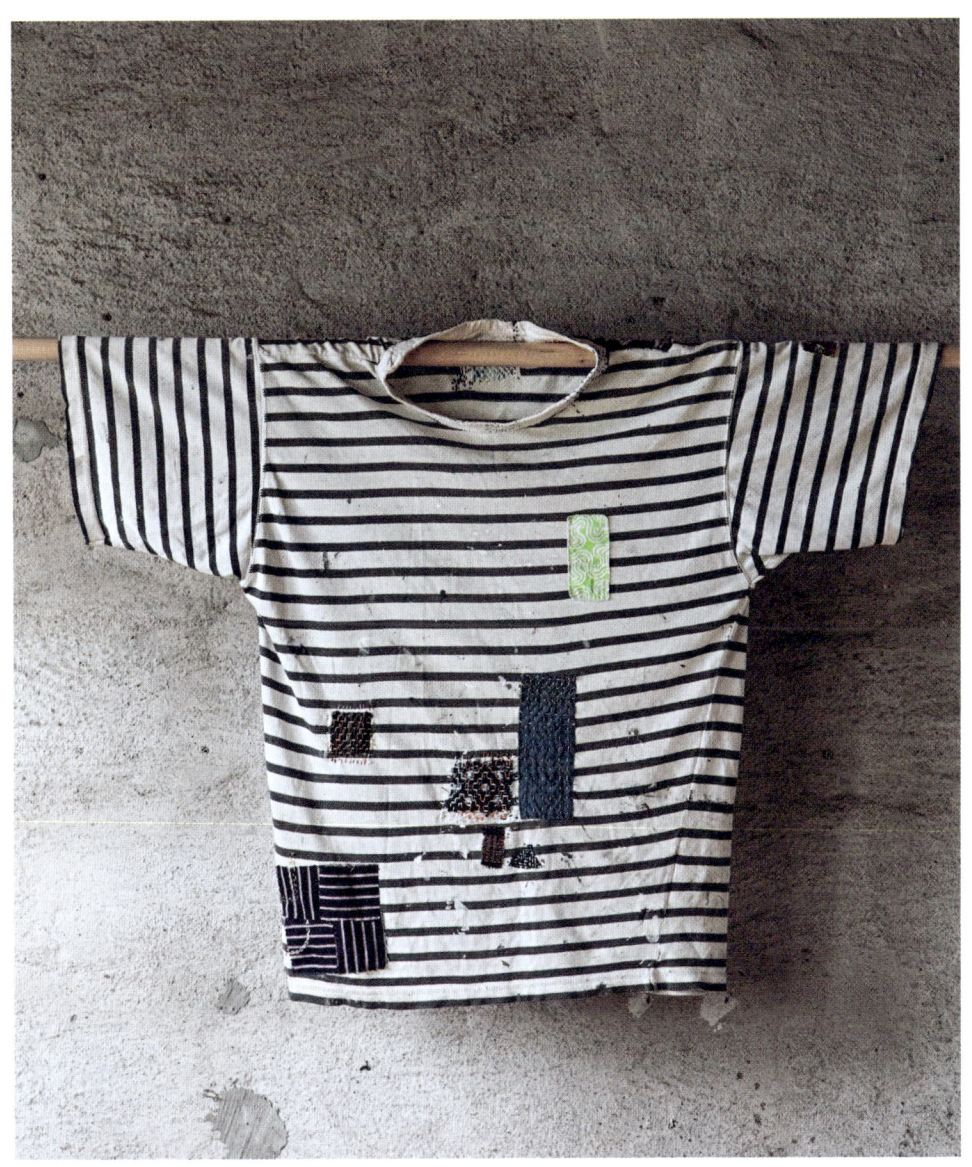

T-SHIRT
A French t-shirt from the '90s that has now been downgraded to a painting t-shirt.

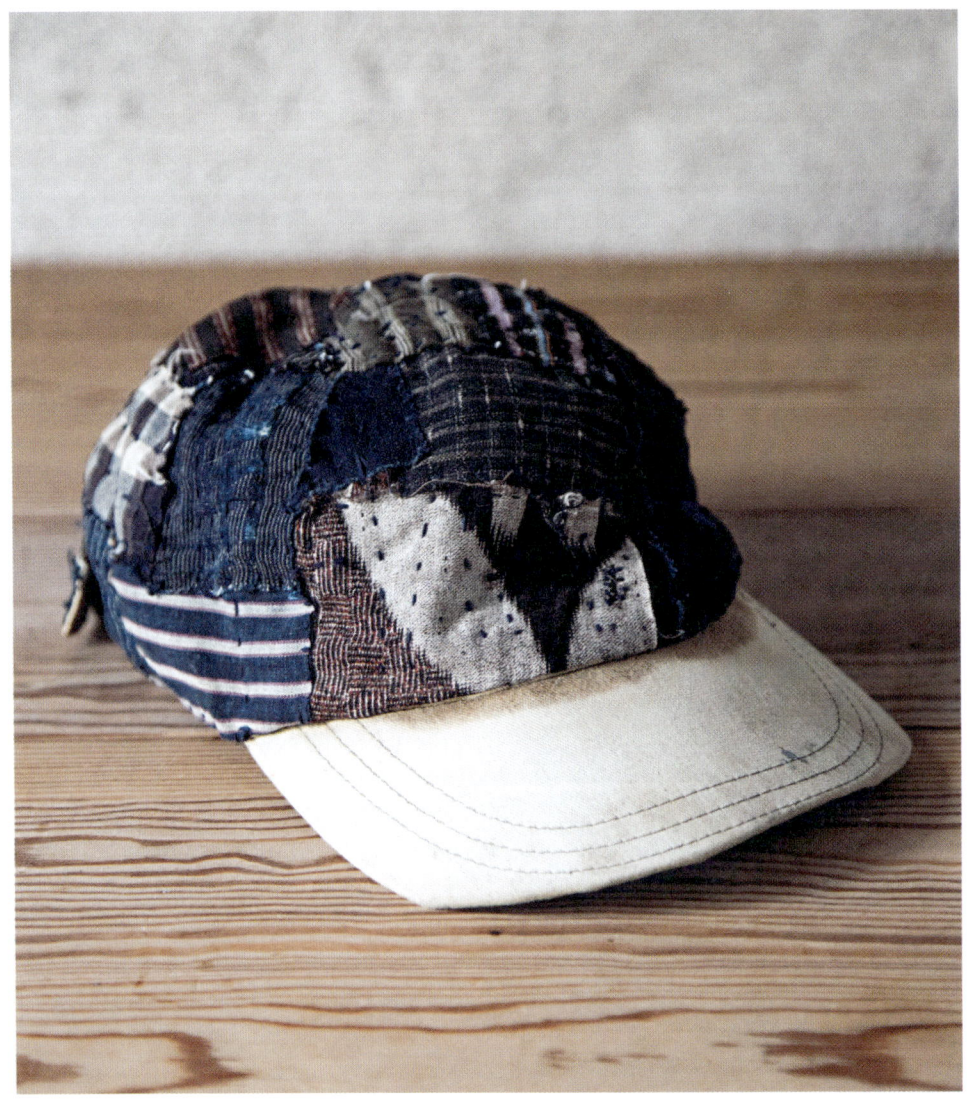

CAP WITH SEWN-ON PATCHES

For a while, Momi trimmed the hedges for an ex-policeman in Malmö, who always wore the same cap when he came out to inspect the work. He thought the brim was a bit too long and cut it off, folded the fabric around the brim's edge and then glued it underneath. When the policeman later died, Momi inherited all his caps and started sewing small pieces of Japanese fabrics onto them. This is now also Momi's favourite cap. 'Now it's like it's him and me together, in a cap! Can you see the sweat on the brim? It's from the policeman!'

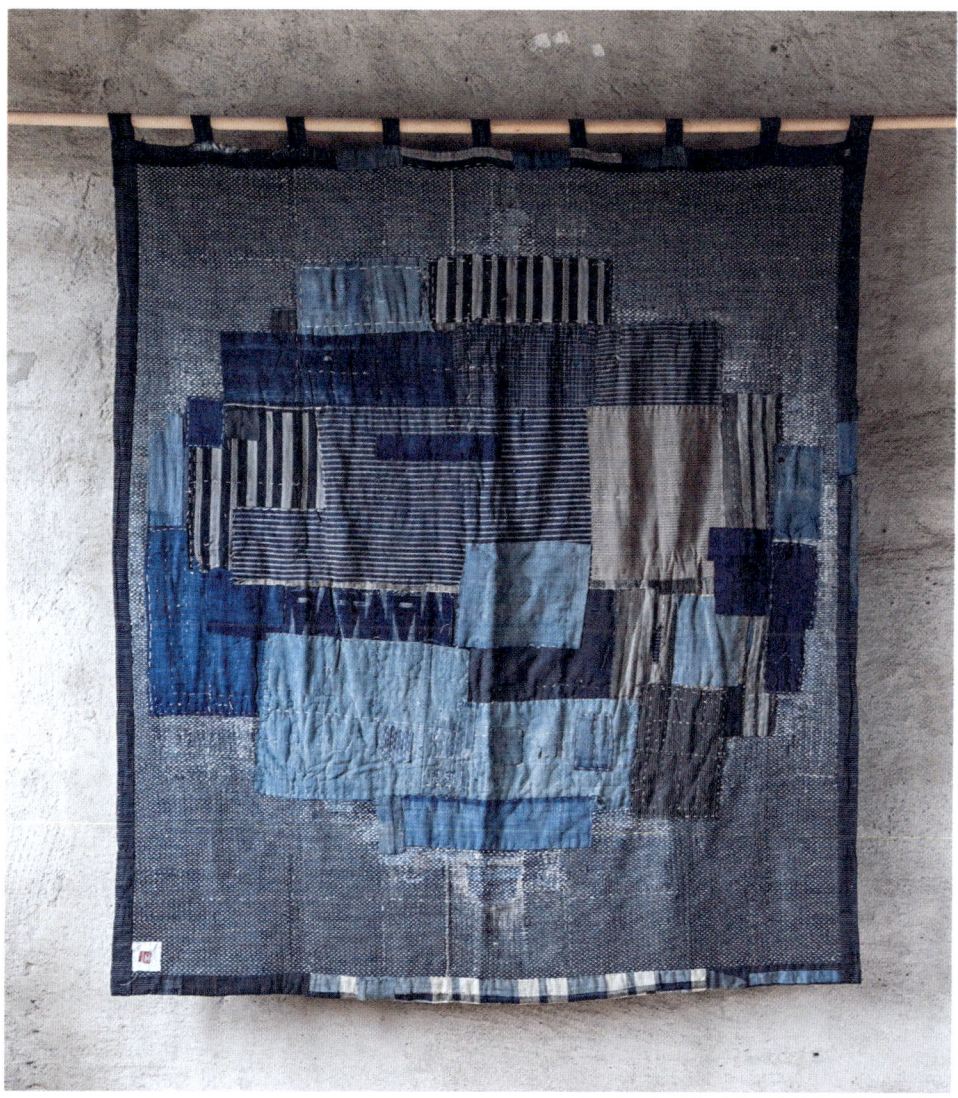

SHIKIMONO, CHILDREN'S BLANKET

This blanket weighed almost 14 kilograms when Momi bought it at a flea market. It was very thick and he thought it was filled with wadding, but when he opened it up it turned out to be made up of 26 different layers of fabric! Some were more worn than others, but Momi particularly liked a layer that was completely covered in sashiko stitches. That became the new front of the blanket, and the large hole in the middle he mended with fabrics from the other layers that he unpicked.

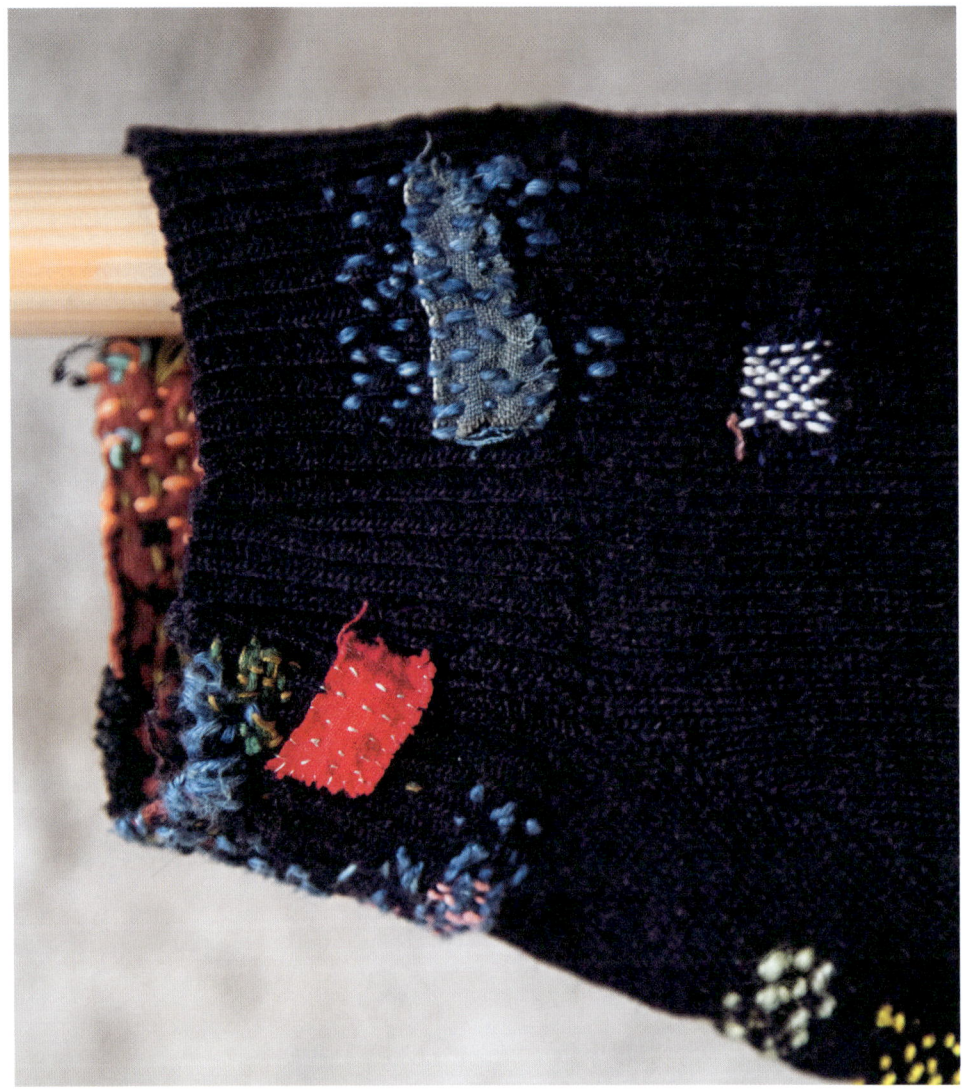

NORWEGIAN WOOL JUMPER

One of many jumpers worn while gardening. This one in particular got forgotten about and left in a corner and when Momi found it again, it had been infested with moths. After a round in the washing machine followed by the freezer, he started mending it. 'The contrast between the colours and the techniques makes this one of my most joyful mends!'

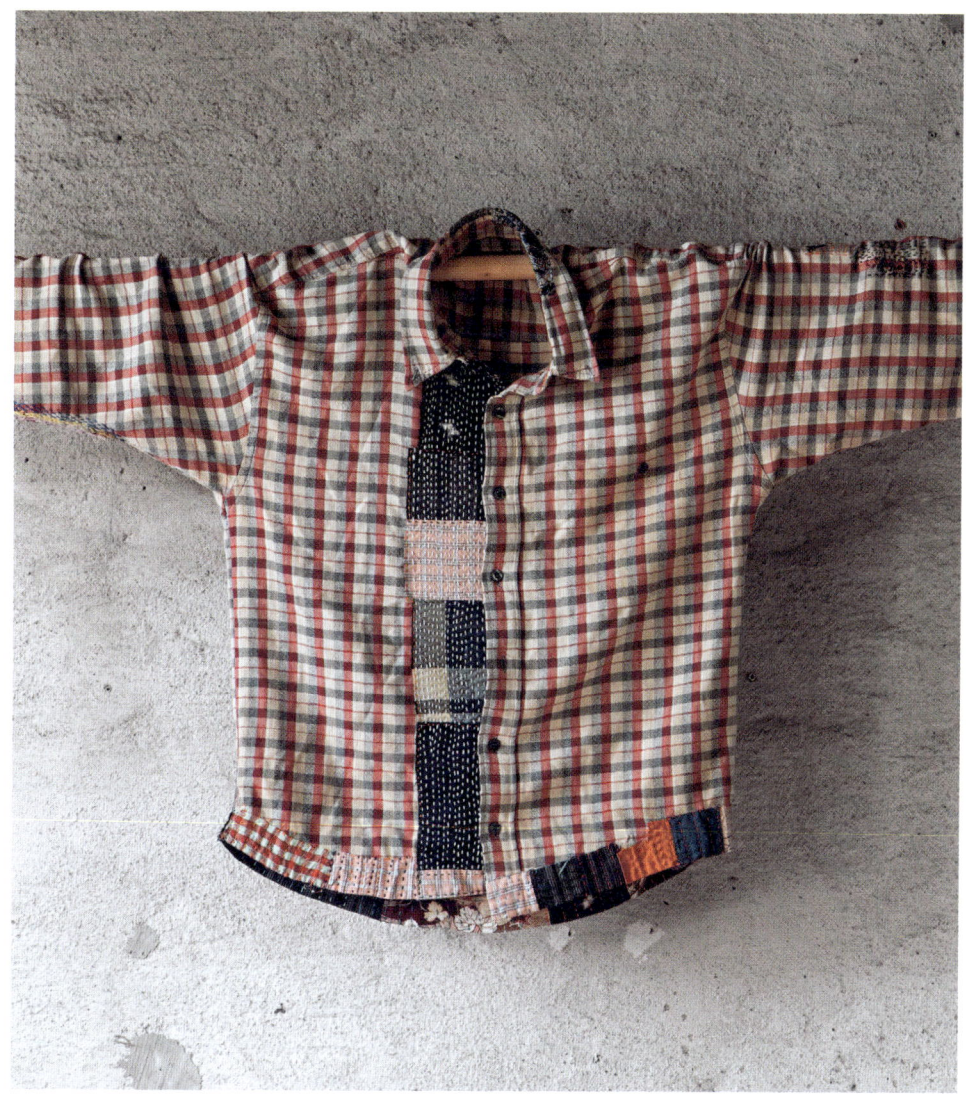

SHORTENED MEN'S SHIRT

Clothes should sit loosely, according to Momi. Therefore he likes to pick garments in size XL, but then they are very long on him and need shortening a little. He usually wears this shirt in the garden.

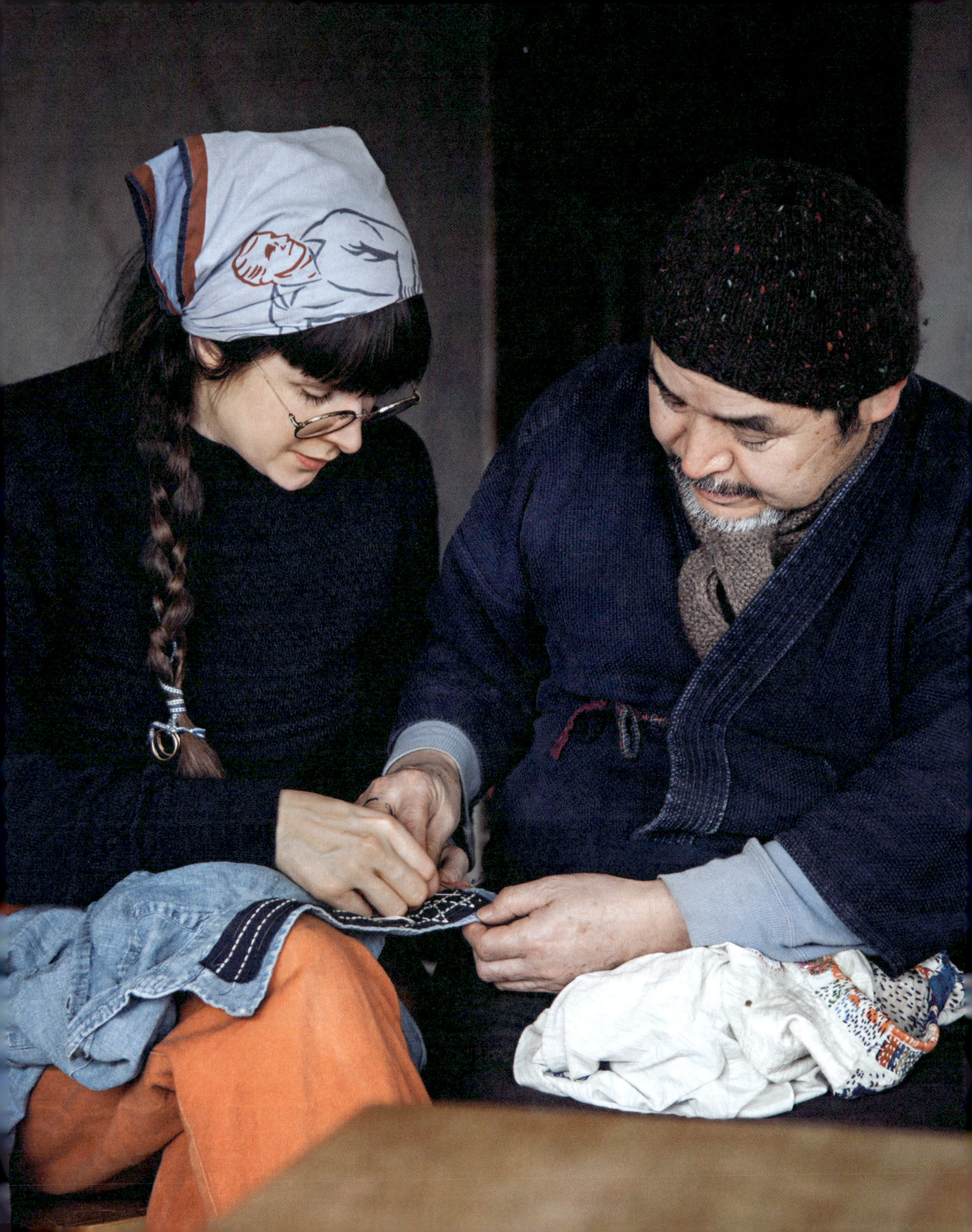

AFTERWORD

Taking inspiration from a craft technique that originates in a specific culture can be difficult to navigate. The cultural heritage can be sensitive and carry a lot of meaning for people – regardless of whether they belong to the culture where the technique was developed or not. The keywords here are humbleness and respect, and it helps if you have read up a little on the history of the subject. Embroidering a wall hanging with a traditional sashiko pattern in rainbow-coloured yarn on a pre-printed pattern is quite far removed from the original sashiko tradition, but it's not 'wrong' per se. It's just a new version of an old theme. If you're aware of what inspires you, you can use that as your starting point and choose if you want to sew as close to the historical sashiko as possible, or not.

Sashiko and boro are cultural phenomena that developed and existed within certain frameworks and saying that you sew 'genuine sashiko' is a bit like saying that you 'paint renaissance art'. You might be Italian, buy oil paint and panels, travel to Florence, paint an exact copy of the painting – but you will never be Leonardo da Vinci in the 16th century and your painting will in best case scenario be a good copy, but you can never paint the Mona Lisa.

In the same way, regardless of whether we're Japanese or not or have all the right materials, we cannot today sew the sashiko that was sewn during long winter evenings in Aomori around the close of the 19th century. It doesn't mean that the sashiko we sew today isn't genuine, but you have to look at it in a contemporary context. Your version of sashiko can be genuine, regardless of what it looks like! You can sew it on a sewing machine, use sequins or tinsel, make plastic moulds out of the patterns or make glow-in-the-dark fridge magnets if you want.

Try to distance yourself from the thought that you might do something wrong. The only thing that is relevant when you create is whether the result is what you had in mind or not. You own your own process, and no one has the right to come and say that there's something wrong with it. And if they still try, you can say: 'I'm very inspired by sashiko. This is my take on it.' Just as we do in this book.

First published in the United Kingdom
in 2026 by
Batsford
43 Great Ormond Street
London
WC1N 3HZ

An imprint of B. T. Batsford Holdings Limited

ISBN 978 1 83733 006 5

A CIP catalogue record for this book is available from the
British Library.

10 9 8 7 6 5 4 3 2 1

Reproduction by Rival Colour Ltd, UK
Printed and bound by Toppan Leefung International Ltd,
China

This book can be ordered direct from the publisher at
www.batsfordbooks.com, or try your local bookshop

Distributed throughout the UK and Europe by Abrams &
Chronicle Books, 1 West Smithfield, London EC1A 9JU and
57 rue Gaston Tessier, 75166 Paris, France

www.abramsandchronicle.co.uk
info@abramsandchronicle.co.uk

© 2024 Kerstin Neumüller & Takao Momiyama
Original title: *Laga med sashiko*
First published by Natur & Kultur, Sweden

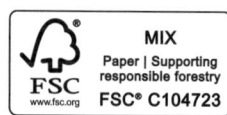

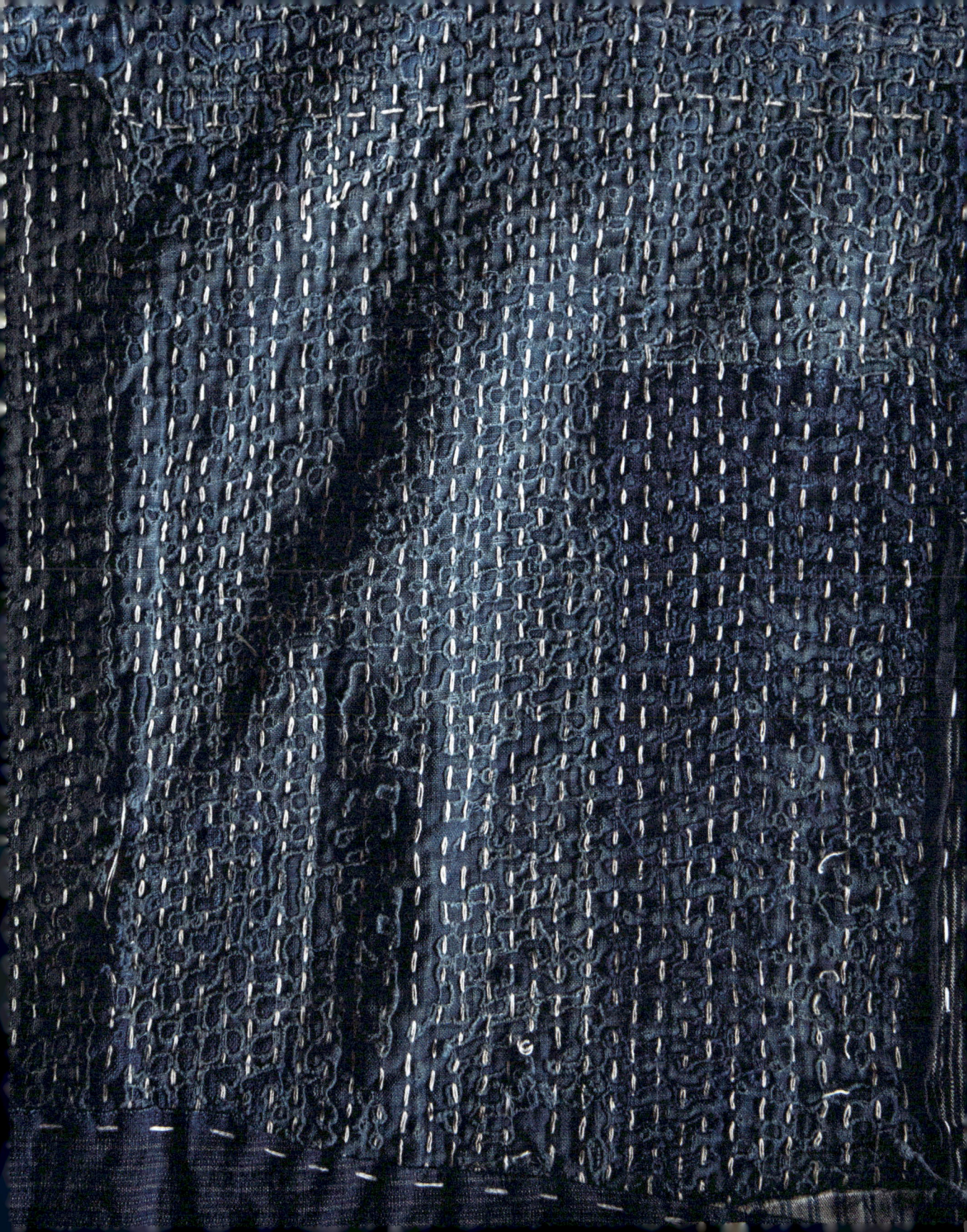

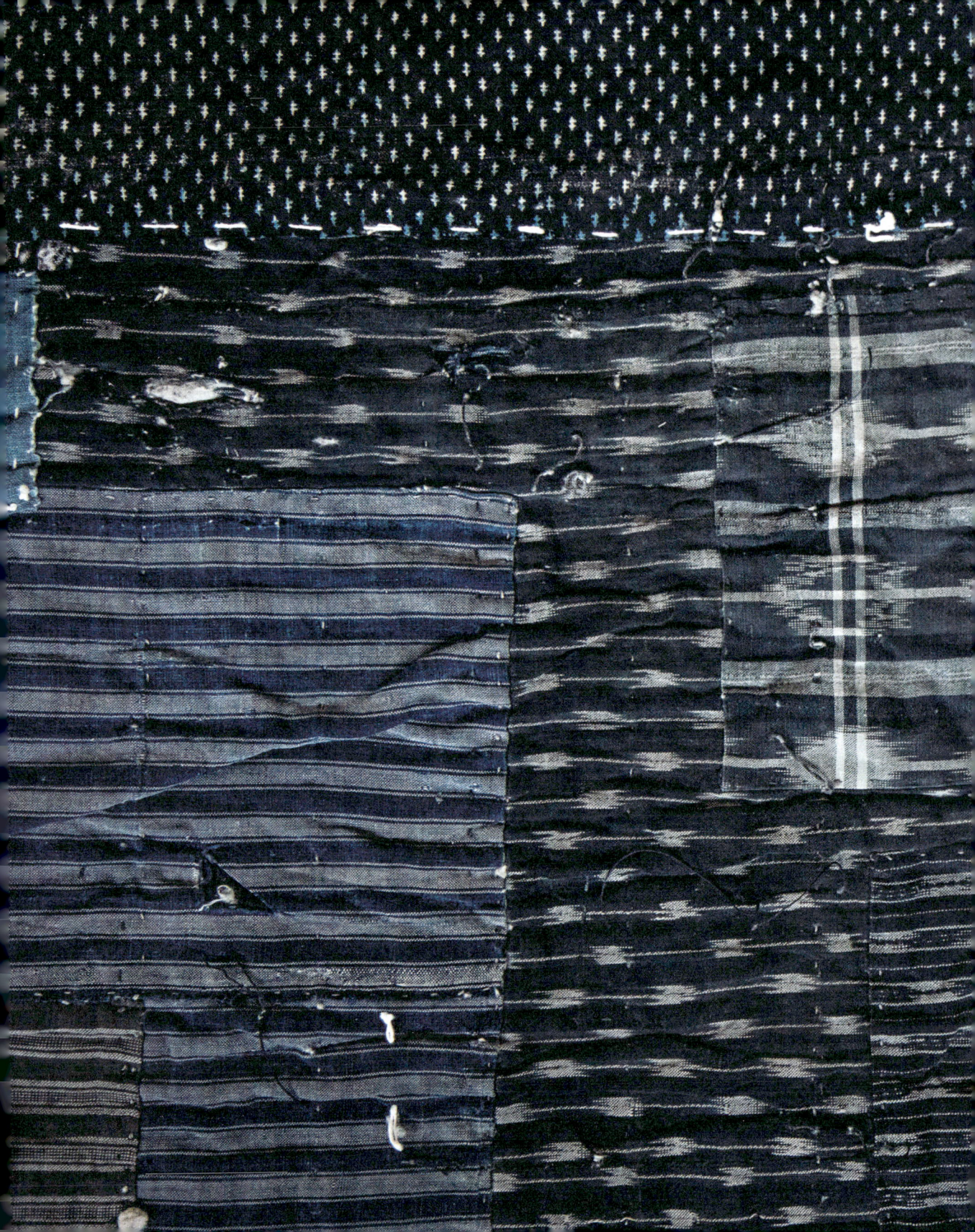